PRAISE FOR *NO ONE CROSSES THE WOLF*

"Prepare yourself: reading Lisa Nikolidakis is a revelation, the kind that makes you gasp and call your best friend and say, 'Listen to this sentence, this paragraph, this chapter. Listen to how she has made sense of the parts of us we ran from.'"

—Mira Jacob, author of *Good Talk: A Memoir in Conversation* and *The Sleepwalker's Guide to Dancing*

"*No One Crosses the Wolf* is a striking, thoughtful, and engaging exploration of the inheritance of abuse—the way it passes through generations, the way it echoes through the lives of survivors."

—Dan Chaon, author of *Sleepwalk*

"This is a benediction as much as a book, a plea for, as Lisa Nikolidakis so beautifully puts it, the cradle of someone else's tongue. *No One Crosses the Wolf* is for anyone who has ever been silenced, anyone who has ever had to learn to be a soft cradle to themselves. As a reader, as a writer, and as someone else who lives in this broken and beautiful world, I honor what Nikolidakis has made. This book will mean so much to so many."

—Alex Marzano-Lesnevich, author of *The Fact of a Body: A Murder and a Memoir*

"When a woman tells the truth by beginning with her body, she cracks open the world. Lisa Nikolidakis's memoir, *No One Crosses the Wolf*, is a force of nature, a story unearthed from under the weight of a father that brings a woman back to life. Sometimes we carry generational burdens that nearly crush us. Sometimes we run like the wind. This book is a triumph and soul song."

—Lidia Yuknavitch, author of *The Chronology of Water* and *Thrust*

NO ONE CROSSES THE WOLF

NO ONE CROSSES THE WOLF

A Memoir

Lisa Nikolidakis

Little
a

Published by Little A, New York

www.apub.com

Amazon, the Amazon logo, and Little A are trademarks of Amazon.com, Inc., or its affiliates.

ISBN-13: 9781542037716 (hardcover)
ISBN-10: 1542037719 (hardcover)

ISBN-13: 9781542037709 (paperback)
ISBN-10: 1542037700 (paperback)

Cover design by Rex Bonomelli

Printed in the United States of America

First edition

To my father: Επιτέλους τέλος.
At last, the end.

CONTENTS

AUTHOR'S NOTE

Memories are knotty and gnarled, complicated by our biases and fallibility. What appears in this book is my truth—the emotional truth of my experiences. Others who appear in this text may have a different take; after all, experience is subjective. My aim was to put my truth on the page as I understand it.

The names and characteristics of some people have been changed to protect their identities.

We look at the world once, in childhood.

The rest is memory.

—*Louise Glück, "Nostos"*

PROLOGUE

It was a call in 2003 that cracked my world open. My younger brother Mike said my name twice, but when I spoke, I heard only the hollow echo of my own voice and the clicks and static of empty sound. A bad connection, I assumed. Next to me, a tapping like nails drummed against a desk; my sleeping hound, Dante, kicked the air behind her, her short legs beating the back of the stiff pleather sofa. The third time Mike said my name, I sat forward and snapped, "You called me, fucker. What?"

"I think Dad's been murdered," he said slowly. His voice sounded split in half, at once high and low, as if two people were trapped inside him fighting to use the same vocal cords.

I shook: my muscles volcanic, every bit of my body rumbling and quaking. An old violence stored deep inside stirred. I stood, thinking that might steady things, but I only swayed in small uneven circles as a familiar float took over me.

Beneath my feet, a ratty beige carpet.

Why couldn't I feel the dense and dusty foam of it?

That woozy drift: the world suddenly dulled. No car alarms or horns, the hum of the air conditioner gone, the scent of recently brewed coffee erased. Even the scrape of Dante's paws hushed. When I was young—five, maybe six—I was sure I'd levitated between the sofa and love seat of my childhood home, crashing to the ground when the clop of my father's footsteps severed my concentration. In that float, imagined though it must have been, I'd felt lightness and joy. This was different; in my living room, the beginning of an untethering I didn't yet understand had begun.

"What do you mean *murdered*?" I asked.

"I don't know," he said. "I got to his house and there were cops everywhere and they brought me to the station. I was down there for an hour, sitting in this waiting room with some jackass I went to high school with telling me how cool my old band was." I hadn't heard his voice crack so much since he was a lanky preteen. I wanted to ship him back a decade to the safety of giggle-grunting along with *Beavis and Butt-Head* and cranking out metal licks on his Fender. Back to a time before the police were at our father's home or the ugly double bump of the word *murdered*. Back to when he was a boy oblivious to what our father was capable of.

"Are you driving?" I asked. "Get over here before you crash."

"I'll be there in ten." He paused. "Lis? The cops said not to watch the news."

I hung up and reached for the remote.

The picture on my ancient Sony sharpened into splotches of red, yellow, and orange on a deep-blue background, like fire sitting on water. Hurricane Isabel spun two hundred miles off the coast of the Carolinas, muddying the Atlantic as she decided whether to head for shore. I didn't care if she destroyed everything. I wanted the anchors to say something of consequence, something to snatch me back into this world. I had to know what happened.

A newscaster in a fuchsia blazer offered advice: "Stock up on water and batteries. Locate the safest room in your home. Check your emergency kit."

My emergency kit had long been stuffed full of booze. The night before the call, I'd celebrated my twenty-seventh birthday with my dear friends Guinness and Jameson, and I'd paid for it all morning with an ache in my temples. I'd finally recovered late in the afternoon, but then Mike called.

I stared at the TV, empty, w e i g h t l e s s.

How many times had I wished my father dead? In eighth grade, I daily pressed my forehead to the smudged window of the school bus and invented capital punishments for him as the landscape ticked by. May a riptide carry him directly into a shark's gaping mouth. May his souvlaki contain hemlock instead of oregano. May a meteor target his car, the intersection where he waited for the light to change reduced to a smoky black crater. I'd wanted him gone, but an external source had to be responsible. If I thought directly about it, if my wishes grew too realistic or personal, the guilt was too heavy to carry.

And still, I shook. My hands, the thin skin below my eyes, the *rectus femoris* muscles that connect hips to knees. *Rectus.* From the Latin for "appropriate" or "straight," as if shaking muscles were the appropriate response, the straightest line the body has to shock.

I made two quick calls—one to the Wood, a bar I hated but worked in, the other to Matt, my boyfriend of seven years. I'd planned on lying to my boss, but when he answered, the same line Mike had said poured out like one soggy word: *Ithinkmyfathersbeenmurdered.* I begged him not to tell anyone and hung up. Next: Matt. The corporate art store he worked at put me on hold, and I chewed on the word *murdered* while an overly enthusiastic recording thanked me for calling. I pictured Matt leaning against a counter surrounded by canvases, talking someone into having their work professionally framed, his dark hair pulled into a loose ponytail. A black tee and torn jeans, the uniform of artists everywhere. When he answered, his voice felt like knuckles stroked softly across a cheek. I envied him. He sat in a moment of preknowledge, hovering in a dull and ordinary day.

"Babe, this is hard to say, but I think my father's been murdered." I paced in my living room.

"What? What? What do you mean?"

"I don't know. That's what Mike told me. He's headed here now." Part of me knew I was in my living room, on my phone, but part of me floated elsewhere.

Matt was silent for a beat before asking, "Should I come home?"

That brought me back to earth. My spine straightened, my voice flat as paper.

"No, I'm fine," I said, though clearly I wasn't. I couldn't articulate what I needed, not then or for a long time afterward, but I wanted someone else to know what to do, to spring into action and make sure I was okay. In short, I needed help, and I didn't know how to ask for it. Maybe more than that, I didn't want to have to ask.

I would repeat that lie for months—*I'm fine*—for years—*I'm fine*—but in the moment—*I'm fine*—Matt must've believed me because he didn't come home.

He did not come home.

I waited for Mike—standing, swaying, time stuffed with stiff talk of cloud formations and barometric pressure.

When the five o'clock news began, my father was the top story. A trembling aerial shot of his yellow bungalow: overgrown grass, neighbors clustered around crime-scene tape, a SWAT team that crawled over his property like bald-faced hornets. Everything stilled. It was as though I were suspended in formaldehyde, a young woman peering out of a jar, the outside world slow and blurry. When I think of that moment now, I do not see my chest rising and falling with breath; instead, I am static with anticipation.

I pressed "Record" on the VCR, making a tape I would never watch but still carry with me each time I move to a new home, and squatted inches from the screen, as if by getting close I'd be able to learn more. When I reached out to touch the image of his house, a space I hadn't visited in four years, a tiny bolt of electricity stabbed my fingertip. My television suddenly seemed absurdly small. Big news should come from a big TV, not from the same little box coated in stickers of glittering hearts and stars I'd had since the fourth grade. Not the TV my father bought me.

The newscasters filled the air with information that didn't help: *We've gotten word that a man lived in and owned the house in this suburban South Jersey neighborhood.* I desperately wanted them to say his name. I wished the anchor would look directly into the camera, fourth wall be damned, and say, *It's over now, Lisa,* so I could know for sure that my father was dead. But I also wanted them to say nothing, our last name so uncommon that anyone watching would know immediately he was related to me. Shame. A shame I hadn't handled in years simmered beneath my skin, every inch of me hot to the touch.

Finally, movement: the front door to his house opened, a toothless mouth. A man with *SWAT* stamped across his shoulders walked backward down the steps, pulling a gurney, while a woman pushed from the other side. Then again. And yet again. *We're told there are three deceased.* Three gurneys were wrenched from my father's home, and at the sight of the third one, the floating stopped. I dropped hard to my knees and let out a sound I didn't know I was capable of—a sharp, inhuman howl. Dante scurried beneath the couch the way she did when thunderstorms shook the walls. She was right. My twitching muscles had started a storm: one that climbed through my legs, rumbled past my stomach, and barreled into my lungs before reaching my throat until, finally, I had no choice but to open wide and let that terrible sound rattle the walls.

∽

For a long time I thought that howl was about the death itself, that even without confirmation from the news, I knew in my body my father was gone. I told myself it was intuition, a familial connection. Blood recognizes blood, like twins who feel one another's pain from across the country. But that's mythology, a bit of wishful wizardry. Once, Mike told me over breakfast that our father had had a minor heart attack. *Is he dead?* I'd asked. Mike said no. *Too bad*, I'd said and continued shoveling my Special K. Not a blip of empathy on my emotional radar and not my finest moment, but had he been dead that day, I'm not convinced I would have cried. Of course, there would have been processing and grieving eventually, and there's no way to guess what that would have looked like, but I didn't shake. My pulse remained steady. I most certainly didn't crumple to my knees.

This was different. I was different, and to understand why—to get to the heart of that unmooring howl—I had to figure out how we'd gotten here: my mother and brother still living in my childhood home in South Jersey, me a quick drive down the road, all of us fifteen minutes from my father's post-divorce house, the one he shared with a woman and two children, the one now on TV with a SWAT team carting away the dead like ghoulish repo men.

∽

When Mike's tires crackled against the driveway, I peeled myself off the ground and wiped my face. The next day, I would find rug burns on both knees, scabbed patches that wouldn't heal for weeks, but I couldn't yet feel them. I blinked quickly, trying to erase the evidence of what had just happened. For my brother, I wanted to fake being okay so that he had the space not to be, but when I opened the door and looked into his bloodshot eyes, there was no hiding from it; we both looked like shit.

I hugged him, the bones of his shoulders sharp beneath my palms.

We flopped onto the couch, stared blankly at the TV. We'd have to wait for the top of the hour, a full forty-five minutes away, to learn anything more. We didn't know the six o'clock news would bring no answers. We didn't know we'd drive to a local pub and play pool, and the late news would mispronounce our last name before delivering the sentence that would take years to unpack: *The bodies of three deceased— two female, one male—have been found in this small South Jersey home, victims of what appears to be a murder-suicide.*

"Oh god," I'd say.

"What the fuck?" Mike would whisper.

My father's girlfriend and her daughter were dead. It was official. Two possibilities wiped out, two remaining: our father was either dead or on the hunt. And if he were hunting, I was sure I'd be next.

PART I

Exile at Home

CHAPTER 1

MYTHOLOGY

My father chose me. Not my little brother Mike, the freaking golden boy, but me. I followed him to our rusty shed, where we untangled fishing poles from spiderwebs and loaded them into the car, their handles digging into the floor by my feet in the passenger's seat, their hooks dangling over the cooler in the trunk.

"You pick music, yes?" he asked. So glad not to have to listen to the Greek songs that hibernated in his tape deck, I turned the dial to oldies, a safe bit of middle ground. Del Shannon filled the car, crooning, *I wah wah wah wah wander*, and we waved goodbye to my mother and brother as we left our suburban home and headed out in search of something bigger.

At Strawbridge Lake Park there was water, yes, and in theory there were trout, fathead minnows, and swamp darters flittering somewhere in the lake, but there was also my father. With his hand clamped to the back of my neck, we trekked through weeds and underbrush until we reached the edge of a craggy alcove, my ankles a skein of scratches.

"Do you know why today you are full of luck?" my father asked.

Because you love me, I wanted to say, but if that were wrong it would have sounded corny, too needy. I shook my head.

"I am the only man who knows this place," he said and smiled. "Now you know too." Other people fishing with their fathers fought for elbow room near the parking lot, their noise scaring off any possible catch, but we were tucked far away from them. Suckers. By early afternoon, our shoulders were worn raw from casting and recasting our lines. When they zipped together over the lake, before their lured and weighted ends plunked beneath the face of the water, I felt close to him. I could almost smell the pleasure he took in those seconds of unison, a lightness and lily of the valley to the air. Together we sat on a felled log and peeled the sandwiches my mother had packed us from their foil wrappers. Before I finished half of my PB&J, I jabbed my straw into the corner of my juice box, slurping the last drops.

"Here," my father said and held out his beer. "You want?"

I took the sweaty bottle, a Michelob pony that looked so cute in my hand, I couldn't make sense of why, when I took a swig, it attacked my body. The inside of my nose burned like Pop Rocks.

"Gross," I said and shoved it back toward my laughing father. I could've lived inside the sound of his laugh.

We got back to fishing, but save for a few nibbles and the drag of a towel I'd hooked that morning, we'd gotten nada. I was sure it was my fault. Whatever we'd joked about earlier, that space of light and air, had disappeared. We'd grown silent, and I felt his stare before I saw it. I could always feel it; his looks seemed like physical entities, invisible creatures that coated my skin. When I turned I found a glare I knew well: my father's brow bent, his flat, brown eyes drained of fun, filled instead with something at once darker and vacant.

"Take off your shoes," he said.

⁓

Seventeen years later, a few miles from that lake, he would kill the family that came after us—his live-in girlfriend and her fifteen-year-old daughter—before turning the gun on himself. My father would be low-ered into the ground in a pale-blue coffin: a murderer. The funeral would be nearly vacant and entirely in Greek, and for years afterward, I'd dream he was alive and coming for me. Upon waking, I'd run Google searches to remember precisely where he was buried. But I couldn't know that then. What I knew was I didn't want to take off my shoes.

∾

"Off," he said again, and if he had to say it a third time, I'd get it some-thing good.

He mounted the flash to the body of his Nikon. It let out a long, high whine.

Leaning my rod against the rough bark of a tree, I dug my toes into the heel of my knockoff Keds and flicked them into the mouth of a nearby bush. I picked up my rod again. The pads of my feet winced against the cool ground, mostly pebbles and fallen sticks, the occasional burst of crabgrass.

"Now roll up your pants and get in the water."

A few hours of daylight remained, and the sun had been pinched behind a plate of clouds most of the day. It must have been March, maybe even April—memory blurs time the quickest for me—but the air was cool enough for jackets, the water frigid. I wanted to say, *No, this is a bad idea, it's too cold*, but when he was like this, I was lucky if I remembered to breathe. It would take years for words that meant precisely what I thought to develop, to find their footing in the loose earth of my childhood.

While my father fidgeted with the camera, I scanned: those people in the distance—the suckers by the entrance—I heard them, but no one stood close enough to see us except a family of ducks that cut the water in a straight line toward the opposite shore. Half of me wanted to join them—to fall in line, stick out my undeveloped chest, hold my head high, and slide off toward the horizon—but the rest of me wanted to peg one with a rock. One of the ducklings fell behind, and the mother circled back for it. My throat tightened.

"Go," he said.

At first, the large rocks of the lake's floor surprised me, smoothed by the current but slick with algae. I used my rod like a flimsy cane to steady myself as I wandered out and clenched the muscles of my back and stomach. As if all at once, my body registered the temperature, a cold so fierce it punched like heat. I paused, my jaw clamped. Surely ankle deep would be enough, but my father nagged me to go farther. When the water slapped the tops of my shins, I turned to look at him again.

"Cast out and act like the big one is on the line." As he spoke, I zeroed in on the bomber jacket that clung to his body, but I knew better than to argue. I obeyed and waited for him to get the shot.

"C'mon, Lisa," he said and raised the camera to his eye. "Make me believe there's a fish." I tilted at the waist, my weight on my back foot. I wondered what he saw as he watched me through the viewfinder. A shivering child? *His* shivering child? Or was I merely scenery, no different than the ripples on the surface of the lake?

"More."

I arched back until my hair swept my butt and held the pose as the shutter ticked again and again.

"Happy," he demanded through the camera.

I forced a smile and tried. Good god, I tried. But when I wiggled my toes and couldn't feel them, my body stiffened. The day had confirmed that the fish weren't biting, but I thought of nothing else: schools of yellow bullheads or, worse, a family of fat catfish slinking along the lake's bottom, hungry for my feet. That's when I felt it, the flaw that made everything worse: the fist in my throat that meant I was going to cry.

What is it about anger that changes the air—even the wide, clean air of a lake? When my father raged, the air hardened and slowed like some terrible charge had overridden the molecules.

"Son of a bitch," he said and held out his sunglasses from the shore. "Here. Put this on."

I waddled over to him, but when I tried to take the glasses, he grabbed my wrist and pulled me closer. "This could be over. Thirty seconds if you do it right."

I nodded. My wrist burned beneath his fingers. Later that night as I lay in bed, I'd trace the oblong bruises, his hand long removed but the pressure of him still there, never gone.

But of course I couldn't do it right, and why it was wrong that day at the lake remains a mystery. Perhaps my muscles didn't flex enough, or my smile looked too fake, the illusion incomplete. More likely, my father's frustration had little to do with me and everything to do with the invisible sack of poison he carried inside himself, one that leaked without warning. I didn't know why he was broken, why other adults weren't, but something in my father seemed wrong. I felt that acutely, and I assumed it had something to do with being Greek. *He wouldn't be like this if he'd never left home*, I thought, but a louder voice told me I was wrong too. After all, if I were better, my father wouldn't be so angry all the time.

Eventually, when he had the shot that satisfied him, he turned, picked up his cooler and rod, and headed back into the woods toward the car. Despite desperately wanting out of the water, I couldn't move. Would he leave me there if I didn't hustle? Had I finally performed so poorly that he was quitting being my dad?

"You coming?" he yelled without looking back.

After a week or so of tinkering in his basement darkroom, my father placed a four-by-six photo framed in cheap plastic beside the TV in our living room. I stared at it from the couch while my mother cooked dinner and talked more to the air than to me through the cutout wall between rooms. A row of fake plants and candles on the ledge behind my head kept her out of view.

"The phone rang today, and I just knew it was going to be bad news," she said. "And sure enough, Marilyn's sister is sick."[1] She paused to poke her head over a dusty silk fern. Curly black hair pulled into a dancer's loose bun, red-orange lipstick, perfect. "I've always been a touch psychic," she reminded me.

I smiled. "I know," I said and turned back to the photo. The day appeared sunny. Clearly at the end of my line flopped a fat one. I looked happy—a kid with a proud father and one hell of a fish.

Later, the four of us piled into the kitchen for dinner: my father at the *head of the table*, even though it was round, directly across from me, Mike and my mother flanking us. I poked my chicken—I hated food with bones—and my mother pointed to the photo.

"I love that picture of you so much." She smiled and stabbed a forkful of lettuce. "Must've been some fish," she added and patted my arm.

"It sure was," my father said and winked at me. I looked down, the nubby end of the drumstick on my plate pointing at my chest as if to say, *You. You have been chosen to keep another secret.*

⌒

We lived in the center of a row of alphabetized streets in South Jersey—on E—and as far as I knew, our neighborhood held one collective truth: at the end of Jerome Avenue, where the tar curved and swung toward Kohomo, a white biplane lay crashed, its snout sunk into the earth. As

---

1   I have no idea who my mother got bad news from that day. Our un-spoken agreement is that she tells me about people I barely know, and I politely *uh-huh.*

I walked to school each day, I looked that way, the airplane taking a bite of overgrown yard. I liked to imagine what happened: an engine failing, maybe even flames, a swift fall from the sky, screams, prayers, no survivors.

A couple of months after the fishing trip, I decided to ask my father about it. He knew everything, after all, and liked to remind us of that often. I found him in the backyard tossing handfuls of seed to the chickens.

"Why doesn't someone clean up the plane crash?" I asked.

He raised one eyebrow, a trick that pumped me full of envy for my inability to do it.

"What are you talking about?" he asked. And when I explained, he said simply, "Show me."

So we walked to the corner together and I pointed. "Down there—all the way down the street," I said.

He tilted his head, gauging my seriousness. "Come with me."

Together we walked blocks, past dogs barking through chain-link fences and creepy houses I'd have run past were my father not by my side. As we approached the plane, it took a different shape, and I stopped.

"You see?" he asked. "Is a boat." His accent often omitted contractions. But he was right. An incredibly terrestrial white boat sat in someone's driveway. My stomach bubbled. I scrambled to save myself.

"Gotcha!" I said and adopted the biggest smile I could manage. He loved a practical joke. Maybe I could earn some points.

But his voice was singsong. "I don't think so."

"Ha, I got you good this time!" I said, less convincing, and he laughed while my insides chewed themselves. How could something I was so sure of—an open secret I was certain we all shared—be wrong? One answer is simple: myopia. I badly needed glasses, and shortly after, I got them—big red Sally Jessy Raphael frames too large for my young face. But there was a complicated answer, too, that turned in my guts:

no matter how sure I was about my reality, my father could shift it in an instant.

"Come," he said, his hand landing heavy on my head. "Is *Hogan's Heroes* time."

I don't remember what we talked about on the walk home. I was good at that—at splitting myself in two—half of me able to *yes* and *mm-hmm* at the right moments, the rest of me floating far away. Once indoors, I beelined past Mike, who waited for our father on the couch; I hated *Hogan's Heroes*—the colors too drab, the comedy a stupid language I didn't speak. I dashed toward my bedroom, the pink one at the end of the hallway, and as I turned to shut the door, I noticed something new: a bookshelf, the first one we'd ever owned, parked outside our bathroom.

Where once there was only tan wall, a fifteen-volume set sat cloth-bound, the corners of its spines curling—red, matte red, the color of stacked bricks. I ran a finger over the gold lettering. It felt like I imagined a snake might: finely textured, woven. Aside from my mother's moldy copy of *If Life Is a Bowl of Cherries, What Am I Doing in the Pits?* and *Zolar's Encyclopedia and Dictionary of Dreams*, the *Britannica Junior* volumes were the first books not from school or on loan to enter our house. I sat down on the rug.

My mother stopped by my side.

"These were mine when I was a kid," she said. "My father gave them to me." Her voice dripped with pride and dreaminess. "I think you'll like them."

Finally, I thought. Sure, I'd read some Judy Blume and basically attended Sweet Valley High by proxy. I'd even snuck in *Flowers in the Attic*. But those were stories, fictions, lies borne of imagination. What I had before me for the first time were facts, and I knew I'd turn every one of those pages until my life made sense.

But so many words were omitted: *fear, weirdos, stomach cramps*. Where an entry on *crying* should have appeared lay only the blank space between *crustacean* and *crystal*. Of course they weren't there. Our collection was written for children in 1957, the same year *Leave It to Beaver* premiered and blasted people's problems with heavy doses of *golly* and *gee whiz*. When my mother received those books, at seven years old, their facts were fresh. But in the mid-1980s, when I couldn't keep my tiny fingers from them, they'd long grown outdated: Cyprus and Somalia and so many other countries not yet independent, the stink of imperialism and sexism printed in a bold serif font, imposing order on my world. What did it matter if the order wasn't right?

When my mother walked away, I pulled Volume B off the shelf and opened it. After getting distracted by a passage on wild boars with an illustration that looked like a pig-beaver, I read the entry on "Boats." It turns out there are light boats and motorboats, sailboats and pleasure boats. I turned up dull facts about gunwales and battens, chines and longerons. But not a single boat could suddenly shift from airplane to sea vessel. I closed the book, the pages hard hugging my thumb while the truth of my young life solidified itself once again: something was definitely wrong with me.

∽

My father was born in a small village in the center of Crete, the low-hanging island beneath the mainland of Greece—the largest island in the country, a crooked smile of land. It boasts beaches and mountains and the cave that was the birthplace of Zeus, as well as the labyrinth that, at its center, held the pacing Minotaur. Olives and grapes spring forth from the hard, dry land, and on all sides yawns the deep, deep blue of the Aegean. Ask anyone in Athens, and they will tell you the same thing: Crete is the jewel of Greece.

But everyone needs out of where they're from.

My father told us about the heroes. Odysseus took off from Ithaca to save Helen and battle the Trojans, even though he'd been warned it would take him years to return home. He wanted so badly to stay with his family, he pretended to be crazy, but the Greeks have a way of tricking people, so off he went, ten years of his life gone, poof. In Seriphus, Perseus was content at home with his mother, but the king outwitted him, so he begrudgingly left to claim Medusa's head, kicking rocks all the way. Brave Theseus traveled over much of Greece, a journey that forms the shape of a Dorito when traced on a map, and eventually killed the Minotaur at Knossos. Even Balki Bartokomous from *Perfect Strangers* fled his life as a shepherd on the made-up island of Mypos with his belongings jammed into a trunk and a sign that read America or Burst. That's meant to be a broken English joke, but *burst*. What a word. As if staying will kill you. To really make something of yourself as a Greek, you've got to leave village life in the dust, but you're a fool if you think it will be easy. If mythology teaches us anything, it's that away from home, out *there*, the world will test you again and again.

According to my father, his journey to the States was no less heroic. He repeated the tale of his adventure so many times that most of the tellings blend together with a roll of my eyes, but I remember one narration vividly. My first-grade class was headed to the Philadelphia Zoo for our annual field trip. Every day, lunch box in hand, I walked alone to the school at the end of our long street, but when I opened the door to leave that morning, my father was on my heels.

"Wait for me," he said and grabbed the screen door before it slammed.

I looked up at him, confused.

"I come today," he said and smiled. My father, a chaperone. It was the single time he volunteered to do anything scholastic.

Pegged to that spot on our patchy lawn, I looked him over: navy tank top, cutoff jean shorts, camera swinging from his neck, a toothy smile with one metallic cap. Why couldn't he look more . . . normal? Later, *Britannica Junior* would lead me down the misguided path of wishing Teddy Roosevelt were my dad—not for his military accomplishments, which bored me, but for his waistcoat and mustache. He never wore a tank top in public; I was sure of it.

"You don't want me?" he asked—half accusation, half wound—and my belly churned. My mother said I had a "nervous stomach," but what made my insides twist was a word I didn't own: *exposure*. My father, with his thicket of chest hair and soupy accent, his short shorts and gold tooth, was my secret. I didn't want my classmates to see me through a lens of him.

And though exposure was a threat, one that nearly doubled me over in cramps, another layer of truth hid beneath that: my father had wormed his way into the only space in my life that was free of him. I was a nerd, and school was my shelter, my respite from home, the singular place where I could count on my father's absence. As I studied him on our lawn, I thought of him not as a chaperone but as an invading army of one who would take up all the space in my life he could find. Like Napoleon, but taller.

"Of course I want you," I said quietly, and his expression relaxed. But as soon as we left, I power walked ten feet ahead of him. Halfway up the street, he barked my Greek name.

"Garifalitsa!"

I stopped, and heat rocketed to my cheeks. He caught up and squatted to my level, put a hand on my shoulder. Shorter than our refrigerator and impossibly fit, he was swarthy, with thick black curls that framed his head like a pillowy helmet. Sitting on the lip of the bathtub, he'd hold still while I uncoiled his hair lock by lock to scissor away half an inch, then watch it miraculously spiral back into place. I thought he looked like Johnny Mathis from the cover of his *Hold Me, Thrill Me, Kiss Me* album, a musty, weather-eaten record that lived in our basement, and though no one has ever agreed with me on that, women clearly found him attractive.

"Are you ashame of me?" he asked, his face so close I could taste the Old Spice on his neck.

"No," I said and looked at his sandals, his hairy toes jammed into them like exotic caterpillars.

"Then act like it." He extended his massive palm. As my hand slid against his rough grip, I was certain no one would speak to me again, that bringing this man on a school trip was like lugging an active beehive in for show-and-tell.

But there he was: on the bus next to me, sitting on bleachers at the zoo, waiting for the big cats to be fed, their roars and grunts rattling our rib cages.

The blinds have been yanked shut over swaths of that day, like so many moments of my childhood. I don't remember the elephants or lunchtime or even the long bus ride home in rush-hour traffic. Instead, what zips into focus is a bronze statue of a monitor lizard on its hind legs mounted on a tall rock, and my father taking photos of me and the girls he was left in charge of. Three of us, one of them the girl I most wanted to trade lives with. Beth was the same height as me, with a bar of her top front teeth missing, perfect bangs, and a leather belt, which seemed to me so fancy that I often picked at the loose threads on my fabric one in her presence, hoping I could pluck it into oblivion.

My father told us to climb onto the rock and huddle around the sculpture, the lizard a few inches taller than each of us and warm to the touch. As he snapped pictures, he started the story.

"You know, this statue is smaller even than the octopus I fight when I come to this country." The girls looked at each other, eyes wide. One of them sucked in a short whip of air.

"Is true," my father continued. "To come to America, I have to swim here. Boats very expensive. Is good thing I am such strong swimmer," he said and flexed his biceps. My classmates giggled.

My father lowered the camera and held it in front of his chest. His voice deepened, as though he were letting them in on a secret. "But when the octopus come, I know I have to be stronger than him, more clever." He tapped his finger against his temple. "I grab him around the neck and his . . . his—Lisa, how you say *plokamia*?" my father asked and wiggled his arm.

Everyone looked at me.

"Tentacles."

He repeated the word, but it sounded like *Socrates*. *Tent-a-cleese*.

"When I grab his neck, the *tentacleese*, they hit me in the face, in the legs." He paused to swipe his rubbery arm at the girls, who squealed with delight.

My father sighed and looked around at the air, at nothing. "Okay, we go see more animals now?" he asked. A classic fake out.

"Wait! What happened?" Beth asked.

My father never needed to be invited to a party twice. He reenacted the fight, grabbing the invisible octopus by the neck, hitting it first with its own tentacles—big laughs there—then poking it in the eye, a Three Stooges move that startled it so much it swam off in a plume of its own ink. Eventually, tired of swimming, my father hitched a ride on the back of a whale—it was a whale that day. Other times it was a dolphin[2], a detail that made more sense to me, since they have built-in handles. He laced his fingers behind his head to show how relaxed he was on the aft of a humpback. Just then, a loose peacock walked behind him and paused before spreading its feathers. They lined up in such a way that it looked like my father spread his own glamorous plumage. By the time he was through, the girls were clapping and laughing and ready for more.

The next day at recess, Beth ran up to me, breathless, and blurted out in a wet, gummy lisp, "Your dad is so cool!"

---

2   Dolphins are whales, of course, but first-grade me didn't know that.

"Really?" I asked, caught between embarrassment and delight.

"He's so funny," she said, and a fleck of spit landed on my shirt.

I wish I'd muttered something under my breath, maybe a frustrated, "You like him so much? Take him," but I'm sure I didn't. I was incapable of speaking a bad word about him. Besides, I was the kind of kid who swallowed her language.

I walked away to sit alone beneath a tree, where I picked up a stick and dragged it through the dirt to dig thin lines. The first set was uneven, so I erased it with a fan of my fingers and tried again. Still crooked. I needed them lined up like roman numerals or the soldiers of some war I'd seen pictures of in one of the *Britannica* volumes, but I kept hitting pebbles that threw off my symmetry. I dug them over and over, and there it was, the speed bump in my throat that meant I was about to cry, but a black ant showed up and my body relaxed. I studied him as he tried to crawl through the lines, his abdomen bobbing up and over the grooves. As he crossed my little desert, I imagined how tired he must've been when he got to the top of one trench only to discover another one dipped before him. I wondered if he assumed this is what the world looked like now, an endless chain of spikes and lowlands. When he reached the last line, his hardship almost over, I dug the blunt end of the stick into his small body and twisted it.

Even then, in grade school, I understood that life with my father was complicated. How could I explain that he owned two spotlights? One was a warm white that froze you onstage like a soloist about to receive a dozen hurled roses and applause, applause. But the other lit you deep red, your body a target of rage, of heat. My mother and Mike got the red sometimes, but if I were present, I provoked him enough to swing the spotlight onto me. I remember him hitting Mike twice, but only my brother could tell you how many times it happened. There's a benefit to being the golden boy, after all. But when my father washed the world red, he could yell until you quivered and cried, or maybe he'd slap you across the face, his massive hand covering the real estate from forehead to chin in one lofty swipe. He could also take whatever you felt best about and sculpt it into a flaw with a handful of words. A terrible gift if ever there was one. Slaps wear off; bruises fade. But withheld love leaves a trench of invisible scars.

How was I to articulate any of that as a child? The world fell at my father's feet in fits of charisma. Who would listen or believe me? People saw only the white light, and I couldn't blame them for latching on to that beauty, that love. He never showed the red one to strangers. If I tried to explain this to Beth—to anyone—they'd look back and forth between me and my father, and he'd compliment whatever they were most insecure about and win them over.

～๑

It took more than twenty years for me to confess the truth of the fake fish to my mother—not because it was our most sordid secret but because she isn't a woman who examines family mythologies. I assure you, I type that without judgment. We simply come at the world with different skill sets and aims. I'm the wrangler of stories. I wrestle them to the ground to see what they're made of, even when they're stuffed with stinging nettles. She lets stories glide by like strangers in a supermarket: barely noticed, forgotten instantly.

In many ways, her choice seems more pleasant to me.

When I told her over the phone that there was no fish, that the whole thing was a sham, she asked the question she always does: *How did I not know?* That makes it sound as though there's some objective truth ready to be plucked from the air, that having lived in the same home means we should have the same experiences and memories.

Of course, that's not how it works.

In some families, abuse acts as a bond. Imagine a family locking themselves in a closet, all hands pulling in unison at the handle to keep their monster out. A team at work. In other families, in ones like my own, abuse is a shell game. Each of us was trapped beneath our own cup, seeing one another in slivers when a hand shuffled us around at its whim. I can't speak for the inside of anyone else's cup. I only know that mine was dark, a space filled with pain and dread, and the best I could do to get by was to flick on my reading light.

CHAPTER 2

FAMILY

We lived in a working-class neighborhood where identical ranches and oak trees lined most of the streets. Occasionally, someone had a two-story house or an in-ground swimming pool, and as far as I was concerned, they were rich. That's all it took to impress me: stairs and water.

We were a nuclear four—my mother, father, brother, and I—with a smattering of cats and dogs over the years. There was a Siberian husky who ran to Alaska, I assumed, to beat the Jersey heat. A golden retriever who I'm told fell through a gaping hole in the living room floor of our first home, one I don't remember, and landed safely in the basement. A scraggly terrier named Muffin, whom I adored and everyone else cursed. Pumpkin, Kitty, and a few others, nameless now because they didn't last long enough to be remembered. I was stunned when someone at school mentioned a fifteen-year-old dog. Even our animals knew better than to stick around.

In its opening paragraph on "Family," *Britannica Junior* states:

> Each member is expected to behave in certain ways
> to other members. These ways of behaving are indi-
> cated partly by the community in which the family

lives and partly by the traditions handed down by the older members of the family. People tend to behave in ways expected of them. Failure to do so usually means that they are not accepted by other people in the community.

Expected drips with danger. Who monitors expectations? Our neighbors, our "community," we knew peripherally: the Bakers next door, a couple that seemed miserable and shut in; the Kellys on the corner, equally miserable and shut in; the weird house next to us that changed owners more often than the pizza shop up the street; the mean old folks across from us with their yappy white dog that gradually turned pink. None of these people were friends. No one watched each other's backs.

Growing up Greek, I assumed that our community had read and internalized "The Kid and the Wolf." In that fable, a child sitting on a rooftop sees a wolf below. He pelts the animal with rocks and sticks, calls him all sorts of names. The wolf, slick as can be, looks at him and says, "It's easy to be brave from a safe distance." It's Aesop's *Say that to my face, bro.*

Maybe people noticed that our family was off. Maybe I felt so isolated because we weren't accepted by others. Perhaps they talked about us at dinner or in whispers beneath linen sheets. But nobody knocked on our door. Nobody called the police. No one crossed the wolf.

Both of my parents worked at a diner then—my father a broiler cook, my mother a waitress—which is how they met. During a late shift, my father left the kitchen and approached my mother's cold marble counter, where he confidently leaned toward her on his elbows and asked for a glass of prune juice. *Obvious reasons*, he joked. And somehow, his battle against constipated bowels charmed my mother enough for her to say yes when he asked her for a date, an event that would take place at a Jersey Shore burger joint drowned in '50s nostalgia. Between my parents' schedules at the diner and ours at school, someone was always in class, grinding out the graveyard shift, or sleeping the day away in recovery after a long night spent prepping or serving food.

Like so many others who ruin family, my father claimed it was the most important thing. *You are nothing without a family*, he said often, then repeated the sentiment in Greek, as though hearing something in two languages solidifies its truth. There was no greater show of unity than a Sunday dinner.

One evening, I helped him in the kitchen. Me: a girl forever peeling potatoes into a garbage can, fishing the slick ones that slipped from my grip out of the bin. Even though my father cooked for a living, he didn't seem to mind it at home; as captain of the stove, he filled the house with the aromas of Greece: stewing fish or chicken or rabbit with oregano, lemon, and olive oil on everything.

While my mother piled our plates and served, my father said, "This fish is with small bones. Be careful." Mike and I nodded, and indeed more of the meal was spent peeling needle-bones off our tongues than enjoying the snapper.

My parents talked about *getting the bedroom ready*—for what, I didn't know—but my father's tone grew clipped as they went on, and eventually, my mother stared at her plate.

After we ate, my father split up two oranges for dessert—one wedge at a time, the rind still attached—and Mike and I jammed them in front of our teeth and smiled wide, dayglow juice running down our necks as we tried to talk and laughed. My parents moved to the living room to smoke cigarettes in front of the TV while I wrapped leftovers and loaded the dishwasher. There were maybe two bites of *fasolakia* (a baked tomato and green bean dish) left—not enough to save—so I scooped them out of the pan with a wad of paper towels. Hours later, long after I'd been in bed, my eyes snapped open in the darkness the instant my father touched the handle of my door.

It was never okay when he was in my bedroom.

I ran the calculus of what I'd done wrong and immediately cursed myself for throwing away food. After all, as we were so often reminded when an untouched piece of liver sat on our plates, there were starving children in the world.

"What is this?" he asked, his voice all growl and bass. I squinted in the darkness, his silhouette backlit from the hall light, and as my eyes adjusted, I realized he was gripping the paper towels from earlier.

"Don't make me ask again," he said.

"There wasn't much left, so—so—so I threw it away," I stammered.

When he stepped forward, I scrambled to sit up and pressed my back to the corner.

My father leaned in and dragged the cold, trashy leftovers down my cheek.

"Don't you ever, ever waste paper towels again," he yelled and left the room.

I waited to hear the sound of his footsteps in his bedroom, to hear the door close. I waited and waited, with tomato stink running down my face, for his snore, the only indication it was safe to go to the bathroom and rinse my face—in the mirror, a girl whose eyes I couldn't meet.

Directly across the street from my bedroom window sat the nicest house on our dead-end block: a half-brick split-level with landscaping. I didn't care about manicured lawns or architecture. What I cared about was Stacy. Seven years older than me, she sported huge, frosted hair and a denim jacket blotched with sewn-on patches. When she left the house, she sped off in her black Firebird, an enormous Screaming Chicken painted boldly across its hood in metallic gold. I thought Stacy had everything I didn't, and instead of hating her for it, I loved her. From my room, I watched her whip her car into the drive, and I did my best to memorize everything about her from the moment she appeared till her garage door clamped shut.

Do you remember that hunger of youth? Ravenous with the need for belonging, wanting so badly to be older, to be liked by the teenagers who barely registered you as human? If I were on our lawn when Stacy pulled up, I straightened my posture and tried to look as normal as possible, praying she'd say something, anything, to me. She never did. Of course she didn't. Once inside, I bet she said, "That weird kid's staring at me again. She's so creepy." She wouldn't have been wrong.

And what did I even want from her? I wouldn't kiss someone for another five years. It wasn't exactly sexual, though it wasn't entirely not. What I wanted was attention. Any kind I could get. And kindness. I wanted her to swoop me up in her denim arms and tell me I could live with her, no questions asked. I wanted love. And the way I wanted it from Stacy confused me so much that I tucked it away for years, certain yet another thing was rotten inside me.

∽

In its four pages on family, *Britannica Junior* does not once mention grandparents, but my *yiayia* arrived from Crete when I was six. She visited like a Greek: for five long years, limping after me with a spoonful of vinegar to drink when anything hurt, cupping my back when I was ill. Hunched, she lit fires close to my fevered body, then placed glasses on my back, my skin pulling in the vacuum the cooling air created. In other words, when I was sick, my *yiayia* laced my back with perfectly round hickeys.

Like *yiayias* throughout Greece, she wore black from scalp to toe, in perpetual mourning for the man she lost. Her long hair remained pulled back in a tight bun unless she brushed it, and when she let it down, it fell in a waterfall below her shoulders. In thick orthopedic shoes, she hobbled on crutches, her joints in the grip of arthritis, her fingers and ankles swollen with knots. We were bonded twice over: my middle name was her first, *Garifalia*, which means "carnations," and she was the only other blue-eyed person in my family—her cornflower irises illuminating how I'd wound up in our dark-eyed clan.

I'd hoped my *yiayia*'s arrival would snap my father into good behavior, but he was typical in her presence: he claimed to love her while treating her like a servant. This woman in her sixties stood all day long, hip dug into the stove, perpetually stirring or baking or waiting for dough to rise, Greek radio blasting on the countertop. Eventually she would sit slowly, her face puckered, and let out a low grunt and sigh, the sound of a body deflating with pain. If my father ever noticed, he didn't let on.

We quickly learned not to tune in to TV dramas with *yiayia*, as she believed—no matter how many times we explained it—that the actors really died in their scenes, and she prayed to the Virgin Mary for their souls while she crossed herself three times. Together, she and I watched *The Price Is Right*, which she called "the big game," and I practiced my Greek with her during commercials. She called me *paidi mou*, my child, a nickname doused in kindness.

But she was the kind of woman neighborhood children mythologized and feared, like a witch or a strange hermit. Then again, in our little patch of New Jersey, anyone who didn't speak English and dressed in black *was* a witch or a strange hermit. In my goth-and-punk teen years, I was called a witch so often, you'd have thought I went to high school in 1692.

And she didn't do much to dispel the myths. *Yiayia* claimed to have eyes in the back of her head—a line she said so often it would've made a great center square on a bingo card—and though she almost never left the house, man, that lady knew when I was up to no good: when I pilfered quarters from my parents' water jug to buy penny candy, when I tried out curse words in the anonymity of the woods by our house. At evening's end, I watched as she removed her teeth and placed them in a glass on the nightstand, stunned by a woman able to remove her own mouth.

Though she adored me, her stay fertilized my shame, a perennial bulb that grew in my chest. I knew it wasn't her fault she'd lived a quiet villager's life, that her world had been small, but I resented that she only made me feel like more of a misfit. I didn't consider how truly difficult it must've been for her: a woman with no education, no husband, no money, and sometimes, no food. It never occurred to me that all those challenges made her the most interesting person I knew. Instead, I was too busy worrying about how she might affect me, how her very presence might spill the secret that I wasn't like the other kids. *At least she stayed in the house*, I thought. My lone friend, Gina, didn't come over anymore. The previous summer, we'd wandered into the basement in search of Popsicles, but when we opened the industrial-size freezer—a perk my father had brought home (or stolen) from his diner job—a full, intact goat head stared back at us. There was a good chance no one would even see my *yiayia*, I reasoned.

But then more Greeks came.

In June 1986, the five of us drove up the terrifically dull New Jersey Turnpike to JFK. My father and *yiayia* led the way in his new-smelling Buick—a car he'd bought himself as a Valentine's gift for my mother— and I sat in the back of my mom's beat-up Ford, periodically kicking

Mike's seat. The acoustics of our car's backfiring resonated over both sides of the Verrazzano, echoing between Brooklyn and Staten Island, and we sat idle and stifled in unair-conditioned traffic, windows up, wavy sheets of exhaust surrounding us. With my hair stuck to my neck, I worried. This new family would be weird. I just knew it. I kicked Mike's seat again.

I was certain I'd recognize my cousins, though I'd only seen one picture of them that peeled at its edges, a photo that showed the boys, Theodoros and Dimitri, standing on a dirt road, hands to foreheads, squinting against the sun. They looked sweet enough, I thought, but no one sends photos overseas of their kids acting like dicks. At the international gate everyone looked alike to my young eyes: olive skin, dark hair, hugging and loud and talking so fast it sounded like wind blowing against my ears. It wasn't until my father jumped up and nearly knocked a woman over with his embrace that I knew who my family was.

His sister, Georgia, was a rougher version of him, squarer and squat, a bulldog of a woman. She flashed a smile at us, her canine teeth prominent and pointed, both of them yellow as tea. Behind her, two brothers who had spent sixteen claustrophobic hours likely tormenting each other and passengers alike were exchanging punches in the shoulder, their misbehavior ignored in the shadow of a reunion seventeen years in the making.

The teenager, Theodoros, strutted in a black tee with a Greek flag on it and a red imitation-leather jacket like the one Michael Jackson had rocked in "Thriller" three years earlier. I bet he thought, *You know what'll make me cool in America?* when getting dressed for his trip, not realizing MJ had already moved on to his military look. With thin eyes and a hooked nose, he reminded me of a terrible Greek rat. Dimitri stood behind him, his cheeks puffed as an autumn squirrel's, his mouth surrounded by sticky blue goo. At maybe ten or eleven years old, he looked softer than his brother, a boy who might take a punch for you.

Georgia walked over to me with a slight limp, bent at the waist, her face inches from mine, and said, *"Yiassou."* I said hello back, and the second I spoke, she snatched me into a hug and rocked her weight from side to side while humming. She smelled of mothballs and meatballs.

The Greeks, to my relief, piled into my father's car. Their luggage filled both trunks and our back seat, cocooning me in a small fort. I must have dozed off because I awoke first to my mother's horn, then to her cursing. I tunneled my head through the baggage to get a glimpse of what was happening. She laid on the horn again, flashed her high beams, and accidentally turned on the wipers.

"Son of a bitch."

"What's wrong?" I asked.

"Can't they see the sign says Connecticut?"

We followed them north for an hour, honking and flashing lights, before they realized their mistake. No, they didn't see the sign. They were instead consumed by family.

$\sim$

According to *Britannica Junior*'s subsection titled "The Family the World Over":

> In all families parents control the lives of their children for a period of time. In this parent-child relationship, the parent has physical strength, the means of providing a living, and the power of punishment. A mother or father can withhold or give affection, which is the basis for the feeling of belonging.

Georgia and her sons were slated to spend the summer, and after a few days of living with them, I couldn't wait for August and prayed their stay didn't turn into half a decade too. Mike moved into my room with me, his twin mattress pressed against the other wall, and though I was annoyed to share my space, his presence let my muscles relax a notch. My father's hands, his breath, would not find me at three in the morning, not with his favorite child sleeping across the room.

Because I was nine in the summer of 1986, my memory of that time is like looking through a fogged windshield: I can see shapes on the other side of the glass, but none of them are precise. I assume we did things as a family—sat around the dinner table, maybe drove to the beach—but I don't remember that. I don't remember the difficulty of nine people sharing a single bathroom or the quiet moments in front of the television. My mother tells me that Pete, the boys' father, was also there, but I don't remember him either, an entire man erased.

What I remember is division.

The adults, none of whom seemed to work at the time (which can't be true), camped in the kitchen drinking coffee, chain-smoking, and laughing, my *yiayia* waiting for everyone's empty and upside-down demi-tasse cups to dry so she could read their fortunes in the grounds. But what no one else seemed to see—not my prognosticating *yiayia* or psychic mother—was that my cousins were bad. Not simply strange, as I'd originally feared, but bad in the way that boys who curse and spit and incessantly grab their private parts are. Boys who make you feel ashamed without you understanding why. Anytime I approached the kitchen table, my parents waved me away and without much thought tossed their new motto over their shoulders: *Go play with your cousins.* I would've preferred driving thumbtacks into my palms than spending time with them.

In ancient Greece, according to *Britannica Junior*, "the father had absolute power over his family and others living in the household." This was neither news to me nor so ancient. My father wielded the phrase "My house, my rules" like Zeus's lightning bolt: a thing to cower before. He was also a fan of the absurd aphorism "I say jump, you say how high!" As a child, I learned there is one right way to make a bed, to weed a garden, to scrub a floor. In the last case, it's on your knees, always on all fours, your face inches from the grout. Whenever my father pulled into the driveway, my mother quickly clamped the phone into its deck, the outside world disappearing the moment he appeared. Even my brother felt his wrath one time at dinner for eating spaghetti wrong—he failed to use a spoon when he was seven or so—and though I often held the majority of my father's attention, Mike, too, must have been screaming on the inside, because he raised his kid fist and gave my dad the finger. The lot of us were so surprised by his outrage that we couldn't help but laugh as Mike ran off to his room, punishing himself.

And though my brother was, indeed, the open favorite, the one who'd pass along my father's good family name, I'd wrongly assumed that favor was a fluke. I did not expect all Greek boys to get away with whatever they wished, but I should've known better. That year in Greek school, two of my male classmates snuck into the ladies' room and tied the strings of two tampons together to make cottony nunchucks, which they hurled at our teacher mid-lesson.

When would the bad behavior of boys stop surprising me?

The thing about these new Greeks is they were mobile. One day, while my mother was at work, Georgia, accustomed to doing her laundry by hand, flooded the kitchen with suds, and instead of using the ropes that ran the length of our backyard to dry her delicates, she strung them throughout the tree in our front yard, its branches draped with large white panties and brassieres—a sea of cotton lingerie lanterns drying in the breeze for everyone to see. Another time, she went for a walk through our neighborhood and began cooking when she returned— an activity that almost never ceased during her stay. Later that night, when she served dinner, a vegetable dish called *horta*, it turned out to be brimming with ingredients she'd found scattered along the road-sides, throughout overgrown fields, and in our neighbors' gardens. *Horti*culture. Weed and grass stew.

Like little brothers everywhere, Dimitri followed his big brother's cues, and for Theodoros, *playing* meant three things: attracting atten-tion, making my insides squirm, or breaking things. With the adults inside twenty feet away, we kids would gather on the lawn. I wanted so badly to contain the damage these two might do, but it was useless. About five minutes after arriving, Theodoros commandeered a bike from our shed and spent hours riding up and down our streets in his "Thriller" jacket, whooping as loud as he could past the homes of every-one I went to school with. He didn't shout words, just long yawps of glee to be out of his village, but he might as well have been yelling, "LISA'S A FREAK AND I'M THE EVIDENCE!" Despite ten years of pains to keep my weirdness hidden, my summer had been claimed by Greece, and I could feel the blue-and-white flag protruding from the center of my forehead, waving at everyone who passed by.

Outdoors, my preferred pastime was flipping over rocks or logs to study the pulsing microcosms that lay beneath, but the boys' hobby was procuring shame. Theodoros and Dimitri ran loops around me on the front lawn, trapping me in a tight spiral. They circled and circled, whispering and taunting in Greek, pointing, giggling, pinching my ass, pointing at my crotch until I wept, frozen and unable to escape them. Eventually I thought of them not as individuals but as Orthrus, the two-headed cattle dog of mythology, a creature hell-bent on herding me into submission. They both made me want a hot shower and the power of Medusa.

But when faced with their parents or my father, they oozed angelic charm, false as a nun in a brothel. Because I was perpetually under my father's scrutiny, I was often in trouble—for things I both did and didn't do. That there was no comeuppance for my cousins, that they were given a Greek boys-will-be-boys pass, forced a raw noun to sizzle below my skin: *injustice*. It burned brighter with each passing second the two of them lived in our home.

One evening, the adults drove to Atlantic City to see a show. Of all the possible events—a good band, a musical, a guy on a sidewalk with a ukulele—they went to see Lynda Carter's stage show. Lynda Carter of *Wonder Woman* fame. Why anyone thought a bunch of Greeks who spoke no English would enjoy that is baffling, although I guess that, technically, she was an Amazon. Still. That meant the rest of us were left with a babysitter, Kristy, an acned, boy-crazed teen who was probably getting five bucks an hour and spoke passable English at best, as her every third word was *like*.

It started with pizza and MTV, a solid combo, but at some point, it grew quiet, the cousins gone, and Kristy sent me to look for them. I found them in the basement, a space that doubled as my mother's dance studio, where she taught five-dollar Jazzercise lessons after her waitressing shifts. With joy, they snapped her vinyl in half, the floor littered with triangular black shards. I yelled at them to stop and told them they'd be in trouble (an empty threat if ever there was one), but they held eye contact as they continued destroying my mother's things. Back upstairs, I did what any frustrated kid would do: I ratted them out. But Kristy was no match for them. She couldn't understand them—who could?—yet she managed to herd them upstairs. She smiled at me—a

See, everything's okay grin of sympathy—but the boys promptly barricaded themselves in my bedroom. The locks in our house were easily picked—a fingernail in the slot and turn—but someone was leaning against the door. Mike and I slapped our hands red yelling at them to let us in. When the door finally opened, Theodoros stood there and smiled, his eyes lit with malice. Behind him on the floor, our toys lay in a broken heap: dismembered dolls, the filling torn from stuffed animals, anything plastic snapped in two. A pain like a hammer hit my temples—my undiagnosed migraines—and as the boys left, laughing, I got on my knees and squeezed my head between the door and the frame, that pressure the only way I knew to grab relief.

But they weren't through. Nope. They went outside and continued their spree, smashing everything they touched and making so much noise that a decent neighbor would've called the cops. Kristy stood on the front step yelling; she might as well have been a bird letting loose a song into the night.

By the time the adults returned, Kristy had been locked in the bathroom for hours. I'd gotten Mike to bed, though he couldn't brush his teeth, and I lay in the darkness, eyes open, waiting. I knew better than to get out of bed after midnight, but I listened from the hallway as Kristy sniffled her report to my parents while my father translated for his sister and her husband. *The parent has physical strength, the means of providing a living, and the power of punishment.* I thought my father would destroy them—grab the boys by their ears and smack them until they wept their apologies. But my father couldn't punish another man's children. I imagine everyone looked at the boys' father, prepared to see an explosion. Instead, he was so embarrassed by his sons' behavior, he took a long walk.

That was their punishment. My mother found this so absurd, she still brings it up, but what was she to do? A woman—some other kids' mother—had no power over Greek boys. I wasn't sure anyone did.

While their father walked our lamplit streets, I heard the boys in the next bedroom, laughing in the darkness.

Mercifully, they cut their trip short, and when they piled into the car for the airport and waved goodbye, the cousins sticking out their tongues, I looked only at my *yiayia* sitting rigid in the passenger's seat and cried quietly. Later in my adult life, when nightmares of my father still plagued me, my *yiayia* would occasionally show up in a dream, her image precisely as it was in 1986, though my subconscious kindly strips away her crutches. She has come to me in my sleep four times, each when I needed her most, and in that dream space she is able to accomplish what I'd longed for while she lived with us: she made my father behave.

Once his family left, my father soured. He couldn't return to Greece; he'd jumped ship during his obligatory military time in the merchant marine. If he were to go back, even for a visit, he was sure he'd never make it through customs, that he'd be shipped from the airport directly to jail like some Hellenic version of Monopoly. I don't know how true that was, but when my *yiayia* lay on her deathbed in Crete some years later, my father did not risk going back. The day she left us in New Jersey was our last with her, and the best we could do as a family was to step into the narthex at St. Thomas Orthodox Church, light a candle, and jam it into the soft sand before an oversize stained-glass Mary. I always lit one for myself too. I'm still not sure if that's allowed, but I didn't think god would mind if I gamed the system. After all, I needed all the help I could get.

CHAPTER 3

GAMES

The children are pale and dimpled, plucked from *My Three Sons* or *The Donna Reed Show*. Predictably, the girls wear skirts, the boys slacks, all of them topped with thick coifed hair and radiant joy. In two of the photos they hold hands—in a circle, in a line—and in the third, three boys grit their teeth and lean in the posture of tug-of-war. *Britannica Junior* lists hide-and-seek, tag, dodgeball, and hopscotch, but most of the pages are filled with games I'd never heard of: ball statue, apple snatch, the worrisome Sitting Down Jerusalem.

The most mystifying definition is "Blind Man's Bluff," which reads: "May be played by groups of 15 to 30. There are so many varieties of this game and so many people are familiar with it that it hardly requires description." It is, perhaps, the laziest entry ever to appear in an encyclopedia. You can almost feel the author sighing, *Ugh. Why bother?* The first line of "Games" is, "Did you ever invent any games?" Yes. Blind Man's Bluff. Because I had no idea what it was. I pictured a herd of children, bandannas 'round their eyes, edging toward a cliff, wondering who would chicken out before plummeting over the ledge. In retrospect, it is lucky I did not have fifteen to thirty friends.

Alone with my stuffed animals, I played hospital: Nurse Bunny and Dr. Bear losing their patients at an alarming rate. Eventually, they'd swoop in and stitch up Quackers, the mallard duck in constant need of surgery. I also ran a perpetual game of beat the clock. Take out the garbage? Get a can of green beans from downstairs? *WATCH HOW FAST I AM.* I'd hustle back to my starting position, panting, certain I'd beaten my previous record, though I never actually timed it. In a black leotard and pink tights, I watched myself in the basement mirrors as I performed pliés and jetés and pirouettes and Stop! Hammer time! until I broke a sweat and awarded myself Best Dancer in the World. Take a bow, curtsy, wave to your invisible fans. The lonely games of a kid who needed desperately to be told she was good.

Together Mike and I set up Monopoly, Battleship, Parcheesi, and, once, the incredibly tedious Mouse Trap. I cheated every chance I got, my right as the oldest, and my brother smartly quit playing board games, so we created our own. At the kitchen table after school, our parents absent, we saw who could stuff the most grapes into their mouth, then slapped our overstuffed cheeks with our palms to spray one another with pulp and juice. Once, in the bathroom, we came up with a more disgusting version and soaked our small socks in the tub before shoveling them in, our chins dripping through giggles with warm bathwater and saliva. But we played best together on the open sand of the beach.

Since the days of my mother's youth, her family has rented a summerhouse on Long Beach Island, New Jersey, a tradition that continues today. I stopped going in my twenties, but as a child, I loved our vacations for their anonymity. The adults, busy mixing gin and tonics and sucking the meat from boiled blue crabs, lost sight of the kids, so I'd wander the island—the overpriced merchant shops at Bay Village, their storefronts crawling with hermit crabs; the disappointing food court at Pier 18, a place that could've been called Everything's Fried; the dizzying kiddie casino at Fantasy Island: poker and claw games and the nonstop clatter of tokens falling into slots. But the real pleasure lay in the fact that no one knew me or my father. By day, we'd tan and swim and dig for mole crabs, not climbing back up the dunes until the ice-cream man showed up peddling Drumsticks and Bomb Pops. But at sunset, we became superheroes.

Before leaving the beach to cook dinner, my mother tied towels around our necks, kissed us on the head, and blammo—I was Wonder Woman, Mike was Superman. Had we known then that in 2013, DC Comics would expand their story line to include romance, we'd have chosen different characters, spat at one another in disgust. But with the sun slung low above the water, the sky blazing pink and orange, we chased one another over sandcastles and climbed the empty lifeguard chairs to jump full of abandon onto the soft sand below. Then we played a game of paddleball, our capes allowing us to make more magnificent saves than our mortal selves could ever muster. Eventually, we wandered home, coated in sand and starving, our muscles ringing from laughter.

But the beach was not without its troubles.

The four of us, two sets of aunts and uncles, their children, and my grandmother all shared a space, usually a three- or four-bedroom home, and on rainy days we couldn't escape one another, so we settled in for naps and games of Rummikub or UNO!, waiting for the showers to pass. My father charmed the family and hid his rage, but his ease was cultivated. Like a pot smoker flushing his system before a drug test, he prepared to pass as good by purging himself of the bad. Like the summer I was ten, the night before we left for the shore. A night my father visited my bedroom.

Sound woke me, a scrape or scratch, and I scanned my room for its source but found nothing. Had there been something in my space, I'd have woken up. Even today, the moment someone is outside my bedroom door—before they touch the handle—I am awake. When I heard the noise again, I sat up, and it took time for the sound to take shape, like looking at a wedge of magnified nectarine, at first just orange but then so clearly fruit. A sliver of my father's face came into focus; he stood outside my bedroom window in the garden, watching me through the slit in my curtains, petting the screen's mesh with his fingernail. When I went to the window, I knew something was wrong: my body heated up.

"Forgot my keys," he slurred. "Let me in." He pointed toward the front door. I followed his finger and saw his van in the driveway. If he'd lost his keys, how did he drive home?

In the dark, I stumbled to the living room, unlocked the door, and ran back to my bed. I thought if I moved quickly enough he might forget I existed.

His silhouette appeared before he closed the door, and I felt the weight of him on the end of my bed. My body burned, hot to the touch, heat like pins pricking every millimeter of my skin. And then there's nothing.

Lisa Nikolidakis

There's no icky scene, not because I won't type it but because dissociation arrived welcome as a breeze. Trauma is a manipulator of time, and sexual trauma is pockmarked with gulches of blank space and overlap. I don't consciously think of this as the first time—factually, I can almost certainly say it wasn't—but it's one in which the before, during, and after remain tethered to memory. Before—the creep of his fingernail against the screen. During—my body on the bed, trapped beneath my father, my mind elsewhere, anywhere but present. After—me motionless, staring at the ceiling for hours, my eyes adjusted to the dark while on the other side of my bedroom wall my father snored in bed next to my mother. If I tried, I could block out the sound of him, so for a bit I hummed a made-up tune and flipped the pillow to cool my boiling body down. I hummed some more but stopped when a new sound arrived: a cricket in the wall by my head chirped. Sure enough, far away as maybe the kitchen, another cricket answered. I pictured them playing their wings like violins and rubbed one of my feet against the other. It was noiseless, my motion, but maybe deeper in the house someone would hear my call and respond.

The next morning we left for Long Beach Island, and that evening we sat in a restaurant shaped like a ship and ordered our favorite seafood—a pile of tender scallops for me. The place was packed, the clamor too loud, so I drifted away again, far from the table. When we got back home, I locked myself in the bathroom and rubbed between my legs until my skin turned raw, red, swollen, and sharp with pain. I rubbed for release. I rubbed to erase myself. I rubbed until I passed out on the tile floor, ashamed of what I was: a girl broken.

I awoke scratching, blood caked beneath my nails, and went to find my mother. From my scalp to the bottoms of my feet, my body was covered in a pink blanket of hives, the itchiness so intense I wanted to climb out of myself and into a cool glass of milk. She took me to the hospital, where a doctor kindly gave me a shot of Benadryl and something else after it, something I barely remember because I was already nodding off. On the edge of the hospital bed, my mother sat stroking my hair. I rolled over and away from her into the greatest sleep I'd gotten in my young life, my brain drugged, my hypervigilance turned off. The world went black for nearly twenty-four hours, and when I came to, I found the family had already written the mythology to explain what was wrong with me: I must have eaten a bad scallop.

⌒⃝

A few weeks after the beach trip, my father again entered my bedroom, and my body stiffened. He sat on the far corner of the bed and for too long stayed quiet, the only sound my pulse thumping in my ears. In my throat, my breath hitched until I felt the bed tremble. He would not touch me that night. Instead, he wept.

"I am so sorry I hurt you," he cried. "I don't want to hurt you. Ever. You must believe me."

"I believe you," I said quietly.

"I need you to forgive. Promise me you will forgive." He inhaled, the sputtering sound of snot. His warm hand wrapped around my ankle, and silent tears dripped from my eyes into my ears.

"I promise you: never again," he said, and he sounded so sincere, so absolutely remorseful, that I said, "I forgive you," and in the dark we hugged and wept against one another's shoulders.

I remember nearly a dozen such apologies from those years, each of them cried and slumped, his head held and bowed until I offered forgiveness. I always did, partly because it got him out of my room, but mostly because I believed him. To see grief so close up, to inspect it and work out the algebra of its accuracy, filled me with shame, as though lying near his shame released its contagion. Perhaps it is because I was present for the very acts that provoked my father's remorse and allowed such devastation to rise up and out of him. I don't know. But I do know that when he apologized, I believed him. I had to. Without the hope he would stop, without the belief he was capable of controlling himself, I had no reason to live.

⌒

I know some folks think of family reunions as joyous occasions—barbecues or weekends filled with sun and booze and reminiscing about the good ol' days—but I am still uncomfortable in a room with my family, the weight of all they don't know worn like a Ghillie suit.

A year or so before the beach trip, my mother's side of the family met at a resort in Virginia, and again my father purged his badness the night before performing his good-guy act. In the back seat of the car the next day, I pressed my forehead to the cool window, the landscape changing from oaks and pines to Eastern redbuds and dogwoods. I hadn't slept in a day and a half. I was ten.

The resort was a dark-paneled hotel, like a ski lodge in summer, a new space to explore, so many places to hide. Quickly I found the horses, animals I still go to when I am stressed, and while I was too scared to ride, I inched close enough to kiss their furry muzzles. Relatives had flown in from all over the world—Venezuela, Germany, the West Coast—and at the party, ever-present predictable food floated by on silver trays: squares of marbled cheese on Ritz crackers, rolls of lunch meat spread out like fans, shrimp hugging their pools of cocktail sauce. No *taramasalata*, no *dolmades*, certainly no animal with a face rotating on a spit. These pasty adults were, somehow, also my family: redheaded and freckled, people allergic to the sun of high noon. I didn't see how I fit in with them.

My mother's sister, Christie, has long been the family organizer, and she'd devised activities, I assume, to keep everyone from drinking themselves stupid or, perhaps, because it would be funnier to watch people try one hand at dexterity while sloshing their cocktails in the other. First up was a game of family Double Dare. Yes. Like the 1980s Nickelodeon show.

In a wide and scorching field, we gathered beneath the July sun as Christie explained the rules for each event. But the last thing I wanted to do was play with my father. We might as well have been tied together in a three-legged race—an event mercifully absent—while he ran at full speed, dragging my kid body along for the bumpy ride. I excelled at disappearing into the background, at remaining unnoticed, but Double Dare was too much; everyone watched my fake fun, my father cheering me on, my isolation never deeper.

As the game broke up, my father still coursed with adrenaline.

"Wanna race?" he asked, but I knew better. I'd seen him sprint, and his speed was superhuman. He'd told us about the time he'd run faster than a motorcycle in Crete. Did I look dumb?

"No way," I said. "You'll win."

"You don't know. C'mon." He smiled. I scanned the open field.

"Where to?"

"The fence." A baseball field away. Better just to do it. I nodded.

"Ready . . . set . . . ," he said, and before "go," he took off.

I ran after him, the cheater, and he got so far ahead that he spun 'round to trot backward.

"Come on," he said. "You're faster than this."

Pushing off harder, I gained a little ground and took the lead, but he took it back almost immediately. We volleyed like that, as though the race were actually close. He let me touch the fence first. A mercy. We collapsed onto the freshly mown lawn.

"You're good, you," he said and smiled, so I smiled back at him, and from a distance it probably appeared to be a lovely moment. But as I grinned, my muscles tightened. From afar, it looked like play, but I knew the truth: it was all part of his game to keep me guessing at what kind of person he was, at what was coming next. As we found our breath, I worked on decoding his hidden message until it came to me so clearly that I had to turn my head so he wouldn't see me cry. *We don't do this for fun*, I thought, staring out at the wide and cloudy sky. My palms were pressed flat against the ground. Blades of grass made my wrists itch. *We do everything to hurt something. We run to crush the grass. We run to crush each other.*

Recently, my aunt texted me a photo from that day. In the foreground, on a mustard-colored couch, sit three adults and two toddlers. Two of the adults smile for the camera—the man with teeth, the woman without. My uncle pays attention to the child on his lap, and to the right of the frame, two more adults in pumpkin-orange sweatshirts hover. I am directly behind everyone, centered and alone, my gaze off to the right of the room, no doubt keeping a lookout for my father. Beneath my eyes sink enormous black half-moons, and my skin is sallow, drawn. I look a bit like the swarthy ghost who's haunting her own family.

As I stared at my aunt's text, part of me wanted to do what I've always done: blow it off, make myself invisible. *What does it matter now?* I chastised myself, but I couldn't let it go, so I wrote back: "Look at my eyes. Zoom in." My pulse quickened as I waited for her response.

"Oh god, Lisa. You weren't okay." I looked at those words until they blurred. Even now, thirty years later, her recognition made me cry. That's how important it is for our pain to be spoken, to be cradled by someone else's tongue.

That weekend, my parents argued fiercely. By the time I was eleven, they fought the way adults do: believing they're successfully hiding it from the kids, not realizing how far their hushed bass travels—through walls, into new rooms, down hallways, and around corners. I don't know what their argument was about, though I can guess. Despite my mother being the best possible sport when his family visited, he picked a fight with her over something trivial because he couldn't acknowledge his truth: when he wasn't at the center of things, he felt small. A venom he didn't understand filled his throat. To avoid choking, he spat it at whomever was closest, swelling with self-loathing disguised as self-importance.

My father left the reunion early—a confusing detail. How did he get home? Did he take the car? If yes, how did we get home? All I know is that later in the day, I was in a suite with the women of my family, my father gone, the air light as helium. Woozy from lack of sleep, I sat down at a vanity with a revolving oval mirror, delighted by how fancy real ladies' things were. I looked on as my grandmother placed a hand on my crying mother's shoulder, a quick touch of consolation, and just as quickly had to look away from that tenderness. I turned my gaze to my own reflection, the sun catching the mirror at the same time, and jumped when I saw it:

in place of my own face, the visage of a haggard old woman stared back at me—a me full of wrinkles and age and hardship.

Instead of seeing myself as the child I was, I looked at a ruined woman. It scared me so much that I tried to explain it to my mother, but she couldn't concentrate on me, on my weird story. She had her own problem, a marriage boiling over, so I snuck out of the room and went back to the horses. I pressed my hand against the warm brown shoulder of a mare and whispered to her, *Everything's going to be okay.*

◌

"Each environment calls for its own games," *Britannica Junior* says. "Children in the country will play different games from those in town. Again, the home and the school call for games of a different kind." At school, I tried to be a cheerleader, as if pom-poms might make up for everything else, but despite my years of dance training, I wasn't one of those girls. They could smell my difference. Year after year I tried out— how funky is *your* chicken?—and every time I found my name on the cut list, even the year my mother was a guest judge. Finally, in eighth grade, they took pity on me and made me an alternate. In my mother's girdle, I squeezed into my sweater and bloomers, hurrahing from the sidelines at every basketball game my classmates played, occasionally used for my sturdiness, a thick base for a pyramid of spirited wafer girls.

At home, my primary game was Amateur Sleuth, which I played every moment of the day, watching and listening to everything closely in order to deduce what might happen next. Footsteps in the hallway: Heavy or soft? My mother's or father's? Bathroom or bedroom? The weight of doors closing, the slight difference between casual and angry. Quietly opening a locked door, or fumbling, cursing. The scent of beer, whiskey, and ouzo, each of them distinct, sour or sweet when leached out of pores. The hum of an electric razor, cologne in the air, the faint wood and vanilla of Old Spice, the best signs my father would leave the house.

But even when he wasn't home, he was. In my mind, every corner of the house was under his surveillance, and those imaginary cameras lived on until my early thirties. Alone in my room or the kitchen or even outdoors, I played as though being watched. I feared if I didn't, that would be the moment my father surprised me. One time I was outside and realized my tank top was on backward. No one was around, so I twisted it right there on the street, but my arms got tangled in the straps, my undeveloped chest exposed, and when I looked up, my father stared at me through our screen door. I turned like I hadn't seen him, casual, a girl out observing birds, but I felt the blood vessels of my face open wide, my cheeks undoubtedly scarlet.

I never heard my father speak of the games of his youth, but there is a game Greek children play called "round round all." Everyone holds hands in a circle, at the center of which one child stands with their back to a chair. The children in the circle sing a taunting, rhyming song, and when they're through, they let go of their hands and sit while someone tries to kick the chair out from beneath the center kid, making them fall on their ass. If they fall, they remain in the center. If they don't, the child who failed to make them fall takes their place. *Children in the country will play different games from those in town.*

In the United States, we'd call the child at the center "it." The Greeks call that child Manolis. My father's name. Manny in English.

Shove aside that this seems like a game of *bullying*. Imagine growing up and everyone knowing a song in which your name is synonymous with *loser*. The entire point of the game is to not be Manolis. Perhaps that's what my father wanted too. He said he came to America for opportunity, but who knows when the idea first struck him. Maybe he was a kid tired of being teased. Maybe so much teasing is what made him a master of it. Wouldn't that be something? So many lives wrecked by a man who never got over his playground ridicule.

∽

There are no card games in *Britannica Junior*'s entries, but my father shuffled and dealt with such ease that you knew he'd played his whole life, most certainly on the last day of Decembers in Greece, where cards are part of the holiday ritual. "Many lands follow interesting traditions on New Year's," my encyclopedia claims, and among my father's annual New Year's customs was being kind. Guaranteed. That made it my favorite holiday, even in those preteen years when everything seemed so wrong.

After dinner, we cleared the table of its place mats and centerpiece, and the three of us—Mike, my father, and I—sat down to a card game that lasted well into the night. For Greeks, New Year's is a time of luck and fortune, with many people practicing *kali hera*. The literal translation is "good hand," and one's hand is deemed good by being generous to children. My father bankrolled us, and Mike and I pawed at our sleeve of quarters, greedily gulping down the soda we weren't usually allowed to drink.

"I'm gonna take every penny you got," I said to Mike, who looked to our father for help, but he shrugged it off.

"She's good, this one," he said and motioned to me with his thumb. I smiled and swung my feet.

We warmed up with easier games—a few rounds of Crazy Eights and Go Fish—the new deck still crisp, but after an hour or so, we moved on to poker and blackjack. My father, as always, dealt.

"Oof," he said after looking at his hand. "These cards is terrible." He winked, and Mike and I dropped more change into the pot. We played for hours, our stacks of silver growing taller and shorter, but my father never let us lose for too long.

When he stood and walked to the counter, we hoped for cake, but it wasn't time yet. Instead, he brought back a pomegranate.

"Ready?" he asked.

We nodded and silently prayed for a massive pile of seeds to spill out from the tough red skin, another sign of good fortune. With a thwack that made our quarters topple, he smashed the fruit against the table's lip. Leaning in, we examined it together.

"This," my father said. "This is a nice one. Our year looks good!" He slid us each a napkin with a handful of seeds on it.

"What you think, Garifalitsa?" I hated when he used my Greek name, but it wasn't the time for protesting. I studied him, his cheerful face, his eyes full of light, and anything seemed possible.

"Yes," I concluded. "Our best year."

"That's my girl," he said and shook my shoulder.

"What about you, Mihali?" he asked my brother.

"Definitely," Mike said.

We played hand after hand until midnight, when we counted down the old year, and the appearance of the *vassilopita* made us stop caring about cards. My father carved the sign of the cross with a knife on the cake's surface before slicing it, and we ate our pieces quickly, searching for the baked-in quarter that guaranteed a year's worth of luck. At the metal clink of it against my teeth, I grinned.

Scowling, Mike helped himself to another slice, his chin dusted with powdered sugar.

"One whole year," my father said and picked me up. He spun me around, my feet swinging out from my body, circling until we were dizzy, locked in a joyous waltz.

"Tell me," he said. "How you get so lucky?"

CHAPTER 4

DANCE

When I was in second grade, my father knocked on my bedroom door and leaned against the frame. From his neck swung a gold chain with a cross, Jesus's tiny feet nestled comfortably in his chest hair, the Greek men I've known never meeting a button that needs fastening. He presented me with a matter-of-fact question: "There is Greek classes at church. You wanna go?"

Of course I was supposed to say yes. Yes, I want to learn everything I can about your language, about your culture, about philosophy and art and basic civilization—all the things the Greeks take credit for. Yes, I want to connect with you.

I nodded, and my father grinned widely.

"You really are the best girl," he said and put his hand to his heart. When he left, I, too, grinned, adding ten, fifty, a hundred points to the mental tally of things I did that would make my father love me.

What I didn't know was I'd just committed to two and a half hours each Tuesday and Thursday for *six* interminable years at the St. Thomas Orthodox Church—a place that comfortably blended belief in god, mythology, and nationalism into the same lessons. A sample chapter title from one of my old textbooks is "Greece Is the Most Glorious

Nation in the World." A few pages later is "The Tortoise and the Hare." At the end of the book is a lesson we'd never reached that featured a shaky line drawing of the crucifixion. I may have drawn horns and a cloud of pubic hair on our lord and savior.

During my sixth and final year of Greek school, our primary jobs were clear and twofold: (1) tell everyone how great Greece is, and (2) dance at the agora, the annual fall festival. According to *Britannica Junior*:

> All the European countries have great varieties of folk dances . . . Folk dances, being of peasant origin and danced originally out of doors or in barns with rough floors, are rarely gliding. They are more a matter of jumping and stomping and other vigorous movements.

I can assure you, we did not glide.

From years of taking dance classes with my mother, I picked up choreography quickly, but in the States, we moved to an eight count. Greeks count music to twelve. The difference might seem small, but it confounded me. One bar of dance could go: step right, left over right, left behind right, step, step, stomp, jump, hop, left over right, left behind right, jump again. If that sentence makes no sense to you, I assure you, it made little sense to me either, but those moves seemed to be in the other kids' DNA, like they'd *opa*'d their way out of the womb.

In class, we spent an hour learning how to conjugate important verbs—to eat, to pray, to conquer—then moved into a large banquet room to practice. In a massive circle, I held the clammy hands of two Georges and stepped foot over foot to music my classmates sang along to. I silently mouthed made-up lyrics, but two truths boiled inside me: I was too Greek for American school, too American for Greek school. As the child of an immigrant, I forever straddled the line between the Old World and the New, one shaky foot in each territory. At least my

Greek classmates were impressed by the pom-poms I brought with me. *Oh, these? I just came from practice.* An easy lie for popularity.

At the agora, the air thick with the gaminess of goat and honey of desserts, my class waited in the hallway for our musical cue. We were the graduating class—the best dancers Greek New Jersey had to offer—and at the strike of bow to lyra, we leapt onto the center of the hardwood auditorium, the crowd whooping and clapping as we circled and stomped and changed formations to highlight the jumping abilities of different boys. As we spun, our arms linked, I scanned for my father, for the proud smile I was certain to find behind the small Greek flags everyone waved. I looked and looked and looked. Later, our dance long over, my mother and I found him arguing with a man in the parking lot.

"You were great, sweetie," she said. I wanted to ask, *How would you even know? You're not Greek!* But she said, "Let's get a gyro," so we stood in line in one of the tents while my father remained locked in disagreement on the asphalt. At the end of a plastic folding table, I frowned and plucked the onions from my pita. Around us, the buzz of families sharing joy.

"You know you can tell me anything," she said.

I looked up and met her soft eyes, then looked toward the parking lot, toward him.

"I know," I said, my voice small. I'd spent six years trying to win his affection through Greece, and it had failed. I ground my teeth and made a decision: this was it. After today, I would never speak Greek to my father again. I didn't have much, but I could deny him his mother tongue, leave him screaming at me to answer him in *his* language. Never. Again.

My mother interrupted my fuming by cupping my hand in hers. "You really were great," she said, but she, too, stared out at the parking lot, her shoulders high.

In the late '80s, my mother balanced waitressing shifts with the dance classes she taught both in our house and at a proper studio called Diana's. After asking her boss for a twenty-five-cent raise that was denied, my mother chucked her apron, gathered the students that weekly visited our basement for Jazzercise, took out a loan, and opened her own dance center in a plaza next to my middle school. A third of Diana's enrollment followed her, and her business was born. Diana's eventually died.

Tap, jazz, and ballet: I'd danced since the age of three. More often than not, my mother was my teacher. I never saw Saturday morning cartoons, my weekends spent pulling on tights and a leotard, preparing to spend the day at the studio, watching my mom teach the toddlers in the morning, the teens in the afternoon, the same songs on repeat for so much of my childhood that I can still recite the pitiful lyrics to "Bumpy Train," or, as I did yesterday, every single word to DeBarge's "Rhythm of the Night." My mother believed in teaching ballet with French terminology, though I misheard it all. As a class we were supposed to repeat *battement*, but I yelled *Batman*. When my mother shouted *glissade*, I heard only the music of my name in her mouth.

In middle school, we had to make a step stool in woodshop, and I gripped a burning pen to carve a pair of ballet slippers into the grain, a gift for my mother, one she still has in her kitchen. More than anything, I longed to be a ballerina-lawyer, to balance grace with argument, a perfect blend of my experiences with my mother and father. I imagined I'd fight for my clients' injustices in a tutu, *en pointe*. In my room, I cloaked Dr. Bear in the black towel my mother used to dye her hair and shouted at him, *Your Honor, I object!* Then I arabesque'd my way to victory.

For the grand opening, we decorated my mother's studio with balloons and flag bunting, its triangles stretching a lipless rainbow grin across the room. I stenciled my mother's logo on her pink wall in black acrylic: four impossibly skinny silhouettes, from the tallest with her leg stretched above her head in *développé* to a woman in a V-sit, her legs forty-five degrees off the ground without so much as a trembling muscle. My mother booked Jazzworks, the award-winning company she belonged to, and gave the people of South Jersey a taste of how great dance could be.

My mother and I used to ride the train into Philadelphia, and while her troupe practiced for three or four hours, I wandered the city blocks, stepping into La Boulangerie for a croissant, ignoring my mother's advice to avoid eye contact with the homeless, dropping my change into their coffee cups. Our house was twenty minutes from Philly, but it might as well have been a different planet. I perpetually hoped she would finish rehearsal and say, *Let's stay here.*

The Jazzworks dancers were nothing like the wholesome Gene Kelly or Fred Astaire I'd grown up watching. They were cleavage and slick-bodied, grunt and innuendo. But with all that talent crammed onto one floor, I couldn't take my eyes off my mother, her movements so quick, so sharp, her body fully in her control. I wanted to be her: to teach thirty-five classes a week; to come home after nine, damp and wrapped in Lycra; to eat half a grapefruit and six ounces of grilled chicken breast for dinner. I wanted to be thin, to see my ribs stabbing through my leotard, to suck in my stomach and walk tall, my neck stretched swan long. I wanted to flip through catalogs like *Costume Gallery* and *Curtain Call* and plan an entire show, execute my vision. I wanted a head stuffed full of choreography, not the dumb stories I made up—something other people could see and applaud.

My mother and I danced together so many times that it's impossible to tally. We'd hit the stage, the spotlights warming us, our sequins and eye shadow sparkling all the way to the back row, then we'd wink at one another before ball changing and *jeté*-ing, hitting our marks, nailing our formations. Sometimes through a gritted smile, we'd *pas de bourrée* near one another and say, *Oh shit*, if we missed a cue, the audience unaware of our exchange, that moment making everything okay. It remains a mystery to me how we could be so in sync onstage and so utterly staccato off.

I thought I'd wanted to be a dancer, to be like her, but what I really longed for was autonomy. Watching my mother grab hers drenched me with complicated pride. She was doing something for herself, something that didn't involve my father. Forget that a-woman's-place-is-in-the-home bullshit. My mother was getting hers. If I'd known the word *feminist* then, I'd have pumped my tiny fist in the air in solidarity. But it came at a cost, that autonomy, one she couldn't see. Of course she couldn't. She was gone more than she was home.

⁓

Mike and I were latchkey kids, though we wouldn't have called ourselves that—didn't even know the term. At first my mom hired a babysitter who lived on our street to watch us after school, but she was off—more likely *on* something—and at our first visit, she baked a frozen pizza upside down and stared into space while smoke filled the room. After that, we were on our own.

In the '80s, there lingered an ever-present rumor about a white van roaming the streets and snatching kids, so our job was to walk home quickly, no dillydallying, but I loved nothing more than moving slowly and inspecting nature. I could lose ten minutes to a leaf shaped like a fish, holding it by its stem with wonder as I made it swim in the air before me. If a robin crossed my path, I'd see how still I could hold to watch it gather pine needles and grass for its nest. I was also an accomplished rock kicker, best in the county.

Though no one had yet figured out that *stranger* rhymes with *danger*, it was clear the world believed that whatever was going to harm you was out there, at the hands of some unknown sicko brimming with evil intent. This wasn't entirely wrong. When I was four, a man called to tell me I'd won a beauty contest and asked for my address. *You're so beautiful,* he said. Once, my father was supposed to pick me up from gymnastics. I badly needed glasses, my vision so nearsighted that everything blurred, and I got into the wrong car. Instead of saying, *You've made a mistake, sweetie*, a man ran his palm up my prepubescent thigh until his fingers grazed my crotch. That man: someone else's father. From middle to high school, grown men flashed me four times that I can remember. One day I cut through a small patch of woods on my bike to buy penny candy and noticed a man hanging around. On my way back, he wagged his cock at me, aggressively grinning at my discomfort. Another time, two boys chased me into a different patch of woods while wielding a knife just to show me theirs. Another boy held a knife to my throat while he pinned me down; he was still so young that he seemed unsure of what to do next.

I could go on. And on.

And on. And on. And on. And on. And on. And on. And on. And on.
And on. And on. And on. And on. And on. And on. And on. And on.
And on. And on. And on. And on. And on. And on. And on. And on.
And on. And on. And on. And on. And on. And on. And on. And on.
And on. And on. And on. And on. And on. And on. And on. And on.
And on. And on. And on. And on. And on. And on. And on. And on.
And on. And on. And on. And on. And on. And on. And on. And on.
And on. And on. And on. And on. And on. And on. And on. And on.
And on. And on. And on. And on. And on. And on. And on. And on.
And on. And on. And on.

Really.

⁓

On my twelfth birthday, Mike and I got home to find a note tacked to the metal hood above the stove:

Hi sweetie. Sorry I had to work. Going to Doris' after.

We'll celebrate tomorrow. Call if you need anything. Happy birthday!

XOXO, Mom

In a crockpot, beef stew, the air sweet and fatty; in the fridge, a fudge-iced chocolate cake plugged with cool, unlit candles. No adults meant impolite gift opening—cards checked for money, not sentiment—and I squealed when I unveiled the Crayola 120 pack. After cake, Mike and I watched *Looney Tunes* and took turns saying, "You're despicable," intentionally coating one another in as much spit as possible, laughing until we begged for breath, our third empty glasses of soda stuck to the coffee table before us.

Later, Mike fell asleep on the floor of his bedroom, surrounded by He-Men. A split-open Castle Grayskull yawned by his stomach, so I covered him with a blanket; nothing woke him up. I studied the wall above his bed, jealous that he had talking animals on his wallpaper. "I wish I were a bird," said a pale elephant. A giraffe with a stubby neck longed to be a fireman. What a defeatist moral to put above a child's bed: *Psst! Hey, kid! Everyone wants the impossible.*

Back in the kitchen, I colored the wings of a Pegasus in flight, each minuscule loop of feather a different hue, pure delight in a fresh batch of crayons. Pegasus is supposed to be white, gleaming white, a white nearly intolerable to look at, but that great horse sprung from the blood of Medusa's decapitated head; I thought he should shine with color. When I finished, I left it on the edge of the couch for my mother, "happy birthday" scrawled in the corner. Hers is the day after mine.

Sometime into my homework, my father's headlights slapped the living room blinds, striping the walls and balloons and birthday. I listened. Everything I needed to know was coded in sound. Sometimes he'd make it all the way home and the only noise was the cough of the engine shutting off; the next morning, I'd find him slumped over the steering wheel and tiptoe past the driver's seat on my way to school. Other times the door closed quickly after arrival, a short bark of metal, and I'd run down the hall, dive into bed, and fake sleep. This time the headlights blew out, but I didn't hear the door. I listened hard, heard nothing. Still, I gambled that I was safe. It was my birthday, after all. The one day everyone had to be nice to me.

Eventually, a familiar thud: the knob of the front door dug into the living room wall, the hole in the Sheetrock long hollowed out. I glanced out the window and saw his van door remained open, its interior light on. A noiseless exit. At first he didn't see me, so I watched. He wavered like a man moving through dream water. He seemed to carry with him an enormous wind, and as he walked past the couch, my Pegasus swung to the ground. When he neared the kitchen, I held my breath, the kind you suck in when you drive past a cemetery, one that makes you feel invisible in your stillness. I hoped he'd hit the wall and turn toward the bedrooms, like those plastic ducks you shoot at the carnival, but he saw me, paused, and propped himself up against the doorframe. Beneath his armpits, the white ribbing of his undershirt bore yellow stains. Like tea, I thought. Or urine.

"Where's your mother?"

"Aunt Doris's." Her best friend. *Wish me a happy birthday*, I thought. *Say it. Say happy birthday.*

"Why arentcha in bed?"

I pointed to the open textbook. "Homework. Almost done."

He muttered something I didn't understand, a hybrid of Greek and English, then pushed his weight off the wall with one hand. I thought maybe that was the end of our exchange, but once semi-steady, he stared my way. He seemed like he'd lost focus in this world. What was he looking at? Me? The half-eaten cake on the counter? Could he see the balloons latched to my chair with curlicued flair?

"You look fat," he said. No affect, no expression. A statement of fact.

I eyed a splotch of hardened yolk on the woven place mat in front of me and picked at it with my thumbnail until the hallway creaked beneath his weight and the bedroom door slammed. An ocean whoosh in my ears, my surging blood. My father had targeted the body I couldn't see clearly, my soft thighs and fleshy stomach, parts of me I already believed to be ten times their size. When I lamented my fatness, my mother would say, "You're zeroing in on sections, but you have to look at the whole picture." And she was right; I dissected myself again and again in the mirror. To this day, I have trouble spotting advertisements with disembodied women—a loose arm that reaches into the frame, a busty torso without a head. I'd experienced myself the same way: in eight-inch hunks of thigh, in tubes of fat blooming above my denim waistline. It would never have occurred to me to see myself as a whole person.

Alone at the kitchen table, I throbbed with disappointment—for the birthday I cared about so deeply, for putting myself in another position to be wounded, for not being thinner for my father. These are the moments I can't quantify. How long did I sit at that table? Minutes? An hour? Eventually, I got up and opened the front door, looked around for loose dogs or people and, seeing none, sprinted outside to close the van door. Once back in, I set the Pegasus on the shoulder of the couch and headed for bed, where I found the drunken lump of my father unconscious on my twin mattress.

We often took turns springing him to life, gently urging him from couch to bedroom, but this was different. He'd never passed out in my room. No matter what else he did in there, he always had the sense to flee, and this hill of drunk dad violated our unspoken pact.

"Dad." I nudged his arm. Nothing. "C'mon. Go to your bed, Dad." He responded with a half grunt, a primitive attempt at speech that hung in the air. I turned my head to avoid the smell of it. My father the Hydra, a creature so venomous even its breath was lethal.

"Dad. Dad. Go to your bed. Dad. Dad." Something in me boiled. With each "dad," my throat grew more taut. I needed my bed. It was mine, and there was no way I could sleep in his; it reeked of sweat and fryer grease and farts.

"DAD!" I yelled as loudly as I could and instantly regretted it. His left eye slit open and swam in its socket. Before I could duck, he backhanded me across the cheek, which launched me into my bookshelf and set off a rainfall of doll miniatures and paperbacks. Afraid he'd follow up one hit with several, I scrambled to the kitchen and waited until I heard him snore again. My pulse thumped in my cheek.

What I did next was new: I called my mother. *You can tell me anything, sweetie.*

When she burst through the door twenty minutes later, she might as well have been wearing a cape.

My mother tilted my swollen face toward the light, her fingers cool and slender against my chin, and told me to stay in the kitchen. I'm not sure how, but she managed to wake him. The fight moved into their bedroom, and I quickly ran to my own, where I backed into the corner of my bed and hid under the covers. I could smell him in the comforter.

An hourglass of regret filled my gut. I'd woken him for a second and seen in his wandering eye that no one was home; my father was continents away. I'd unlatched the hook on his kennel and run, but my mother had called him back to his body from wherever he drifted. In waking him, she'd flung open the kennel door with abandon. Of course the animal would be set loose.

Their bedroom door whistled open and crunched into the closet behind it. The doorstops in my house had long been snapped off. My door jerked open seconds later.

"You hadda tell on me," my father slurred and tore off my blanket. "You little bitch. You couldn't sleep on the couch?"

My mother swooped in and grabbed him by the shoulders.

"Don't you dare talk to her like that," she yelled, but he wafted her aside, a gnat, and she fell into my dresser. A row of drugstore perfume bottles tipped over like dominoes, each of them landing with a delicate glass tink. She bounced back up. *Stay down*, I thought, trying to will the thought into her mind. *Stay down*. I didn't understand then that she rose to keep him away from me.

"This bullshit," he yelled. "I pay the bills in my house. Sleep where I want. My house!" He staggered down the hallway, repeating "my house," a refrain that sounded like an echo losing its reflection the farther away he got from my room. The wooden steps of the basement groaned as he made his way underground.

My mother's face flushed, her eyes wide. She squatted in front of me and stroked my hair, her voice at once wobbly and strong.

"It's going to be okay," she said. "Stay here. Promise me. Stay here." I nodded, and she tore after him.

But as soon as she was out of sight, I snuck down the hallway, through the kitchen, to the top of the basement stairs, and positioned myself three steps down, enough for me to see my parents while keeping my body hidden. Within moments, the yelling turned to shoving, which made room for my first experience with the inevitable: my father drew back his fist and punched her in the stomach, in the ribs, in the arm. That sound, the flat clap of skin on skin and my mother's cries—if I could erase a memory, it would be that. I wanted to glide down the stairs in one quick move, leap onto his back, shout for him to stop. I wanted to be strong enough to stop him and be her hero, but I didn't move.

I never moved.

⟡

I didn't sleep that night, and in the dark my hands shook as resolution poured out of me: I would be less sensitive, not take things so personally. I'd fall asleep wherever there was space. I didn't need my room, like some baby. I didn't need my mommy. I was twelve, damn it. Time to start acting like an adult!

I want to whisper to twelve-year-old me that none of it was my fault, but I couldn't have heard that then. My world only made sense when its failings were my own. If only I could have behaved better, spoken finer Greek, been less sensitive. If, if, if. I hung my hat on that puny conjunction because *if* it were my fault, that meant I had the power to stop it, to stop him. Power. Control. I couldn't admit I had none, so I believed I had it all.

I sat up in bed, feet pressed to carpet, and slapped my own face. I had to toughen up. Still crying, I slapped again, numb to the sting of my own palm. To be a daughter—to survive being his daughter—I had to grow a shield. I'd be a rhinoceros, thick with dermal armor, my skin deflecting any pain thrown at me. No more crying. No more running to my mom. No more feeling anything. If I grew my armor thick enough, I thought, I could survive anything. And soon I'd be ready for battle.

CHAPTER 5

ARMOR

As a dancer's daughter, I'd been sculpted from sequins and spandex, and for most of my freshman year of high school, I was between costume changes, still wearing cutesy sweatshirts and pastel-colored slacks—the skin of a girl I was determined to shed. *Britannica Junior*'s "Armor" entry shows a picture of an Etruscan soldier in a helmet—inspired by the Greeks, of course—topped with a red-and-black plume. An ancient warrior's mohawk.

The moves I made were so cliché, I may as well have worked from an Introductory Course on Depression and Angst checklist:

- ✓ Find a girl whose face is pancaked white; ask her for music. Discover The Cure, The Smiths, Nine Inch Nails.
- ✓ Rent *Sid and Nancy* roughly two million times.
- ✓ Steal your father's clothes. Disappear into his enormous pants and flannels. Do not think of this as symbolic.
- ✓ Shave half your head; dye the rest black.
- ✓ Black lipstick, black eyeliner.
- ✓ In fact, black is the only color now.
- ✓ Let your grades slide into the sea.

- ✓ Let your hygiene do the same.
- ✓ Look infectious.
- ✓ Buy a tarantula.
- ✓ Find new friends. You will know them by the rainbows of their hair, the crunch of their skateboards against blacktop.

Overnight, I became a different girl. I showed up for school the next day as someone who frightened people more than she was frightened herself. When my mother came home the evening I changed my look, she paused by the couch and said only, *Why?* before making her way to the kitchen. If my father noticed, he never said a word, but he also never visited my bedroom again. My armor was working.

I spent uncountable hours locked in my bedroom, three of my pink walls now black, the single wallpapered surface covered by my Sharpie with lyrics and drawings and the names of the boys and girls I loved. The truth is, I loved them all: people I'd never spoken to, their bright faces and goofy grins circled in my yearbook. Ultimately and sometimes only for a moment, I loved everyone who wasn't me.

I met Michelle on my way to steal a pack of smokes from the store. She was a grade ahead of me and looked like a young, stoned Meryl Streep. I had the Winona Ryder *Beetlejuice* thing going. We didn't make sense on paper—like the sun befriending the moon—but after so many years of abandoned or, worse, no friendships, it was platonic love at first sight. Ravenous for affection, we fell into one another. Before long, we could communicate with the telepathic acuity teenage girls possess: one glance from across a room, and we understood each other perfectly. It freaked people out, our closeness, and often they asked if we were witches.

We said yes and wiggled our fingers at them. *A pox on your family*, I added, and we laughed as they shook their heads or backed away from us slowly.

She introduced me to the skater boys and artsy girls we went to school with: the fellow misfits I was convinced would make my life complete. I'd never figured out how to make my father love me, but it was so much easier with teenagers. If you have drugs, you have friends. I wasn't in the business of quality control; I only knew if I was holding, I'd have company, and eventually they'd switch from using me to get high to genuinely liking me. I'm embarrassed to admit it worked well, as far as pathetic plans go, and soon enough, my circle of friends ran twenty deep, as though the god of friendship had extended a plentiful palm to make up for years of drought. The people whose names I'd scrawled on my wall now joked with me, the lot of us chummy as sitcom neighbors.

I was too caught up with my own life to ever wonder what was wrong with theirs, though sometimes slivers of their injuries slipped into conversation. One afternoon, sitting cross-legged in an open green field, one of my friends confessed to me that another friend of ours had molested him when he was a child. I want so badly to write that I comforted him, that I said, *I'm so sorry that happened to you*, or held his hand and suggested reporting it, but I didn't know how to help him because no one had shown me what help looked like. A nasty fact lingers around that memory: I couldn't bear the proximity of his truth to mine. My body bolted awake with heat, and as he spoke, I began to sweat, a fire lit in my stomach that doubled me over. I bent forward and pressed my forehead to my ankles, a dancer's retreat. As he continued speaking, I thought, *Liar. Why would you ever hang out with the person who hurt you? I'd never forgive him.* Forget that I still craved my father's love and forgave him every time he said he'd never hurt me again. What a thing a mirror is: impossible to gaze into when it holds the answer we don't want to see.

⟜☉

Parents often think that fighting in front of children is the worst thing they can do, but I loved it. I'd prayed for their divorce, even when I hadn't believed in god, and when their arguing grew constant, I could see a glimmer of light in the distance. What would a life without my father look like? How much space would there be in our house once he stopped hogging it all?

I also loved their fights because it let me gaslight them. I stole money from my mother and blamed my father and vice versa. Eventually, I grew bold enough to do it with them in the room, my parents screaming at one another while standing by the kitchen counter, as I sat a few feet away at the table, ready to strike.

Her: *Where do you think you're going?*

Him: *Out.*

Her (pleading): *We're supposed to see the counselor today.*

Him (screaming): *I am a man. No one tells me what to do in my house.*

Me (slips Mom's wallet out of purse and onto lap; continues watching fight; fingers a twenty out of its slot and into pocket)

Her: *It's like you want us to fail. You promised you'd try.*

Him: *Roar!*[3]

Me (gets up and leaves, noticed by no one; checks mirror for reflection, for breath; confirms she is not a ghost; goes to buy weed, friends)

End scene.

⟜☉

But as their arguments escalated, so did our tension around my father, a man on the edge of detonation. On a fall afternoon, our street lined

---

3   Of course he didn't actually say *roar*, but this feels emotionally true.

with oak and maples that carried gold and orange and umber in their branches, I walked home and saw my father's van sitting in front of our house. I slowed down. I stretched five minutes into fifteen, and when I finally entered, there he sat at the kitchen table. I said, *Hi, Dad*, but he didn't answer, so I moved in closer and stopped fast in the doorway, leaned against its frame. When he aimed the rifle at me and smiled, my first thought was that I'd never before seen a gun in person. The barrel seemed long enough to poke me from where he sat, though he was probably ten feet away. Or maybe he was closer. I'd never been good at determining the space between things, and the rifle seemed to fill every inch of it, the air in the room wavy as heat rippling off asphalt.

Nice of you to join me, he slurred, but drunk was a language I spoke fluently. I forced a smile and asked, *What are you doing?* I tried to sound casual, like this was something that happened every day. To freak out—to show fear—meant to escalate, and I wanted to keep him calm as a pond.

He didn't answer. Instead he tried to put his elbow on the table and missed. He tried again and landed it, then propped up his face, the other hand gripping the rifle, the barrel still pointed at me but winding in slow circles like it was too heavy for him to hold. He said, *I'm waiting for you. That's what I'm doing.* The most normal words in the world, but his tone was razor wire. *I have one question, and you better not lie.* Pause. A pause so long, I couldn't tell if he were making up the question or maybe had forgotten what he wanted to ask. But then he spoke: *Where is your mother?*

I had no idea where my mother was. I was certain that she lived at some combination of the studio, home, and the grocery store—that she could be someplace else never occurred to me—so I said, *I don't know.* It was the truth, and the truth should've saved me because that was his offer. Instead, he grabbed the rifle with both hands and steadied his aim.

Thick like the thieves, you two are, he said, and I noticed something out of place, something shiny, a tear tumbling down his cheek. I focused again on the barrel. He said, *You lie, always on her side*, and I didn't know what he meant because I wasn't lying, wouldn't dream of it in that moment, so I mustered a weak, *I really don't know, Dad*, and he inhaled deeply and moved his finger to the trigger. *This is it, this is it, this is it*, I thought. I wish I'd run, knowing now how much harder it is to shoot a target in motion, but I was stuck. Flight, fight, freeze. I don't know how long it lasted, but I stood there waiting to die in that silence until his voice broke it with a Bond villain's articulation: *We're gonna wait here till both liars come together. First I'm gonna shoot you, then her. To teach a lesson.* I opened my mouth but nothing came out—not a plea, not a prayer, no language at all—so I clapped it shut again and waited. Slowly, he crumbled into a weeping lump at the table.

After some time, he looked at me again and pleaded, *Tell me the truth.* I already had, and it hadn't helped. *I don't know*, I whispered again, because I really didn't know anything in that moment. Eventually he slid his finger off the trigger, though the barrel was still on me, and after a space of time I can't measure, he got up from the table with his gun and at first stumbled past me, like I wasn't there, then turned to add, *If you tell, I'll kill you both.* Only when I heard the choppy grunt of his snoring did I decide it was finally safe to let go of the wall and take a breath.

I stepped into our backyard and plopped down on a rusted, partially reclined chaise and stared at the sky, the color so perfectly blue it felt like an insult. My hands began to shake, and soon all of me quaked—my vision, my breath, my muscles. A steady train of tears found their way from the corners of my eyes to my chin, where they dripped down the front of my shirt until my chest was soaked through. Even though I had no idea what to do or how much longer I had left in this world, I knew I needed to change my shirt before my mother came home.

Survival is, at times, the act of telling necessary lies. We believe whatever we must in order to make it through another day, another hour, another minute. I believed that if I didn't tell, that if I kept my father's secrets caged within my body, he wouldn't hurt us more than he already had. I believed he was in control of his meanness—he'd walked right up to the line but turned back while there was still time. Scare tactics, nothing more. He wouldn't hurt me like that, right?

⁓

After the gun, the checklist grew:

- ✓ Shoplift.
- ✓ Drink.
- ✓ Do drugs. A lot.
- ✓ Get a back tattoo from some dude in Philly. No parental signature. The fish on the cover of Ginsberg's *Collected Poems* will develop scar tissue from how deep he digs the needle in.
- ✓ Erase Mike. Surely he's still there, but my days after school are spent either (a) getting high with friends, or (b) burrowed in my bedroom.
- ✓ Hate your mother. Don't understand that age difference doesn't matter; self-esteem and identity can be stripped away from adults and children alike. Don't know that she once asked your grandmother if you could stay with her, and your grandmother had said no. Don't know that your mother is a master minimizer; she likely tells herself that it isn't that bad, that it's probably her fault, that she can make things right. Don't know any of that, so do what your father taught you: turn mean as a viper. Think, *She's weak. Too weak to leave.*
- ✓ Fuck everyone.

⁓

Like so many teenagers, I was glad to get it over with. No more lying about my experience. I'd never once felt my body valued, so why would I value it myself? And once I gave it away to some nobody whose name I didn't know on the floor of a motel room, the path was cleared for Chad.

When he approached me in the hallway at school, I couldn't hear him over the swoosh of blood in my ears. He had to repeat what he'd asked: Would I trade boots with him? I looked down at his: knee-highs, covered in buckles and zippers, worn and badass. Right there, we swapped. *Britannica Junior* claims, "The weight of a suit of armor was considerable, although not so much as is often supposed . . . There exist complete suits weighing as little as 41 pounds, helmets as light as two pounds. Even so, a warrior had to accustom himself from youth to the weight of the armor." Perhaps Chad had been used to them, but the weight of his shoes made me feel like Godzilla, and for the rest of the week, I smashed my heavy feet down in the halls with a new sense of power.

Chad was so thin he could clip a necktie to his collarbone. He introduced me to the Beat Generation and Bauhaus, and he forever smelled of spearmint. Like so many boys his age—he was three years older than me—he (mis)read and quoted Nietzsche too much, though I loved it—his attention, his believing I was smart—and we passed each other hundreds of notes in the hallways, many of them filled with the awful poems we'd written for one another. His oily hair was longer than mine, and of course he played the guitar. In his bedroom closet sat a coffin he sometimes slept in. I was doomed.

He never called me his girlfriend, a word I ached to hear him say, even casually. He never used the word love, though we dated, I think, for nearly a year. Instead he wrote me riddles and acrostics and every manner of innuendo to keep me wondering how valuable I was.

Chad's mother worked at a bar down the street, so he usually had the house to himself. One night, he said he wanted to play a game, and because I only knew how to pacify, I said yes when he slid my panties off, yes when he blindfolded me. His hands were bony and cold, calloused at the tips of his guitar-playing fingers, and he used them to lower me onto the mattress. When he slid the first thing inside and said, *Guess*, I didn't understand the question, and then almost immediately I did. I didn't say no or scream or even squeeze tight my thighs. Instead, I let him place object after object inside me—a Sharpie, the metallic coil of a light bulb, the chilly neck of a beer—and laughed right along with him while I guessed.

It's important to ask here: What is less than nothing? Absence and annihilation. Zippo and zilch. Emptiness and void. A goose egg, a duck egg, a big fat zero. Naught and nonbeing, nonentity and nothingness. Extinction and obliteration and (fuck you, Nietzsche) nihility. That is what I thought of myself.

⁂

Shortly after Chad and I broke up, I spread my legs—for a boy who drooled when he kissed, for two strangers at the beach who took turns, for the guy who removed his prosthetic leg and smacked my ass with it in a baseball field. A pair of cousins high-fived over my back as they thrust their cocks into me, and once I woke up on a bed in Philadelphia after having been roofied, a used condom stuck to my back like a barnacle. The Boy with the Absurdly Bright Eyes. The White Boy with Dreads. The Girl I Genuinely Loved but Fucked Over. The Boy Who

Lived Conveniently Nearby. The Boy I Most Seriously Liked. The list is incomplete. I don't remember them all—the people I let inside, often without condoms—and I'm sure I couldn't have told you then what I was chasing, but I can now: in those brief moments when men jack-hammered against my thighs, I mistook sex for the possibility of love. It was one-sided, of course. A slut is a disposable thing in the World of Teenagerdom. But I believed no one would ever be into someone as unlovable as me for long, so I took all the minutes I could get and held them as close as I could.

Someone asked me yesterday how I managed the aftermath of empty sex, and I had to think about the answer for longer than expected. Of course, I continued to numb myself with weed, but that isn't the whole of it. Pot doesn't magically erase emotional pain. I regulated the emptiness by buying into the Myth of the Cool Girl. The Cool Girl watches you at band practice for hours at a time, never once showing her boredom. She takes up as little space as she can. Watch her fold into herself over and over until she's small enough to slip into your wallet. She laughs at jokes like, *What do you tell a woman with two black eyes? Nothing. You already told her twice.* She laughs at jokes at her expense when she'd rather kick you in the balls. The Cool Girl doesn't acknowl-edge her feelings or needs. She damn sure doesn't speak them aloud. If she does, she's instantly a nag, a drag, needy and clingy, overbearing and hysterical. In all my years, my needs had never been considered. If you'd have asked me what I needed, *really* needed, I would not have been able to tell you. Instead, I'd have been aloof, super chill, cool as an October midnight, but internally I'd have berated myself for feeling so awful all the time, for feeling anything at all.

∽

On the road, we hotboxed the Volkswagen—me, Michelle, and the Boy I Most Seriously Liked. Packed with the pings and dings of varied games, the arcade at the mall had The Addams Family pinball machine, our favorite, and we lined a rail of quarters up the machine's glass, a warning to any other interested parties that we weren't going anywhere.

I'm sure we were too high—weren't we always?—and sometimes all we could get our mitts on was schwag, a pile of seed and stem, on the worst days laced with something we hadn't signed up for. Maybe it was the noise, the constant clang in the air, or maybe it was the flashing lights, but the Boy I Most Seriously Liked, the coolest boy for miles, took two steps back from the game during his multiball and promptly passed out. Michelle and I looked at one another, then squatted by him, calling his name and lightly slapping his cheeks. When he came to, he looked around for a second before his eyes rolled back until only their whites showed, then passed out again. The third time he fell, we wedged our shoulders beneath his and got him outside, worried that at any moment the cops would show up. Michelle couldn't drive stick, and I was still too young to have a license, but she sat in the driver's seat anyway and ground his gears so violently that he finally said, *I'm driving*, and slid into position.

The Boy I Most Seriously Liked was fine the next day. He'd slept off whatever signals his brain had cross-wired and never mentioned it again.

But I was never the same.

The instant he'd hit the floor, my vision closed in. I was certain I was next and could feel my body ready to give way: my pulse a drumroll, my neck sweaty, my senses overwhelmed, but more than any of that, I remember the heat of the arcade closing around me like a fist. My brain flashed two neon words: COOL AIR, COOL AIR, COOL AIR. I wish it subsided when I got home, but I lay in bed all night, eyes with soft focus in the dark, my thoughts so rapid that I couldn't get a decent breath. Pressing my body to the wall didn't cool me off, so I snuck down the hallway and stood before the thermostat my mother kept at seventy-five, a device off-limits to anyone but my parents. I slid the lever to the left, and eventually the air fell to a crisp sixty-eight. Somewhere in the neighborhood of five a.m., I fell asleep.

I chastised myself. *Who psychosomatically faints*, I thought. *That's so dumb.* I possessed no language for what was happening to me. The world was still six years away from Google searches, and I sure as hell wasn't going to tell someone what my mind and body felt like. They'd institutionalize me; I was sure of it. Even I thought I was a crazy—a freak, broken. I also thought I was the only one. A few years later, I watched an infomercial starring a famous country-singing duo's struggle with anxiety and panic, thirty minutes of television that sped up my pulse. Finally, I could name what was wrong with me.

I envied the Boy I Most Seriously Liked. For him, one night's sleep erased what he thought of as a fluke, but for me, I'd seen a strong, fit young man fall like a guillotine's blade: swift and heavy. It reminded me instantly that I was nowhere near as tough as I was pretending to be. The dam had burst on my anxiety, and for the next decade, I would have multiple panic attacks a day. Because I didn't know what was happening, I couldn't figure out my triggers. Everything seemed to set me off: being indoors or outdoors, crowds, lines, tight spaces, pinball, and most of all heat. *Britannica Junior* notes that "heat and temperature are not the same thing," but I was no scientist. My body registered them identically: as a threat.

∽

One night I came home late, tripping my tits off, and Mike and his friend Kevin, my honorary brother, were the only ones awake, watching cartoons with the lights off. They were twelve, that gross age when boys forget showers exist and live for farts, and I breezed past them and into my room, where I found myself way too high and intensely bored. I joined them on the couch, where I proceeded to talk for three hours straight, pausing only to let them catch their breath between laughs.

For one million dollars, I couldn't tell you what I said, but my brain was on fire with the energy of LSD, and eventually I tired myself out enough to pass out.

The next day, Mike knocked on my bedroom door, and I groaned my acquiescence. He said, "That's the first time you've talked to me in years. It was nice." And then he left. I still think about that, about how easy it is to turn your world so far inward you forget to acknowledge the people near you. Not forget. That things can get so bad, you're unable to see anyone outside of yourself.

I hadn't shunned Mike willfully, but I can't help but think of how badly a little brother needs his big sister to notice him. How alone he must have felt during those years when I walked past him without so much as a word or a nod. Were we all living overcome by the sensation of invisibility, of isolation? It's as though my father had managed to swallow whatever chains once bound us together, and the four of us, each in our separate rooms, were certain our anguish was ours and ours alone.

$\sim$

Addiction is an ouroboros: when you've slid down the dark side of a high or a bender, you'll swear this is it, the end—*last time, bitches*—but the next day the comedown smashes into the reality you were trying to avoid all along and boom! You're drunk or high again, gagging on your own snaky tail. I hung up my LSD shoes (where they promptly melted down the wall); I knew if I tripped again, I might not return. Instead I got high on weed and pills and wrestled my self-diagnosed anxiety disorder. I spent every moment I could out of my house or, if I were home, locked in my room.

One day, my mother knocked on my bedroom door, and I yelled, *Go away*. Par for the shitty course. But she came in anyway and told me someone was waiting for me in the living room. When I got down the hall, I found two uniformed officers standing in the center of the room. My mother said, "Sit down," so I parked it on the couch. I recognized one of the cops as the traffic guard at my high school.

"Your mother's worried you're going down a bad path," Officer Patchy Goatee said.

My body revved with heat.

"I know your friends seem important now, but if you keep acting like this, we'll have to take you to Lakeland," Officer Traffic Guard added.

Lakeland: our county's institution for the insane and infirm and delinquent juveniles. In grade school, our choir visited the elderly there to sing carols, and my voice barely registered behind the terror I felt at the sight of their IV tubes and bedpans. In high school, we sometimes drove down the abandoned dirt roads of Lakeland's campus at night to get high. When we arrived in a clearing, Michelle shut off her headlights and honked the horn three times to provoke an urban legend to life. The patients were supposed to swarm the car, but, to our disappointment, they never did.

I held my wrists out in front of me, a bluff called.

"Go ahead," I said.

"You think this is some kind of joke?" Officer Patchy Goatee yelled. "You know what goes on there? Shit you can't imagine. It's scary."

"I'm not afraid," I said. And for once, I wasn't.

"Get your act together, little girl," Officer Traffic Guard warned. "You've got a good mother here." He paused to look around. "Your parents have given you a nice home. They care about you. Don't throw that away."

I looked at my mother, crying. *What a pussy*, I thought. Then I stared the cops down. *Do something*, I thought. *See it. Notice what everyone else misses. You're trained for this. See it. See the danger. See it. See it. See it.*

One of them shrugged at my mother while the other patted her on the shoulder. Gestures that said, *We tried. Good luck with all that.*

Once they drove off, I sneered at my mother. "You want me outta here? Ship me the fuck off. I'm ready to go."

She wiped her cheeks. "Jesus Christ, Lisa. I'm trying to help you." Her gaze turned toward the carpet. "I don't know how to help you."

༄

It is difficult for me to imagine now where my family was, but I had the house to myself one summer night. Mike likely slept at Kevin's. My mother probably performed somewhere far away enough that it required an overnight bag. My father left for work so late, I felt sure he wouldn't be back before sunrise. I never had people over, but I invited Michelle and the White Boy with Dreads to my house. Together we drank a fifth of vodka and a case of beer, then smoked an eighth of weed. In short: we were plastered. I found myself in the shower with the White Boy with Dreads before we moved our awful sex downstairs. While he was on top of me, he asked only one question: *Why are your thighs so fat?*

Eventually, the three of us passed out on top of the covers in the basement bedroom, the lack of light making it impossible to see. I snapped awake at a sense I hadn't felt in a long while: the presence of someone in our space. When I opened my eyes, I found the silhouette of my father in the doorway, backlit by the fluorescent lights. *Britannica Junior* notes, "In making the materials for the atomic bomb, great quantities of heat were generated." At the sight of my father, my body burst with fever. I thought one thing so clearly I can still hear it in my mind: *We're dead.*

I elbowed Michelle and the White Boy with Dreads, the three of us sitting up and staring at the shape in the doorway.

From the dark, my father asked a question: *You guys want cheesesteaks?*

I coughed up a meek yes. When I went upstairs, the evidence of our party was everywhere: empty bottles and glasses knocked over, cigarettes spilling out of the ashtrays, our clothes on the kitchen floor. I got dressed and straightened up, my body on the cusp of explosion, when a knock at the front door produced our dinner. We sat on the living room sofa, something I don't remember playing on the television, while my father joked with us. I felt Michelle staring at me and made eye contact for a telepathic conversation.

Michelle: *Duuuuude. What the fuck?*

Me: *Duuuuude, I know.*

Michelle: *Can we leave? I want to leave.*

Me: *No way. Eat the sandwich.*

Michelle: *Should I be scared?*

Me: *Yes.*

⁓

Villains aren't clad in black, twirling their mustaches as they hatch a plot to make your life miserable. They aren't obvious. What a relief it would be if that were true: we'd be able to spot danger every time it approaches. But abusers are maps with no lines drawn in. *Here there be dragons.* There's no way to predict where you're going or to mark where you've been. There's only the possibility that you'll be rewarded or punished, and your behavior has little to do with the outcome. If you're a child studying a blank map, if you keep looking at it for clues and finding none, you remain adrift, disoriented, unsure of what could come your way. You tiptoe around the blank map, certain you don't want to be the first to mark it up. To leave footprints on that blank canvas would be to show a direct line from you to trouble. Better to remain still, invisible. Better to let the map remain as mysterious as it wants.

⁊

That cheesesteak night is the second-to-last memory I have of my father in our house. A couple of months before I turned sixteen, my parents' divorce was finalized on the grounds of "extreme cruelty." If there was some after-school-special sit-down to announce the break, I do not remember it. What I do remember is their fights no longer stayed behind doors or carried on in choked whispers. They argued anytime they crossed one another's path, and for all the weakness I'd thought my mother bore, it was clear she'd shed that skin. This new mother had opinions. This new mother yelled back. My father still stormed and shouted, and this is when we all should have been most scared; leaving an abuser is the most dangerous time. But sometimes I sat in the kitchen and watched them go round after round and smiled. For too long I thought I'd smiled because I was a rotten teenager, but I know now it was a grin of relief. Finally, something truthful was happening. Finally, I wasn't the only one fighting my father.

My mother tells me now that she knew he had a gun, though she doesn't remember how she found out. The court-ordered day he was supposed to leave came and went, and it was clear he had no intention of going. Instead of vacating, he yelled a refrain I knew well from my childhood: *This is my house.* He told my mother he'd destroy everything before being forced out.

So my mother went to the police, who at the word *gun* were ready to act. She set up a signal with a friend. If she called her friend and said, *Let's go to the movies,* that was the friend's cue to call the cops. She was explaining this to the friend when my father pulled into the driveway, so she said it again and again: *LET'S GO TO THE MOVIES LET'S GO TO THE MOVIES LET'S GO TO THE MOVIES,* and like that, the police were there to drag him away. My mother says my brother was at a friend's house, which is where I assume he always was; he's absent from so many of these memories, a boy smart enough to spend as little time at home as he could.

I sat on the lawn, knees to chest, and watched my father carry his belongings to his van. I didn't believe for a minute it would be so easy. Unless the cops planned on living with us, he'd be back. I was sure of it. I yanked swatches of grass out by their roots and listened to him yell at the air. *This is America! A man has a right to a home. I pay the bills. Who are you to tell me to leave MY house?* Later that day, a neighbor changed our locks for us, but for months afterward, I swear I heard his keys jingling against the brass, trying his best to get back inside. I will never know if he was there. I was too terrified to look.

It seems strange that you can shrink a family by one member and experience its growth. So many people think of divorce as the most damaging thing you can do to children, but all I'd ever wanted was a home free of my father. My mother tells me I was four years old the first time I asked if we could move. For her that is a charming story, a kids-say-the-darndest-things moment, but what I hear is a plea for sanctuary, an appeal to escape. I assure you that even as a toddler, I did not mean for us to move *with* him. I only ever wanted to be away.

Still, with our father gone and our mother often at work, Mike and I again grew closer. We spent embarrassing stretches of time hacky-sacking on our front lawn, listening to Nirvana and Pearl Jam and Beethoven and Bob Marley. We were eclectic weirdos, the both of us, and we'd been set free. I slowly shed my armor, and the meanness I'd carried for so long melted away in an epiphany. My rage had long made me feel closer to my father, and moving toward kindness was another rejection of him, of all he'd taught me to be.

For the first time since we were much younger, Mike and I shared the common spaces of our home, laughing until we cramped on our couch at *Mr. Bean* and *Whose Line Is It Anyway?* and playing spades with Michelle and Kevin at our kitchen table. At night, our mother might bring us a bucket of KFC or a bag of cheap tacos, and we'd scarf the grub down with greed and gratitude. Our family size may have shrunk, but Mike and I grew into pals, and after so much time spent in solitary, I'd really missed my friend.

CHAPTER 6

GROWTH

There's danger in believing you have one central problem—an obstacle that, if removed, will allow happiness to bloom. People think, *I'll be happy when I'm thinner, when I'm richer, when I have a better job or partner*, but they don't realize it's so much more complex. Yes, my father had been removed from my space, but without him to focus on, I had to figure out how to live in the ruins of my body. I possessed an abundance of energy that had once been given to him. And taken by him. Where was that to go after he was gone? The wrecking ball of my father had hurled into me for just shy of sixteen years. I was a building demolished.

Mike says he'll never forget the calm after our father was taken from the house; there was "kind of a blaring silence" in my father's absence that Mike felt immediately. I don't remember silence. Instead, I hear the electric hum of amps and chords, my brother rapidly becoming a guitar wizard. He'd always been like that. Good at things. Get us a video game, and he'd have it mastered in a day or two. He found a free piano in the classifieds and somehow managed to wedge it into his bedroom. By the end of the day, he was playing Vince Guaraldi's "Linus and Lucy." A week later, he filled the air with cartoon noise when he had the opening to Liszt's *Hungarian Rhapsody No. 2* down. I have no doubt that if he unearthed some ancient instrument at an archaeological site, he'd hold it before him and spin it around for a moment before playing you any song you requested. Our gifts are different, but the primary divergence is that his is audible. You could hear his growth. I had nothing so clear with which to measure my own. As *Britannica Junior* makes clear, "In most living things, even the biggest changes take place by such small steps that a difference cannot be seen from one day to the next. It takes weeks, months, or years before changes in growth become big enough to see."

But I did make some changes: I graduated from high school at seventeen, looking more like an edgy hippie than a goth girl. Shortly afterward, I quit smoking pot. It had become untenable: every time I got high, I had a panic attack, my body erupting with the need to escape itself. I wish I could write that the anxiety eased up once I stopped, but it seemed to get worse without something to numb it.

While my graduating class adjusted to college life, I remained aimless in South Jersey. I'd planned to go to art school, but I hadn't done anything to make that happen. Not one college application. I wound up dragging my feet around the campus of a local community college. In my gut I knew something greater had to be in store for my life; I just couldn't figure out how to make it happen. While I was at the community college, my sculpture professor submitted my work to Moore College of Art & Design and greeted me with a surprise in class: I'd been offered a full ride. In the same semester, my history professor pulled me aside one day and, exasperated, asked, *What are you doing here?* She offered to pull some strings and get me into La Salle University. I said no thank you to both of them. The history professor shook her head. *Why?* she asked. And I told her the half-truth: *I'm lost.*

The rest of the truth was I wanted to major in drinking. In those earlier party years, I only drank on weekends, but without marijuana to calm me, I turned devoutly and daily to the bottle. Drink helped me achieve the silence that came so naturally to Mike. It also helped me sleep, and for the first time in my life, I was sometimes getting six or even seven hours—double what I'd been accustomed to. I didn't know then that passing out and sleeping aren't the same, that the body rarely gets to REM while intoxicated. I drank to soothe my brain's Muppet energy, but the booze kept it activated while I lay in those deep black funks.

In my third semester of college, I stopped showing up. I didn't care about my classes and didn't know what to do with my life or how to sit through a lecture without feeling the familiar rush of fight or flight. My mother reminded me that without a college degree, I'd inherit nothing when she died, a clause in her will that says more about her own regret than anything else. She'd dropped out after one semester to work, to care for people, to marry a charming line cook with a thick accent and pork-chop sideburns. I assured her I'd go back someday when I was ready, but I didn't tell her that she never had to worry about me throwing my life away for a man. Not only was I certain I'd never marry, I also had one rule when it came to dating and sex: no Greek men.

⁓

At nineteen, I splayed on the living room sofa in front of the TV with Cheetos and a palpable lack of ambition. I'd been lounging in the AC for months, ankles slung over the back of the couch, gaze fixed on *Tom and Jerry*, *Looney Tunes*, and in especially low moments, *The Brady Bunch*. One day I heard my mother come in—it was her living room, after all—and I didn't bother to greet her. In fact, her presence didn't fully register until she shoved my elevated ankles to the ground and said, simply, *Get a job*, before walking into the kitchen. It was as though the thought hadn't occurred to me. She was right, of course. I needed to do something.

With no experience, I applied at a soon-to-be-open steakhouse, following my parents' footsteps into the restaurant business. The general manager hired Michelle and me, and when we had our soft opening for friends and family, one of my buddies asked, *Notice anything about everyone that works here?* I looked around at the hive of terribly uniformed women and shrugged. He cupped his hands in front of his chest and laughed. I folded my arms in front of mine. It turns out that the GM was being sued for sexual harassment at three different restaurants. One night while I stood at the service bar waiting for my order, he came up behind me and ground his pelvis into my ass. I knocked him on his, then held out a hand to help him up. *Touch me again and you won't get up*, I said. *Got it?* He nodded and never bothered me again.

At the first table I waited on sat the owners I'd yet to meet. They huddled in a corner booth full of paperwork and self-importance, and as I approached and heard them talking, the muscles in my neck tightened. They were speaking Greek. I introduced myself, but they kept right on yammering, not bothering to acknowledge I was there. I knew how it felt to be a Greek ghost, and years of standing next to my father when he picked me up from Greek school rushed back: tugging at his sleeve, his hand nudging me away so he could make his loud talk with other men. I leaned back against the railing, my tray held at the hip, and waited. *How badly do I need this job?* I wondered. When they finally looked up, they decided to talk about me in Greek. *Pretty*, one of them said. Another added, *I'd fuck her.* He had the tone of a man choosing tile for his bathroom, bored of looking at samples.

"What would you like to drink?" I asked, the pen shaking in my hand. When I returned, I set their scotches and iced teas on coasters and took their lunch order. We were trained to repeat everything.

"That's two Caesar salads, one with salmon, one with chicken, a mushroom and swiss burger, medium rare, crab cakes, and a New York strip, medium. Is that everything, gentlemen?"

They grunted their agreement.

"Great," I said, chipper as a puppy before switching to my low-pitched voice. "Also, *miláo Elliniká, malakas.*" *I speak Greek, you bastards.*

They looked at me, stunned. I wondered which of them would tell me to get off their property. Instead, Bored Bathroom-Tile Boss said, "You will never be fired."

Dangerous license to give a girl without much to lose.

$$\sim$$

Britannica Junior notes, "Growth gives the ability to move forward, to make right decisions, and, above all, to keep on growing." I wouldn't have known a *right decision* if it came up and shook my hand. In fact, I would've shoved Right Decision aside to get to the creep lurking behind it: Wrong Move.

I worked at that terrible Wild West–themed steakhouse/nightclub—yes, you read that right—for a year, but I'm lucky if I remember one third of it. We drank during our shifts and after, a pint glass full of rum perpetually sweating next to my register, and every once in a while, we guzzled so much that we slept on the bar mats, waking to our shifts the next day, our bodies stiff and foul with sweat and booze. I knew the smell leaching out of my skin well. I smelled like my father. When I did make it home, I passed out with the TV on, grateful for the *Law & Order* and *CSI* marathons that made me feel less lonely.

And still, I looked for love, my inhibitions as loose as they had been when I was fifteen. At training, a young woman with anime eyes and I shared our love of Ani DiFranco, and that was it. We dated for a year, sneaking off during our shifts to make out with one another, but when she wasn't around, I turned to old habits. I slept with a surfer boy who disappeared first by fucking a woman twice my age, then by moving to Hawaii. A professional hockey player with all of his natural teeth took me back to his place, and a year later I'd find myself in a different bar standing next to a life-size cardboard cutout of him, unable to remember much else about the night. There were hookups with two line cooks—one in my car, and one in the wee hours of the restaurant biz, maybe four a.m. He did a line of coke off my ass before doing what he wanted to my body, and halfway through, his supposed ex-girlfriend—a gal I'd gone to middle and high school with—pounded on the door of his shitty apartment with her fists and feet. The guy tried to play it off the way terrible men do. He threw out a line as old as the planet—*That bitch is crazy*—and when I imagined her slapping her palms raw in the cool summer evening, she looked like she had in seventh-grade homeroom: blonde hair tucked into pink-ribboned ponytails, her teeth stitched straight by silver braces. She stayed so long, I couldn't leave, so I sat there in the aftermath of sex I hadn't wanted to begin with, blurry with booze and disgusted with myself.

The next morning, I awoke in my own bed and found my car parked parallel to the house in my mother's garden. I did not remember driving home. I often didn't. Still, I must have climbed into the driver's seat, put one hand on the wheel, and cupped the other over one eye to curb my double vision.

That I was never hurt, or never hurt someone else, seems to me an ill-deserved miracle. Not everyone is so lucky. A bartender friend of mine passed out at the wheel and died in the crash, leaving behind a wife and toddler. Another fellow bartender did five years for vehicular homicide. I knew dozens of people who'd lost their licenses to DUIs—including Michelle. As a bartender, I was trained in the art of judging when someone had drunk too much, and I coaxed people's keys out of their hands before shepherding them into taxis. Then I got wasted and drove myself home, my car fueled by arrogance and apathy.

While I was certain the Wild West–themed steakhouse/nightclub would kill me—the drinking, the hours, the bullets mysteriously dug into the walls of the basement—I had trouble quitting. The money was too good to walk away from. To put that into perspective, I made more at nineteen years old than I do now as a professor. I made more than my mother. I made so much money I didn't have time to spend it. I'd get home from a shift and dump a sack of cash onto my dresser before passing out and waking up in time to do it again. Eventually, I took the cash and bought a Jeep Wrangler off the showroom floor because that was the kind of girl I wanted to be: fun, laid back, beachy. In one of its more poetic moments, *Britannica Junior* states, "The growth of a greyhound can be stunted by not feeding it properly, but it cannot be made to grow into a Pekingese." I wanted so badly to be a Pekingese: to be fancy and prized, to be worth something, but I wasn't even a hungry greyhound. I was a lost and thirsty mutt, wandering the bars of South Jersey, searching for something or someone to latch on to.

And then I met Matt.

∽

Michelle was a year older than me and had already become a regular at the dive bar where the mom of Chad, my terrible first boyfriend, worked. Affectionately (or derisively) nicknamed the Wood, it was a long, dank room with no windows and carpeting on the walls, which absorbed the constant stream of smoke that filled it. Three beers on tap, country in the jukebox. Attached to the Wood sat a grimy liquor store, where a beautiful young man named Matt worked. I'd join Michelle at the bar after my shift was over, and Matt would be perched on a stool or throwing darts, spending what little money he'd earned on thirty-two-ounce mugs of Yuengling Black & Tan. I hated it there so much that I kept my head down, drawing pictures on bev naps and growling at anyone who tried to talk to me. When I was in particularly salty moods, I'd put a tampon on my bev nap. No one talks to Tampon Girl.

Michelle liked Matt first—she searched for love with the same promiscuity I did—and I worried that I'd sleep with him. Michelle, the closest thing to love I had in my life, would be lost. But when she asked him out and he said yes, he stood her up. After that, she said, *You want him? He's yours.*

I was slinging drinks at a TGI Friday's, a place I'd applied to with the misguided notion it would be a wholesome spot to work, one that would never let me sleep on the floor of the bar, too drunk to make it home. One night after I closed—restocked the Coronas, wiped out the liquor wells, fridged and wrapped the fruit trays—I headed to the Wood. In the parking lot, I took off my sensible bartender's shoes and changed into four-inch heels that made my fishnetted legs look longer than they were. My shift had been a grueling one, the bar filled with couples, pairs of folks touching, smiling, giggling.

Entering the Wood I saw Matt perched on a stool, back to me, talking to an older woman. I walked up behind him, wrapped one leg around his waist, and physically pulled him away from her. A mutt marking her territory. Two nights later, we went on our first date to a Philly jazz bar, where I kept up with the pace he set, matching him in beers and shots. We listened to the house band tear up standards, an ancient man wailing notes on a B3 that rattled our ribs, and we spoke with our faces so close that the rest of the customers disappeared. We'd both been searching for someone who understood how terrible South Jersey was, who knew there was more to life than high-school bullshit. We talked art and theater and travel and thought we were absurdly sophisticated. When we discovered our first albums had been the same—Men at Work's *Business as Usual*—we looked at each other with relief. We were two sentences torn from the same paragraph.

At the end of the night, he parked his van on a dark street, and my nerves shook words out of me at a rapid speed. I prattled on and on about books and movies and the world in general—anything not to leave space for rejection. Instead of being scared off, he was charmed;

a ripple of adrenaline shot through me when we kissed, our long hair tangling like fine spiderwebs. When I stood to leave, he locked the sliding door and sat in my path. My stomach flipped. Would he rape me if I ended the night at a kiss? But he laughed—a joke, you see?—and we made plans to go out the next night. Something was different about me with him; I made him wait a month before sleeping with him. When we finally did have sex, I was brownout drunk. I remember music, the scent of vanilla candles, blue holiday lights tacked and flickering along the perimeter of my ceiling. The stiff and dirty rug of my childhood bedroom pressed into my back. But my mind didn't record the sex. Years later, I'd admit this gap to him, and his face would slump with disappointment. No concerns for my fragmented memory or the Black Haus that helped get me there. No wrestling with consent—a word that was still a zygote in 1996. Instead, he said with sadness and regret, *Man, I was good that night.*

Two months after our first date, Matt and I sat on my bed, and out of nowhere, he cut the air with it: *I love you.* My body trembled, an old familiar fear boiling beneath my skin. *You don't mean that,* I insisted and pressed a pillow into my stomach. *I do mean it,* he said and inched closer, our knees touching. *Maybe you mean it right now, but you don't mean it for real.* I studied the crease in his jeans, the knob of my ankle, anything but his face. *I am for real,* he said. *The day you walked into the Wood, I turned to Marty and told him I was going to marry you.* My pulse galloped. *Promise me,* I said. *Promise you won't change your mind. Promise you won't leave.* I hated myself for begging, for being so incredibly uncool, but I didn't have a choice. I had to be certain. He cupped my face with his palms and said, *I am always going to love you.* I looked at him for the first time since he'd said it: eyes blue as hydrangeas trained on mine, his lashes waving like seagrass when he blinked. He'd seen me drink and cry and be mean to others and starve myself thin. Still, he wanted me. Me, the unlovable girl. *I love you too,* I whispered, and in my mouth it felt like love does when you're twenty: permanent as a name in cement.

~

My father called Mike to brag that he was getting married. Less than a year had passed since the divorce, and my brother reported that, like his fiancée, our father was a born-again Christian now. I rolled my eyes so hard their sockets ached. I thought of the ruddy icons that had hung in his bedroom beneath an enormous framed painting of Crete: the alien-thin hands of the Virgin Mary, the inescapable eyes of Jesus. Saint Stylianos, protector of children, with his flowing beard and male-pattern baldness, had deeply sad eyes. Everything was a show. For my father, how you appeared to others—devout, funny, cunning— mattered more than how you acted, and this façade was linen thin, a clear and foolish attempt to make my mother jealous. When Mike told her of his plans to marry, she said, *God help that poor woman*, but that poor woman had some sense: she broke off the engagement a couple of months later.

My father bought himself a tiny yellow bungalow about fifteen minutes from my mother's house and invited Mike and me over for dinner. In retrospect, I'm not sure why I said yes. Maybe I wanted to be there for Mike, to make sure he didn't have to face our father alone. Maybe I was curious about what kind of home he'd built for himself without us. Both of those are likely true, but I know what's truer, and it stinks: despite everything he'd done, I still wanted him to love me.

There were familiar remnants scattered throughout his place, as if he'd gone to a garage sale in his former life. A rainbow-striped mug I'd once used for hot chocolate rested on the coffee table. The broken stereo system from our basement sat fat and useless against the wall. A framed picture of our *yiayia* rested in the hallway, an icon of the Virgin Mary next to her. And above the couch hung the item that most reminded me of my father: a painting, the same one that had been in my parents' bedroom throughout my life, displaying the clichéd pride of Crete: a cluster of grapes in one corner, a creature with the body of a man and the head of a bull in another, dolphins all around. My father also had a dog, a scruffy mutt who badly needed brushing; a cat named Joshua; and a tank full of boring fish. I don't remember what we ate or talked about or how long we stayed. I only remember the heat of my body. I folded myself in half at the edge of the couch, the dog's head resting on my bare feet, and prayed to cool down.

The second time I visited him, I picked up a six-pack and went alone. In my quest for growth, I'd been wrestling with an enormous word—*forgiveness*—and I was losing. I spent my early twenties twirling that word like a flaming baton. I asked everyone I met what the word meant to them and learned that many people have staunch and empty clichés at the ready: *He's your father. You have to forgive him. He's the only father you've got.* I said, *Sometimes not having a father is better than the one you've got*, and they looked at me like they'd met a monster they'd only heard tales of: the ungrateful daughter.

As I type this, *The Book of Forgiveness* by Desmond and Mpho Tutu rests on a stack next to my laptop. It is still a difficult word for me to tease apart, but here's what I know: no one automatically deserves forgiveness—not because of their blood or some allegiance to duty or propriety. The notion of forgiveness as something you give away is insidious. Why must we give anything more of ourselves to those who've taken so much? According to some, forgiveness is something you take for yourself, and, boy, that sounds great, but I don't know what that means. Truly. How does one take forgiveness *for* another person? Perhaps they mean one needs to begin by forgiving oneself, and I believe that to be true in most circumstances, perhaps all circumstances, but in the case of child abuse, in the case of terror, in the case of a girl like me who was once so little and helpless—you tell me where forgiveness lies.

Still, I wanted to try. I wanted to move past my father, beyond him, out into the world without a paternal Greek monkey on my back. I handed my father a beer, and we clinked cheers, then settled onto his couch to watch *Jeopardy!* To this day, it might be the best game I've played from a living room. I was on fire. My father looked at me in awe and said, *You were always the smart one.*

I wanted to yell, *I KNOW*, but I smiled instead. He sighed deeply before speaking. *I'm sorry*, he said. *For everything.* He rested his warm palm on top of mine. I pulled my hand away and looked at him. Wide eyes, a slight and soft smile. He looked so sincere that I choked down my tears with a swig of lager. *It's okay*, I said. *Me too.* I didn't yet know how not to apologize for things that weren't my fault, and in fairness, I still believed I was responsible for his behavior. As I drove away I thought, *Maybe it'll be different now*, but I hated myself for hoping so.

A few months later I was in bed with the flu, alternately sweating and shivering, my body filled with a thousand exploding matchheads, when my phone rang. My father. *What can I do?* he asked. *Nothing*, I moaned. *C'mon. Let me help.* I thought about it, my brain swirling with fever. *If it's not too much trouble, avgolemono*, I said. My favorite soup in the world, a tart and creamy egg and lemon broth I am certain can cure any ailment. To this day, my father made the best one I've tasted. *You got it*, he said. *I bring it tomorrow.* When tomorrow came, I craned my stiff neck every time an engine sounded on our dead-end street, but none was his. That call was the last time I heard from him for three months. The next time he called, I didn't pick up. *How stupid does he think I am?* I thought and dug my nails into my palm.

Ｃ❯

You'd think I'd have been dying to get out of the house I grew up in, that I would've moved out the day I turned eighteen, but I didn't. Despite being a handful of years older than me, Matt still lived with his parents, too, and we'd been alternating staying in his attic bedroom Greg Brady–style and my childhood bedroom. One evening, we went to a local bar and drank ourselves so stupid that when we got back to his house, I saw my first opossum and proceeded to stagger behind it for five blocks before Matt persuaded me to let it wander into the night alone.

In the corner of his bedroom, Matt kept a coin bank in the shape of an oversize Moosehead beer bottle, and while he emptied his pockets of change, he jumped from one foot to the other and waved a hand behind his head like fleshy antlers. He bellowed what was supposed to be a moose call while I choked for breath between fits of laughter, and in that moment, I had never loved anyone more.

In the morning, I awoke to Matt standing over me, and my body flinched.

"What the fuck?" he said.

I sat up quickly. Every internal alarm I possessed rang.

"What's wrong?" I asked and wiped my eyes.

"You stole my money, that's what's fucking wrong!" he yelled.

I didn't bother to point out I made triple what he did, or I'd picked up the bar tab the night before.

"What are you talking about?"

Blue veins snaked down his neck. He picked his pants up off the floor and shook them at me noiselessly.

"I had a bunch of change last night, and now I've got nothing. You're a goddamned thief."

Flag on the fucking play. I wish I'd stood up, gotten dressed, and walked out for good. My body told me to leave. It pumped me full of cortisol and said, *Run, run, run.* But I couldn't run away from love.

"Uh, you put the money in your bank last night. Don't you remember? You made moose noises." I watched the blackout veil lift and let in enough light for the memory to come into focus. He sat next to me on the bed and gripped my hands.

"Oh my god," he said. "I'm so sorry. I love you so much." And he looked so sincere that I choked down my tears with a hug. "It's okay," I said. "Me too."

But on the inside, I burned. I burned until later that night, when we went to the bar and pint after pint of cold beer soothed my fire.

A few months later, I signed a rental lease for a big house in a dodgy neighborhood, maybe ten minutes away from my mother but in the opposite direction of my father. Matt, Michelle, and I moved in together, and for a time, I was certain my life was turning around. I had autonomy and space and money. I had a kitchen big enough to cartwheel through twice. I had a dog, a basset-beagle named Dante, who never stopped barking or devotedly following me around. My father was out of my life. I had a man who loved me fiercely—who told me how important I was. I made his life so much better. He couldn't live without me. He left love notes tacked under the windshield of my car while I worked and bought me flowers for no reason. In short, I had everything I'd ever wanted.

But something simmered inside me. Yes, I had everything I'd wanted, but I felt terrible most of the time. *What is wrong with me?* I wondered again and again. *Why can't I just be happy?*

❦

I was freshly twenty-one the last time I visited my father at his home. He wanted me to meet his new girlfriend and her two kids, and enough time had passed since the forgotten soup incident that I'd softened back into another attempt at forgiveness. The holidays strummed our sentimental strings, so on Christmas Day, Mike and I met up at the yellow bungalow. I wore a hangover that seemed determined to skin me alive.

Indoors I was met with the humidity of holiday cooking: some fowl in the air cut by a sweetness, a pie maybe, and a bit of must, the living room scented more like an attic. The dog was gone, but the cat curled into my lap as I looked around. Sitting on the floor, a boy of six or seven years old pulled apart his brand-new action figures. I said, *Hey, whatcha got there?* He kept right on ignoring me to line up his new robots. Mike said, *He's really shy. He barely talks to me.*

The new girlfriend staggered from the bedroom, and I sat up straight. A short, braless woman with knotted ashy hair and a mismatched sweat suit slurred a hello. When she paid attention to her kids, her voice was sharp, a paper cut of demands. *Get these kids some food, for Christ's sake!* she yelled into the kitchen. I didn't know a woman could boss my father around. Listening to her bark at him, I smiled uneasily.

I wish my initial impression had been kinder, but I was skeptical of any woman who'd date my father. I hadn't considered how hard her life must have been or all the damage that could've led her to him. I hadn't yet sharpened my empathy.

After we'd awkwardly made small talk for a bit, the daughter came out of her room with a craft box and knelt at the base of the Christmas tree. She pulled a small sketchbook out of her stocking, lay on the floor, and started to draw. She had a couple of years on her brother, and her light brown hair fell straight as spaghetti past her shoulders and onto the back of her pajamas. She reminded me so much of myself that I instantly wanted to hug her. Instead, I slid down on the floor next to her. *I'm Lisa*, I whispered. *Whatcha drawing?* Unlike her brother, she looked at me for a quick second before going back to work, her face round and pale as a plate. *A horse*, she said to the paper, and indeed the hooves of an incomplete animal came into view. *You're pretty good*, I said, and the tips of her ears lit up pink. *Can I draw too?* She tore out a sheet for me, and I dug through the nubs of pencils in her box to find one with a point. *What should I make?* I asked, and she thought for a few seconds before she said, *An elephant.* I drew my very best one before handing it over. When she tried to give it back, I said, *It's for you*, and she smiled. The room spun with heat.

Are those all of your pencils? I asked and shook the box of scraps. She nodded, and the room spun again. *You don't have any other art supplies?* She shook her head no. *I'll be right back*, I whispered. I told my father I'd be back in thirty and sped with my window down in the cold December afternoon to my empty house. I took the stairs two at a time to my bedroom and boxed up everything I had: charcoals, oils, acrylics, pens, pads, brushes—everything I could to make my world stop reeling.

I spun with guilt. Jesus, did I feel guilty. I could see in her eyes that same desperation to be saved I'd felt my whole life, like it was a language only we spoke, and as much as I wanted to help her—to grab her hand and tell her we were making a break for it, that we wouldn't stop driving until we hit the Pacific, I obviously couldn't kidnap her. At twenty-one I thought of child protective services like Jesus or Santa, some omnipresent entity that magically knew when things were too bad and appeared out of the ether like Boyz II Men sliding into frame in matching white linen suits. I didn't know you could call *them*. Whenever people spoke of child services, it was always, *DYFS showed up*. It was never, *We called DYFS*. And besides, I'd done my time with him and survived. She seemed smart; I was sure she'd make it too. I was overreacting. Yup. That's it. Mountains, molehills.

Only now can I see the brutal truth I couldn't consciously touch that day. I boxed up my possessions to buy my way out of what I felt in my hot body, in the spiraling room: I was deeply relieved I wasn't her. It wasn't my turn anymore.

When I handed the girl my enormous bag of supplies, she stared at me blank-eyed. *It's for you*, I insisted. *Merry Christmas.* One by one she removed the brushes and paints and lined them up on the floor. I grabbed a beer from the fridge and gulped it down. I couldn't stay in that house. I had to get out. I drank another beer, made up an excuse about a stomachache, and waved my goodbye to the room. I was nearly out the door when I heard my name, and I turned to find the girl right next to me. She wrapped her arms around my waist. As I hugged her back, I tilted my head toward the ceiling, my throat tight as a zipper.

I pulled away from my father's house that night and wept on the empty holiday roads on the way to the bar. There I drank and drank and drank until I flooded my brain enough to put the memory of that little girl on a raft, one that floated into a dark estuary of my mind, one I'd wall in behind a psychic dam. Repression is a beast. It yanks the curtains shut on anything too hard to face and leaves in its wake nothing but darkness. Once the sun sets on those hidden memories, they need not see the light again.

Eventually, Matt and Michelle joined me by a fireplace, and we hugged and laughed and toasted the holiday with pints of Guinness. By the end of the evening, a blackout shade had been drawn over the day, the last time I set foot in my father's house while he was alive. I forgot that little girl, that tiny mini me, and didn't think of her again until I was forced to.

∽

A couple of years later, on the millennial New Year's Eve, amid the false panic of Y2K, we pounded beers, half certain our appliances would shut down in unison, planes would plummet from the sky, the planet would take a long blink into darkness. Mike and I had a party at our mom's house, the house he still lived in, and there were ten or so friends on the lawn, but I stood behind the screen door and watched as Matt, Kevin, my brother, and the other boys lit their fuses and split the night sky open with peonies, crossettes, and Roman candles. With names like Sky Bomb and Shellshock, I knew I was safer indoors. When the phone rang, I glanced at the number on the LED screen. My father. We hadn't spoken since I left his house that Christmas night feeling guilty and sick. Still, I was tipsy, generous. It was a new year, after all, and maybe even the end of times.

Hi, Dad.

Can you put my daughter on the phone? His breathing sounded labored, like he'd run to call me. The muscles around my ribs spasmed.

It's me, Dad, I said. I watched a wayward firework snake its way onto our neighbor's roof, the guys exchanging high fives in the fart trail of smoke it left behind.

I need to talk to my daughter. Go getter.

Dad, this is your daughter. I'm your daughter. I turned away from the party and sat on the arm of the couch. Twenty-three and still so easily made small by him.

No, he said.

No. If only. I'd wished for that "no" so many times; if it were possible, I'd have willed it into existence.

What do you want?

I wanna talk to my goddamn daughter! he yelled.

I hung up. He called again, and again did not believe me. The third time I answered, I pled with him.

Dad, it's me—really. I am your daughter. I swelled with exasperation, my breath shallow, my chest taut. Even now it is difficult to explain why I needed so badly for him to recognize me that day, to say my name, to say the word *daughter* and mean me. When I think of the mountain of needs we have as humans, that one seems so incredibly basic, like food or shelter or clean air. I needed to be seen and heard by him—two things I'm not sure I'd ever been before. For so many years, my father had been my entire world, but it was as though whatever relationship we had left was being held together by a small pin, our lives rigged and held in place by a half-inch piece of metal that finally succumbed to the weight of it all and snapped in half. Heat worked its way up my torso, the prickly wave of it rising up the back of my neck.

You know what? I asked and didn't wait for an answer. I held the phone in front of my face and slapped my words into the mouthpiece: *Fuck. You.* I slammed the receiver into its cradle, grabbed a new beer, and walked past the ringing phone to the lawn, where the boys were counting down the clock and still lighting the night on fire. Around me, rockets whistled and whipped through the air, exploding like brilliant dandelions over our quiet street. No one noticed I was crying.

When midnight struck and the world kept going, Matt pulled me in by my cheeks for a kiss. At least I had him, and he loved me so much it sometimes seemed to cause him pain. He'd told me he would die without me. If we fought and I left the house to collect my thoughts, he'd show up wherever I was. Once I went to Atlantic City after a bar shift with my coworkers, and half an hour later, Matt was there, watching me from behind a slot machine. My work bros asked, *What the fuck, man?* But I knew he loved me voraciously, like a man starved. That made him the new core of my world and allowed me to ignore the rest. Fuck my father.

I sat on our concrete steps and lit a smoke and thought about the call. *Britannica Junior* claims, "In growing up, every human being becomes a different person while, somehow, at the same time, staying the same person. As a person grows he keeps meeting new problems which he did not have before." In being so mean to my father, wasn't I being my shitty teenage self again? Wasn't I acting just like him? Did it matter he'd had it coming? Was it possible to be the bigger person with him? Did he deserve that? I wasn't convinced I had new problems. He'd been out of the house for years, and still I had to deal with the surprise of him, with the disruption.

On the lawn, my friends and brother drunkenly bellowed the refrain from a song, a victory cry for having cheated technological death. My tailbone grew numb against the steps, and I forced a smile, one that felt at first like trying on an uncomfortable mask, but eventually my face began to feel like my own. *Fuck. You.* Those are the last words I spoke to my father before he died. They weren't the most eloquent, but they'd slowly gathered momentum over my lifetime, formulating stroke by stroke until I had first one letter, then two, then finally two punchy syllables that summed up exactly what I'd desperately needed to say to him for so long.

$\sim$

When I was in high school, a counselor said to me, *It's clear you've been sexually abused.* I imagine I stared through her, her face I don't remember, unable to touch that part of my life. If I even thought of my father in the doorway of my bedroom or, worse, the weight of him on my bed, I grew so hot I had to leave, take flight, run outdoors. When I visited him that last time on Christmas, I did not possess clarity. I didn't look at his replacement family and consciously think, *They're in danger.* I did not look at the daughter and wonder if he visited her room at night too. Instead, I hoped for all of them that he'd learned his lesson, that all the promises he couldn't keep with me were finally coming true for a new family.

But what was there to stop him from continuing his march of terror? No one had ever stopped him before. He must have thought himself invincible.

According to my father, *a real man* made his own rules. Over the years, he'd received dozens of traffic tickets for proceeding through stop signs and red lights, for doubling, tripling the speed limit. When I was a child, a neighbor's dog wandered the streets freely and barked too much; my father killed it with poison. Three years before I was born, seven children at two different grammar schools complained that a man had exposed himself to them in the early hours of a January morning, and my father, freshly married and twenty-one years old, was arrested and freed on $600 bail. Another time, he was picked up for the same gross crime in a sporting goods store at the mall. No registry existed then. His grand punishment was probation, a warning, a talking-to, and he promised never to do it again. But that didn't matter to him. Laws were for some other poor sucker. Nothing was a crime if he decided it wasn't. Nothing was a crime if he didn't get caught.

PART II

Battlefields

CHAPTER 7

CRIME & PUNISHMENT

My beloved *Britannica Junior* observes, "It is commonly believed that most crimes are committed by the poor and members of the underworld." I'm sure the author meant the mob, but I immediately think of Hades, the god who, among his brothers Zeus and Poseidon, drew the short straw for what was his to oversee. In the underworld, Tartarus—the space where the dead spend eternity—is broken into three sections: Elysium, Asphodel Meadows, and Fields of Punishment. Depending on who you read—is it Homer? Edith Hamilton? Greekmyths.com?—your understanding of the underworld might vary, but I like to imagine Hades as the bouncer at the world's worst nightclub. He looks you up and down, decides you're a foxy and ethical little thing, and points you toward Elysium, a space behind velvet ropes, the VIP section. You and the immortals hang out, complimentary ambrosia bottle service. But maybe Hades sees you and thinks, *Meh. You're fine. Nothing special.* You'll scuttle your ass down a poorly lit hallway, and out you'll pop into Asphodel Meadows, the Chipotle of the afterlife. But if you're my father, Hades doesn't need to look. He feels you coming and summons the torturing Furies with his mind. He knows precisely where you belong. Welcome to the Fields of Punishment, motherfucker.

Oh, how I wish I believed that—that I believed in damnation of any kind. I think of death as eternal darkness: you're here and then—snap—you're gone. But if you happen to believe in some sort of hell, do me a favor; place my father there now. Tell me how he burns, how he jumps and winces at the devil's pitchfork. Tell me he's returned as a dung beetle, a worm, roadkill. Tell me he weeps at his sorry state. Tell me he has no power at all.

⁐

I stared at the TV, empty, weightless.

When Mike's tires crackled against the driveway, I peeled myself off the ground and wiped my face.

"Is it too early to drink?" I asked.

"Nope."

I popped open two Yuengling Lagers, and though we each took an initial sip, the beers remained untouched after that. We flopped onto the couch, stared blankly at the TV. More hurricane preparedness. We'd have to wait for the six o'clock news—a full forty-five minutes away—to learn anything more. Perhaps we were weighing where to begin, but it was oddly quiet for that first minute. I kept thinking about the gurneys Mike hadn't yet seen, rolling them through my mind like a grisly highlight reel, when a thought so obvious occurred to me, my heart sped up.

"Oh god," I said. "Mom."

⁐

I thought of pink, of "Moon Shadow" roses and drive-through strawberry milkshakes, of tutus and ballet slippers creased with wear. We knew where our mother was: at her dance studio, either manning the front desk or stretching her class to Earth, Wind & Fire, but it is impossible for me to picture her without pink, a spring color, a color of such obvious innocence the metaphor stings to type. As a teen, I used to say with the greatest sneer I could muster, *Pink is red's bastard cousin.* Red, still my favorite color, that of blood and Japanese maples and a Cy Twombly painting about Homer's *Iliad* that once made me cry. Beneath the furious red smear of Twombly's oversize canvas, a faint script reads, "Like a fire that consumes all before it." I ached to be an unfeeling force, one not pained by life or people, instead consuming the world with abandon. I'd long suspected I felt things too intensely, that all that feeling was, indeed, my deficit. To be fire. I'm not sure I considered what that would do to a person, how they'd sting from the slow sizzle of their own body.

"We have to call her, right?" Mike asked.

We faced each other on the couch. I never wanted to admit we looked alike. Everyone thought my brother resembled my father, but it was undeniable: both of us had olive skin, oval faces, and brown hair that lit up like copper in the sunshine. Our elbows slung over the back of the sofa, knees bent into figure fours, pillows hugged on our laps. My brother, this odd mirror.

I picked up my cell, but as soon as my thumb sunk into the first rubbery key, I lowered it again. My mind dropped back a decade and a half to my twelfth birthday, the day I told on my father, the day he pummeled my mother with his terrible fists as I watched, frozen.

It's painfully obvious the answer was yes. Of course we should have called our mom, but we didn't know much—only that something had gone grievously wrong at my father's house. On the surface, I thought, *Don't ruin her night at work, not with speculation.* The child taught not to have needs in action. But a few unspoken fathoms beneath that rested my twelfth birthday and the fundamental fact of my young life: there were unbearable consequences for telling the truth about my father.

"Let's wait until we know what's happening," I said. I patted the couch, and Dante jumped up between us. "I'm confused. How'd you wind up at the police station?"

Mike spread his fingers and examined his palms. "I didn't tell you, but I've been working with him." He'd graduated college a year earlier. In fact, both of us had, despite our two-and-a-half-year age difference. After a couple of years behind the bar befriending industry lifers who'd wished they'd done something else, something more, I'd finished my degree at Rutgers. I'd always known I'd go back when I was ready, and despite how fun it looks from the outside, slinging drinks made me yearn for something bigger.

"You know, for extra cash," Mike added.

Working with him. When I was still in middle school, my father left home one day in his Buick and returned in a shiny black van. He honked the horn, and we poured onto the lawn for the spectacle. On the van's side, an enormous airbrushed octopus clasped cleaning supplies in its tentacles: a feather duster, a bottle of Windex, a wavy white rag. In a crescent moon above its head floated the words: M&M Janitorial. M&M, my father's and brother's first initials. My father named the new business for himself and his son. He didn't understand that the laws of teenagerdom decreed "janitor" the lowest work a man could do. On our lawn, my father glowed with pride. How easy reinvention is. No discussion necessary. One day you're a line cook, the next you've got an octopus van filled with steam cleaners and one-gallon jugs of citrus-scented deodorizers.

"I went to clean the big office—his oldest account—and there was a sign on the door that said M&M Janitorial: Your services are terminated. So I called a bunch of times and he didn't pick up. Plus, I tried to call him a few times this week already. Finally I drove over there."

I stared at Mike's trembling chin, at the curls poking out from beneath his hat like tangled brown ropes, and folded my arms into my stomach, seeing my father's face in his.

"We should get some food," I said, not because I was hungry but because I didn't know what else to do. We ordered cheesesteaks and picked them up from the same corner pizzeria I'd frequented my whole life, the one I was banned from in my teen years for stealing, of all things, the collapsible bar that holds toilet paper in place. A pack of pervy, first-generation Italian brothers owned the shop, and when we walked in, I stared at the TV hung high in the corner, the local news crackling through the speakers. I wondered if they knew. Paying at the counter, I couldn't make eye contact.

The drive was five minutes each way, but it felt wrong being outside, out in the world, in a world too beautiful: seventy degrees, the cloudless sky blue as frosting. Back at my house, we slathered our sandwiches in ketchup and mayo until globs of pink dripped out the sides of the rolls. I flipped the channel to *SpongeBob*. Kind, stupid, happy SpongeBob. Mike's steak was gone in two minutes. He'd long been an inhaler of food. I took three or four bites and had to force those down.

"What did the cops say?" I asked.

He sighed. "Nothing. More than one body. They think one is his. Don't watch the news."

"I watched it," I admitted. "Three dead, but they didn't say who."

Mike nodded. I'm certain we were thinking the same thing. Four people lived in his house: my father, his girlfriend, a teenage daughter, and a younger teenage brother. Someone was still alive.

Mike dragged his fingers along Dante's spine. "He's dead, right?"

"I hope so," I said quietly.

People say you can tell a lot about a person by how they react in a crisis. I hope this isn't true. After all, who knows how to act in the throes of shock? And why should that be the measuring stick a person is pressed against? I tried to come at our confusion as though it were a logic problem, one that could be reasoned out. My sleepless nights spent watching *Law & Order* and *CSI* showed. I went into detective mode, and we ran the unthinkable scenarios.

I'd only met the girlfriend once on that visit to my father's at Christmas. She'd made a terrible first impression, and I felt like an asshole for thinking so.

"Dad said she was blackmailing him into staying in the relationship," Mike said.

"What? How?" That made no sense.

"I don't know, but he locks his cash and meds up in a safe so she won't take them. Like even his cough medicine."

"I mean, what if she downed a fistful of Vicodin and a pint of vodka and pulled out a gun?"

"Maybe?" Mike asked.

"Maybe," I said and felt gross for speculating. "What about the boy?"

The son played the part: death metal T-shirts, perma-scowl, eyes averted—not at all different from me at that age. Thirteen seemed young enough not to think things through, young enough to feel trapped, eighteen so far off there's no exit in sight. And he'd been in trouble before, the kind of kid the principal knew by name and on sight. Maybe all that clichéd angst had grown into something more powerful. Maybe it had turned into rage.

"You know him better than I do. Is it possible?" I asked.

Mike shook his head. "I don't know how any of this is possible."

I looked at SpongeBob and my stomach cramped so hard I almost puked. The daughter I'd blocked from my mind. If her life with him had been anything like mine, if she'd been pushed and poked and pinched, backed into corners, her muscles trembling, then yes, yes of course she could've done it. One evening, when my mother and brother weren't home, my father bounded in drunk and did to me what sexually abusive fathers do. Mercifully, my mind has blacked most of that out, but later that night, long after my father had been snoring the song of the blotto, I went to the kitchen and got the biggest knife in the drawer—what I now recognize as a chef's knife. I snuck into my father's bedroom and, weeping, held the wooden handle between two fists directly above his chest. I cried so hard I could barely see, my focus shifting between him and the painting of Crete above his bed. I couldn't do it: if I missed, if I only nicked him and woke him up, he'd kill me. That and that alone stopped me. In retrospect, that knife could barely cut chicken.

So: the daughter. Maybe in bed at night, her eyes barely focused in the darkness, she'd planned when she would take a gun from the safe in the basement. A twisted part of me thought she was brave if she did it, if she actually stood up to it all and ended it in a way I couldn't. I did not consider that one of the bodies had to belong to her mother or brother. I thought only of my father and her enormous relief, how the first good breath she'd taken in years must've felt as it sank into her lungs, her deepest bronchioles opening like a tree springing back to life.

But I couldn't say any of that to Mike. The years of my father in my bedroom, the heat of him: I'd yet to unpack that from its emotional Tupperware. I'd burp-sealed those memories ages ago. I'd be damned if they ever came loose.

"I don't think it was the daughter," I said. "Women poison. Guns belong to men."

Mike nodded at my confident bullshit.

When I think of us talking out those scenarios, I see two kids terrified to face Occam's razor. Did either of us really believe that woman or either of her children had killed their family? In the moment, I guess it seemed possible, but in truth it was so much simpler to pin the blame on near strangers than it was for us to consider our own.

"If it wasn't any of them, I'm fucked." He knew what I meant.

I couldn't speak it, could barely hold on to it in my mind. What if our father had murdered his family and was at large?

"Does he know where you live?" Mike asked.

"I don't think so." Right then: that's the moment we should have called our mother. He most certainly knew where her studio was. Later I would picture her sitting at the front desk, smiling on the phone, filing pink three-by-five index cards into a pink plastic box. If she saw her ex-husband crossing the parking lot, would she know to run? Had she ever run from him? I suppose that's what divorce is, a marathon's papery finish line.

"It's almost six," Mike said.

I flipped the channel back, the cheesesteak on my lap cool and congealed. I slid it onto the table and leaned forward. When it began, our father was "breaking news." A perfect phrase, really. News that breaks you open and apart.

As they replayed the footage of the SWAT team and the gurneys, I looked away and at Mike, a hum whirring through my body like a bell had been struck. I wonder if that makes sense to someone who's never had the body go numb with trauma, but that's how I felt: struck. The bronze of me clapped, my body ringing.

The footage was the same, but a new piece of the puzzle came out: *The bodies of three deceased—two female, one male—have been found in this small South Jersey home, victims of what appears to be a murder-suicide.*

"Oh god," I said and sat back.

"What the fuck?" Mike whispered.

The girlfriend and the daughter were dead. It was official. Two possibilities wiped out, two remaining: our father was either dead or on the hunt. And if he were hunting, I was sure I'd be next.

The only theory on crime that *Britannica Junior* posits is that of Italian criminologist Enrico Ferri, a man whose name I always misremembered as Ferrari. Ferri classified criminals as such:

> (1) the born—those feeble-minded or with criminal traits; (2) the insane, who usually commit crimes of violence; (3) the habitual who lives a life of crime—today's professional who makes his living by crime; (4) the occasional or accidental who commits crime due to certain circumstances; and (5) the passionate who commits crime because of a violent emotion of the moment.

Perhaps my father was born with criminal traits. It seemed such a part of him to get one over on people; it was as much a personality marker as being chatty or good at poker. But was he insane? Crazy like a fox, yes, but he wasn't headed for a straitjacket or padded room. He certainly wasn't a hired assassin, and even though Ferri's dated ideas have long been dismissed, I can't help but think of the last two items on the list. Was what happened in that house a terrible accident due to circumstances? Or was it his Greek passion that roused another violent emotion? How many of those had I seen over the years? But more than any of Ferri's theories, I was convinced the toxicology report would help us understand. We'd see a blood alcohol content never before registered, his veins coursing with amphetamines and crack and cocaine and every drug in existence. No matter what else we found out, if he were dead, there'd be some outside factor to blame. I was sure of it.

✎

As the news moved on to other stories, Mike and I sat silent, the room grown the grainy blue of dusk. I wish we'd had words for one another—assurances, kindnesses, affirmations—but we came up empty. There's no established etiquette for shock. Instead, without speaking a word, my brother and I leaned into each other's shoulders, the sides of our heavy heads pressed together. I imagine we both meant for it to be a brief moment of tenderness, but nearly instantly, we fell asleep. Or maybe we passed out. I suppose the mind can only handle so much before it shuts the body down, and our tolerance for grief was identical, genetic.

CHAPTER 8

ETIQUETTE

"Everything we do, or say, or choose; how we do it, the way we say it; every impulse we follow, is right if according to the rules of etiquette. It is wrong if against the rules."

—*Britannica Junior*, "Etiquette"

A peal of notes from the high end of a piano dragged me back to this world: my ringtone, "Tubular Bells" from *The Exorcist*, a choice suddenly steeped in gallows humor. But it wasn't like a horror movie, no hazy moment when sleep still clung to me and I thought it had all been a dream, when I ran naked into the forest, into the basement, boldly, stupidly. Instead, my muscles were leaden with the knowledge that my world had been irrevocably changed. Mike and I were still on the couch, lit only by the blue glow of *Jeopardy!*, the news over, the earth turned eastward enough to blot out the sun. Looking down, I noticed my sleeping brother's hand cupped to my leg above my knee, so I hooked my thumb into his sleeve and flung his arm back onto his body. Caller ID unknown. I stood to shake off the accidental intimacy we'd just shared, worried whoever was on the other end of the line would complicate our lives even more.

"Is this Miss Nik . . . Nik . . . Nikodalikus?"

What is it about Americans that renders them temporarily dyslexic when faced with a Greek surname?

"I'm the medical examiner for Camden County," he said. "We believe we have the body of your father, but a gunshot wound to the head and decomposition will make the ID difficult." Those are the words he chose—stiff, gross—and I didn't get hung up on the details. That would come later. What I heard was, *We can't be sure it's him.* What I heard was, *You're still in danger.*

"We need more information. Did he have any tattoos?" he asked. He sounded like a man with a mustache. I pictured the "Time to Make the Donuts" guy winding the cord of a landline 'round his sausage finger.

"No."

"What about birthmarks?" I looked at Mike who, groggy, watched me pace.

When I was a child, my father liked to scare me with stories of the devil. Unlike my Catholic classmates' Satan, our Orthodox devil didn't come to you with temptation; it was your failure of wits that led you to his lap. Our devil was a trickster; the Greek word *diavolos* means "slanderer." He'd fool you with his words, mixing enough truth with fiction that to pick his rhetoric apart would be like tweezing droplets of oil from a pot of boiling water. But there was one surefire way to spot him. Alone on our sofa, one of our ten VHS movies in the gargantuan VCR—*Ghostbusters* or *My Favorite Year* or *Romancing the Stone*—my father sloped toward me and asked: "How do you know the devil when you meet him?"

"Look for the hidden sixes," I answered and swung my feet. There was no greater thrill than pleasing him.

"You got it," he said and leaned back, smiling.

"Shave his head. Look for the sixes," I said. I imagined the cluster of numbers looped in a wheel on his scalp like the recycle symbol.

"Miss?"

"Sorry. Bad joke."

"Can you think of anything that might help?" he asked. I wondered if he looked at my father's body while he talked to me. Could it really be him? Or was the ME seated in an office, a stately room lush with mahogany and gold-framed watercolors? Everything I knew of death came from TV procedurals, which is to say I knew nothing. If those shows were at all accurate, it was more likely the ME stood surrounded by cinder blocks the color of slate, oversize bricks painted dull to discourage emotion.

I closed my eyes. I didn't conjure a specific moment—no Thanksgiving dinner or bottle-rocketed Fourth of July—but forged an amalgam: a lifetime of my father layered into a single image, one drenched in khaki and brown, even his skin tawny, like a man made of the desert. I squeezed my eyes tighter to examine this phantom, and his mouth dropped open. I tried to close it, to will it shut with my imagination, but I couldn't draw the father in my mind silent. Instead, his lips parted like a cartoon, the space above the tongue marker black, a character caught mid squawk. And then I remembered the shine of him.

"He had a gold tooth," I said.

"Good, good. Which side?"

A fifty-fifty shot and I still didn't know. Top row, for sure. I looked at Mike and pointed at each side of my face.

"Right?" he asked, unconfident.

"I don't know," I admitted. "It's hard to picture it."

"Do you know who his dentist is?"

I laughed, a small, ugly sound. My own teeth were rotting out of my skull. One dentist believed my shitty teeth were a side effect of childhood trauma. Another shamed me for the state of my mouth, convinced whatever's wrong in there was obviously my own neglectful doing. They were both right.

"As far as I know, he never went to one. He didn't believe in them." Was it possible for a grown man to have possession of all his teeth without seeing a dentist? Isn't it more likely he'd lied—another myth to illustrate his strength—and, like the rest of us, fidgeted in the chair while they jacked him full of Novocain?

"Maybe he went and I didn't know," I confessed.

"Oh," he said, and before he spoke again, a long silence dangled between us. "Are you estranged?"

Estranged? I'd never considered the word, and my mind emptied. *Estranged. C'mon, English major! Gather your synonyms: stranger, alien, foreigner, irrelevant.* My father had been a stranger to me even when we were close. He was an alien in this country who'd gotten his green card when he married my mother, a foreigner most certainly, but never irrelevant. Never that.

I repeated the word into the phone: "Estranged." It felt long in my mouth, a pulled taffy of sound.

The ME sighed audibly. "Does he have any other family?" Translation: *Is there someone more helpful than you I can talk to?*

I told him there were people in Greece—sisters only, I thought— but in this country, it was just Mike and me.

"As the oldest, you'll need to make some decisions regarding the body." I stopped pacing, my internal brakes jammed. How could I make decisions if we didn't even know it was him?

"Like what?" I asked. Poor, patient Mike. I should've put the call on speaker.

"Well, you can claim the body and make your own arrangements, or you can not claim it."

I turned away from my brother and patted my thigh. Dante followed me to the kitchen. "What happens if I don't?" I asked quietly.

"The county disposes of it."

"Would he have a grave, or do you cremate?" I asked and dumped a scoopful of food into the dog's bowl.

"We'd bury the body, and no. No grave. Just a number."

I pictured the burial at the end of *Amadeus*, bodies sewn into cheap linen sacks and flung into a mass grave, shovelfuls of lye heaved on top.

"Miss? You should talk to your family about it, but ultimately, it's your decision."

"Okay," I said, even though nothing was okay.

"Well, have a nice day."

He actually said that. Nice etiquette, man.

⁕

There are people who in times of crisis turn to meditation or prayer. Others strap on their Nikes for a night run or head to the gym to go nowhere fast on an elliptical. We went to the bar. At a stoplight on the way there, my mind zeroed in on that word again: *estranged*. I stared at the glow of the red light. I'd later come across the word in Alexander Pope's translation of the *Odyssey*: "To rest and joy Estrang'd, since dear Ulysses sail'd to Troy!" A line almost odd for its glee. Had my life grown more restful or joyful without my father? And the ME seemed to have used it as a noun, as though *estranged* is a state of being or a vacant island, but I was certain it was a verb, an action. A horn blasted from behind us, and I hit the gas. Did that mean it was something done *to* me? Or had I done it to myself?

Fortunately, the bar was slow, and we had the back room with the pool tables and TV to ourselves. My body thrummed, a vibration so internal I was certain if you held a stethoscope to it, you'd hear my skin scream. I needed booze, and I needed it fast. My favorite bartender, Phyllis, a surly and smoky grandmother, was on duty, and before I asked for it, she placed a Guinness in front of me. I told her to back it up with Jameson. *If ever there were a night for double-fisting*, I joked. It didn't land. Why would it? It felt like everyone knew what was going on with us, with our father, but for her and the six lumps on the stools at the pub, it was just another weeknight.

We waited for three people to join us: Matt, Michelle, and Kevin. Reflexively, I chalked the tip of my stick while Mike racked the balls, and I thought of a night years before I could legally drink when my father picked me up from Greek school on his motorcycle and took me to a crumbling dive for baskets of fried shrimp and clams. From the booth, I watched him make the rounds, speaking the language of back claps and belly laughs as I dipped my greasy grub into a hill of tartar sauce. I watched as he leaned into various women, their slender arms tracing his muscles when they giggled. He disappeared for a while—ten, twenty, thirty minutes—so I looked on at the bar crowd with an anthropologist's excitement. One woman tilted her head to light her smoke, shielding her lighter from a wind that didn't exist. Two men cursed and laughed in the same breath, on the cusp of a fight or a hug. Nearly everyone who tossed back a shot slammed the empty glass against the grain of the bar when they were through. When my father returned, he placed a cherry Coke topped with an atomic knot of maraschinos in front of me and a quarter in the jukebox. Joe Cocker's "You Are So Beautiful" played, the only American song I'd ever known my father to love, and he spun me around in a pantomime of slow dance before my billiard lessons continued. His vocabulary wasn't advanced: no "object ball" or "Angle A" talk. Instead, he stood across the table from me and tapped his finger against the precise spot I needed to smash with the cue if I wanted to sink the eight. *Don't forget*, he reminded me every freaking time, *the Greeks invented geometry.* Later, after we'd played for hours and I buzzed with caffeine and sugar, we climbed atop his black-and-gold Honda motorcycle for the half-hour ride home. On the highway, we swerved between cars: sixty, seventy, eighty miles per hour, my body gripped to his like a koala, the wind boxing our ears.

Mike and I didn't talk; we played, and I ran the table, three of the best games of my life. I owned it all: the breaks, the rail rides, the bank shots. The eternal field of the green felt small, manageable. I worried in playing so well—in playing so well at *that* moment—I was more connected to my father than I ever had been, that he was there beside the table, guiding my hand like he'd done when I was a child. I asked Phyllis to keep the whiskey coming.

Michelle and Kevin arrived within five minutes of one another, and though Michelle's hug helped a little, bringing them up to speed did not. The story sounded worse with each retelling. Michelle said, "Whoa." Kevin shook his head and asked, "The fuck?" then whistled. "Damn."

On greeting people in a social setting, *Britannica Junior* instructs, "If you are a girl you need not make a curtsey if this is not customary among your friends, but you should bow a little as you shake hands—and let us hope *smile!* One thing not to do is stand like a ramrod and look glum."

Matt came in and kissed me on the cheek, and stiff as I was—stiff from everything happening, stiff from his choice not to come home—he was still the love of my life. But the love of my life had no words for me. Just, "Hey, babe." I had no smile for him. I focused on my shoes before walking to the back bathroom and locking the door. I pressed my palms against the cool porcelain sink. In the mirror, I saw some other girl: a young woman instantly aged. I stared and stared, my reflection unflinching, but quick as a hiccup my image shifted. I saw my father's face in my own—the ruddy skin of his chin, the blue of my own eyes turned dark as dirt—and I ran out of the room. I didn't rejoin my friends. Instead, I hung back and hid behind a column in the center of the room, my breath shallow, my heart galloping.

I wish I could write that seeing my friends, my love, dimmed the pain, or I felt the shortness of life and ballooned with gratitude for their friendship; I decided right then and there to live every day like it was my last! I'd stitch *carpe diem* or *everything happens for a reason* onto pillows. But I wasn't filled with inspirational quotes, and nothing felt precious.

When my friends experienced their own shock, when they reached into their pockets and pulled out nothing to say but "Whoa" and "Hey, babe," something calcified in my gut, a pebble that grew quickly into a rock. It wasn't the whole of me; no, it was small, but I felt it rattle. Next to our pool table stood the three people I loved most in the world, and I wanted to smash their faces with my stick. As I looked on at their silence, I began to understand the rock acutely. It was rage. Here were our friends showing up in our ugliest time of need, and what turned loudest inside of me was rage. I hated myself for it.

But I didn't know what to say either, so I kept playing pool and drinking, looking ramrod glum between shots. I hadn't eaten but a few bites of the cheesesteak; I should've felt a little buzz after the second beer, but instead of that welcome blur, everything seemed to sharpen, as if the more I drank, the clearer the world around me became. None of these people were up for this. *Soon enough*, I thought, *I'll be in this alone.*

When the eleven o'clock news came on, I tiptoed to turn up the volume and sat back on the felt of the table, flanked by my brother and friends. Matt slung his arm around my shoulders, and the weight of it didn't register. Our father was the news of the night, and I thought I might vomit, but I choked it down and twirled the slick pool cue between my thumb and forefinger. The same footage as before played, footage I seemed to have memorized, but this segment was longer, replete with interviews with neighbors. One woman looked into the lens and said, *He seemed like such a nice man. We're in shock this could happen here.* Another: *We liked him. He was so friendly. Just goes to show you . . . you never know about people.* Clichés looped from centuries of crimes. I wondered, what makes people so willfully blind to danger? How could someone meet my father—or live with him—and not see the slither beneath the man? The rock in my stomach turned, and my rage blasted into focus; I wasn't angry with my friends or Mike for not knowing what to say. I seethed because they were surprised.

And it wasn't fair, my fury, but trauma's currency isn't equity or logic. Its agony is steeped in solipsism; you can't see past yourself, your pain. There'd never been a sit-down with friends or family in which I told them about the father they couldn't see clearly. Sure, I'd howled for years in every way I knew how: with my gothic armor, with one-inch X-ACTO scars on my arms, with drugs and booze and sex. But I'd never said, "Hey, Mom: Dad is sexually abusing me," or, "Michelle, if I'm late coming home, my dad might punch me in the ribs." To speak my fear out loud was impossible; I'd done it once—on that birthday when he'd beat my mother. The cost for telling was simply too high.

And now, waiting for the news, I knew I'd been right. The cost actually had been too high. I hadn't imagined it. He could have killed me, killed us.

Mike's elbow bumped my ribs, and I looked up at the TV. There, for the first time, we had confirmation: his name, our impossible-to-miss last name, spelled correctly at the bottom of the screen in bold yellow letters.

Our father was dead.

⁓

Within seconds my phone buzzed: our mother. How much adrenaline must've surged through her when she saw the news—when she imagined she'd have to break the unthinkable to her children?

I walked outside to answer and opened with, "We already know."

"Oh Christ. Is Mike with you? Are you guys okay?" she asked, her voice like a breaking tide.

"Yes," I said. "We're fine. We're at the bar."

"Don't drive, Lisa. Please don't drive tonight. Let me come and get you. You can both stay here."

"Okay."

"I can't believe this is happening," she said. "I can't believe what he did."

The rock in my gut swelled.

"We'll be there soon," I said. "We've got a ride."

Back inside I said only, "Mom knows," before picking up my pint and downing it. I swiped my keys off the tabletop. "Let's go."

When we pulled up, I stared at the front door, at the chipped brass knocker that hung in the center of a tangled twig wreath. At the end of the house, the window of what used to be my bedroom glowed dull with amber. I wondered if it had always glowed—if even without a light turned on the remnants of all that had happened in that room caused it to blaze.

Through the living room's bay window, my mother reclined on her sofa, eyes closed or pointed at the ceiling. She looked beautiful. I turned away and stared ahead at the mouth of our wooded dead end.

"Tell her I'll call her tomorrow. I can't."

Mike shifted to look at me. "Dude, you should at least come in and give her a hug."

He was right, but I wasn't sure what would happen if my mother embraced me. I might cry forever, but I also might be vicious. I didn't know what would come out of me next.

"Give her one for me," I said. "I'll see you tomorrow."

He walked in and they embraced, a hug that rocked and had so much meaning in it, my muscles tightened with ambivalence: the urge to run to her and spill the truth of it all slammed into my need to stay silent. When I look back, I recognize that not joining them was a choice I made—the first of many ill-advised ones to come. Surely I could've gone to my mother, could've curled up in her lap and wept and tried to split my grief into three equal measures, but that wasn't how we'd ever lived. We'd managed our lives, our pain, our secrets separately. I'd long ago learned not to burden my mother with anything.

At the time, it didn't feel like a choice. My brother still willingly spent time with our father. And my mother had never seen clearly what he was capable of, even after he'd beaten her or me. That she could be shocked by him felt like a mammoth betrayal: the same betrayal I'd been carrying for years and hadn't begun to sort out, the betrayal that earlier had hardened into a rage rock in my gut. Where were the people who wouldn't be surprised by this awful new violence of his?

⁓

Snippets of the end of that night are blacked out, like a poem whose words have been struck through. At some point, I went inside my own house and got another beer. Michelle headed to bed, I guess. I've lost Matt entirely in this memory. Did he even come home? Did he go to our bed? Did I lie when I said I'd be up in a minute? I don't know. What I do remember is spreading out on the floor of my cavernous living room, Dante curved like a comma against my stomach. I stared at the ceiling and repeated a single word to myself: *murderer*. In poetry classes, they teach you about the importance of syllabic stresses; it's how you find the music of your words. But *murderer* seemed to me three even stresses, each syllable a fist pounded in the other palm. From the floor, the room spun ever so slightly, and I repeated the word until I could name how it made me feel: numb. This wasn't the numbness I invited with drink; this was an old hurt ripping through my body. It was the numbness I'd felt all those years ago when my father visited my bedroom, the numbness I'd needed to survive the heat of that man. But I wasn't ready to face those old memories. No, I shoved all of that into some boozy part of my mind and instead focused on another truth: as I'd suspected for an instant at the bar, I was in this alone.

⌒❨

The next morning, I awoke fully clothed and facedown on the floor, half a warm lager slanted and clamped in my palm, the fibers of my beige carpet pushed deep into my cheek and nostril. I rolled over and flinched when I saw Matt standing above me in his work clothes, the men of my life forever watching me. He offered his hand, which I grabbed to rock myself upright, my joints cracking like Bubble Wrap. The stink of alcohol leached out of my pores.

"I could call in sick," he said and squatted next to me. "Spend the day with you." I wanted him to force a smile, to fake a little normalcy, but the lines of his forehead rippled with worry.

I shook my head and the living room unsteadied, our house bobbing on an invisible river. I didn't want to talk; the inside of my mouth burned hot and foul. I looked away and said, "You should go. You need the money. Plus, I have to work too."

He squeezed my calf. "Maybe that's not the best idea."

Somewhere inside me lived a reasonable person. I could feel her screaming for help, clawing at my rib cage, but she was small, a thimble-size girl whose mousy voice got drowned out by my shouting brain, the much louder irrational voice that overrode every internal argument. *Don't be a pussy. Go to work or they'll think this ruined you. Staying home means your father wins.*

"I'll be fine," I said and got to my feet. "I can't sit around here. I need the distraction."

Matt didn't look persuaded, but he didn't argue either. Instead he glanced at the clock and leaned in to kiss me goodbye. I offered my cheek. As soon as he was out of sight, I wiped the wet remnants of it off with my sleeve and sat back down on the floor, arms folded over knees, head pressed to forearms. I had to go to my mother's house.

⌒❨

How do you begin an inconceivable conversation when your life has existed in the silent gaps? We had never been a family that spoke truthfully about hard things. Could we start now?

I went upstairs to get dressed—torn jeans and a crinkled Misfits tee, a Phillies hat I'd found at the bar to shield myself from eye contact—and flipped on the TV. I punched in the numbers for our local news station but accidentally hit the wrong keys and wound up on a public access channel. On-screen, a group of half a dozen or so people sat in the familiar circle of a support group. To this day, I don't know what to make of the coincidence: they shared and discussed the difficulties of having parents who'd murdered someone. Zapped into my bedroom was the support group I needed most, a new group I was part of, but instead of listening—it seemed so unlikely, so mathematically impossible for it to be on my television at that very moment—I turned it off, afraid. If I randomly chose a channel every day for the rest of my life, I am certain this wouldn't happen again.

In my mother's driveway stood a reporter, just one, confirming my worst suspicion: yes, everyone would know about my father. Everyone would know about me, about what freaks we all were. Such an old fear, but I couldn't separate the old from the new. When my father died, everything felt present—every memory risen to the surface at once. Everything felt present but me.

Dashing past the journalist, I mumbled, "No comment," and barreled into the house, where my mother hugged me hard, my body so numb I barely felt her touch. I joined my brother at the kitchen table, our faces carved and thin from lack of sleep. How many tense meals had we shared with my father in that kitchen?

"What can I do?" my mother asked.

"Nothing," I replied.

"That motherfucker," she said and paused before adding, "Food? Have you eaten?" I hadn't.

"How about a smoke?" I asked. It had been six months since I quit.

"Please don't start smoking again. Not after this long."

I put my head down on the table and spoke into its chipped wood. "Did either of you talk to the vulture on the lawn?" I asked. Neither had.

As my mother sat down, I felt the pressure of the room change. She and my brother were exchanging a look. That's a superpower of trauma: you feel those molecular shifts.

I lifted my head. "What?"

"We have to decide what to do with the body," my mom said. Her voice was tender, worried something might set me off, which is precisely what made my face go hot. I wasn't a wisp of spun sugar. Didn't she know how strong I was? How much I'd survived? And like that, my sneering teenage self showed up—unwelcome by all.

"Let him rot," I said.

"That motherfucker," my mom said.

Mike shifted in his seat. "I think we should have a funeral."

"Why?" I asked unkindly. I knew the answer. He was close to our father. Somehow.

"It's the right thing to do," he said.

"He doesn't deserve the right thing," I said and took a deep breath before careening into a tirade about funerals being a celebration of life.

"What the hell would we be celebrating?" I yelled. "He's a fucking murderer. And a coward. Let the county claim him. He deserves nothing from us. Nothing."

"Honey," my mother said. "You don't want to regret this decision later in life."

I snorted. "I won't. Ever. But if you two want to have a funeral, fine. I don't give a shit."

For a long time, I wrote and rewrote that scene, then scolded myself afterward: what an asshole I was. My father was gone, and there sat my grief-stricken family, forced to walk on proverbial eggshells by me. I was a volatile force, a block of dry ice, a thin line of mercury. Some part of me knew we were all going through this, but my pain overrode my empathy. My pain overrode everything because I didn't understand what was happening inside me. I had gotten the worst of my father in life; wouldn't he have the last laugh if that were true in death too? I'd joked years earlier that all he'd leave us was a legacy of debt and a bad reputation. I didn't know the inheritance tax I'd pay would be in rage dollars, and I certainly didn't know I would have to pay for years.

It is a painful thing to learn that opposing ideas can be true at once. We love to view the world in binary terms, but I'm old enough to know now when a binary surfaces, that's a signal to take a beat—to think harder. Most of the world exists in the gray, and that day when I left my mother's house, I knew two things to be so incredibly true, I felt like an idiot for not recognizing one of them sooner: yes, my father had been abusive, but he'd also been a sick man. How obvious that is in hindsight: the swollen ego, the grandeur, the rapid mood swings, the inability to keep his cock in his pants. I'd believed I'd known the worst of my father, but this new violence—those goddamned gurneys— revealed a new man. What would a man like him keep in his home? What would a man who'd killed hide?

CHAPTER 9

MAN

Britannica Junior claims, "Man is the highest form of life on the earth."
I am willing to wager that the person who wrote this did not inherit a
crime scene from his father.

As the days after my father's death ticked by, I grew frustrated by
my confusion. Did we get a lawyer first? When did the ME confirm
the body was his? When did Matt stop sleeping in our bedroom? Who
gave us the key to our father's house? I began listing the events in a
notebook, trying to keep the order straight, a sheet of loose leaf I still
have. Number 11 is "my inability to create a timeline."

Trauma throws you underwater instantly. Sure, you can open your
eyes, but you damned sure can't see anything clearly.

We inherited a lawyer—the same one who'd represented my mother
in her divorce—and he advised us to find any paperwork that might
prove useful, so Mike and I drove to our father's bungalow together and
sat parked at the curb. A ribbon of crime-scene tape waved from the
railing above the steps. Mike broke the silence.

"I don't want to go in there."

"I know," I said and cut the engine.

"The scientist studies the evidence left behind," *Britannica Junior* says. "Experts piece together the fragments of skeletons—a few teeth, a broken skull, a few long bones—and make a model of what they believe man looked like in the past." I knew, of course, what my father looked like in the past, but four years had slipped by since I'd seen or spoken to him, and I was certain something terrible must've happened to provoke his violence. Nothing happens for no reason; everything is causal. I was determined to piece it together.

I paused on the steps before his front door, opened a can of Vicks VapoRub, dabbed a bit in the divot below my nose, and encouraged Mike to do the same. If *Law & Order* had taught me anything, it's that you never get used to the stench of death, but those endless marathons didn't prepare me for smelling it for the first time. Had Lennie Briscoe been by my side, he'd have cracked wise about how green I was.

The smell: sulfur and mothballs, rotten fish and rotten eggs and rotten cabbage. Rot, rot, rot. Death soaks into everything, and you take it with you when you leave. To this day, I can sniff out decomp like a bloodhound.

And though the smell punched us, standing in the house felt like being choked. Neither of us wept; instead, we surveyed. In the living room and hallway, the police had cut and removed hunks of carpet in imprecise lines, leaving behind dozens of nylon fibers that stretched toward our ankles like worms. A rectangle of wall in the hallway had also been taken, and we took turns pointing when we discovered flecks of blood—on the floors, the walls, the ceiling. In the bottom of the bathtub, a sea of dead black blowflies sent me quickly back to the hall-way, and I turned into the bedroom—the daughter's bedroom. My body throbbed: the crime techs had left behind her mattress soaked brown with blood, the room splashed with spatter. Mike looked over my shoulder.

"Jesus," he said, and I walked back to the living room. The living room seemed safer.

A school of mismatched freshwater fish eyed me. I opened their tank and sprinkled in some flakes, watched them rush to the surface. *Had the police fed them?* I wondered. I lifted a newspaper off the coffee table. September 10—five days ago. The last day someone had been alive to bring in a paper—if they got the paper every day, that is. The tenth was a Wednesday, and some folks only get the midweek and Sunday editions. It was barely a clue.

Or was it? My birthday is September 13. Had my father awoken that morning and felt the loss of me so acutely that it pushed him to violence? Was it his final cryptic message for me? *This is what happens when you cut off your father; you clean up his horror.* A troop of flashing lights crowded my vision, and I shook my head, a lesson from cartoons in how to make the swirling canaries go away after being hit over the head.

I would never have a precise time of death; in place of that clock, I'd have words pilfered from an autopsy report: *bloating, discoloration, skin slippage, infestation by maggots of all stages of maturity without pupae.* Words I'd carry for life.

"Lis, where should we start?" Mike asked.

But I was stuck in an internal loop: this horror had occurred either on my birthday or the day before. As I stood there in my swamp of grief, part of me genuinely wanted it to have happened on my birthday—to be as full of self-pity and sadness as a person can. What had happened was unfathomable, but I desperately needed it to be as awful as possible, for the narrative to leave no loophole for the kind people who'd try their best to console me. I wanted no one to say, *At least it wasn't on your birthday*. Eventually, I'd figure out the date doesn't matter. Whether it falls on my birthday or not is inconsequential. My neural pathways have forever linked the two.

"Lis?" Mike said louder and stepped next to me, so I did what I do when things seem impossible: I went to work.

"Okay, man. Divide and conquer. You want up or down?"

"Up." Why he'd want to stay up there was beyond me. At least there was no blood in the basement.

"Fine. Look for anything important, anything valuable," I said. Our father had been the kind of man who'd stash money in a wall before handing it over to a bank.

"You think we'll find something?"

"Who knows." But I hoped we would—bound stacks of hundreds, tens of thousands of dollars in compensation for having to be in that house, for having lived with him at all. "If you need me, holler."

Crossing the kitchen toward the basement door, I paused before the stovetop, a stainless stockpot on one of the burners. When I peered over the lip, I found more dead blowflies and three bloated ears of corn bobbing in water white as a cataract. They'd been cooking dinner. Corn. How could things go so wrong when sitting down to the food of picnics and county fairs? I bowed my head, my breath yoked in my throat.

☙

Even as an adult, I find basements endlessly creepy. It could be fully furnished, packed with La-Z-Boys and flat screens, meticulously clean, nary a spiderweb or dust bunny. Doesn't matter. Once you go underground, anything can happen.

Britannica Junior states, "The early homes of man furnish other important evidence. In caves beside old river beds, in shell heaps along the ocean shores, and in great earth mounds farther inland, scientists have uncovered tools, weapons, kitchen utensils, carvings, and beautiful paintings."

In the basement I found no utensils, carvings, or paintings, but there were tools, and there were weapons—sort of. I reached into his open safe and pulled out a piece of a gun—the slide, I think—and stared at the other gun parts that lay on the shelf. My anger swelled. Eleven boxes of ammunition sat there too. How could the cops leave that behind? I don't know guns, and I'm sure the parts were unusable without their triggers, but still, why not bag it?

A small desk stood stacked high with papers, the filing drawers nearly bursting, so I sat down, ready to find some answers. First, I spun in the chair to take in the room. It seemed like from the day my father first came to America, he started collecting other people's trash; the basement was where pilfered things went to die. Chairs: a smattering of mismatched ones, their veneered arms rubbed down to a splintery grain, some with one leg off kilter, others cast aside for aesthetic reasons. More nonworking vacuum cleaners than any sensible person needs collected dust against a cinder-block wall. Countless incomplete sets of dishes and photographic equipment, some of it antique, lay piled everywhere, every dark crevice crammed with junk and insects. One of my feet involuntarily thumped against the concrete floor.

Although I did find two insurance policies and the title for a Chevy Blazer, the other discoveries were far worse: dirty letters and sex toys, private fantasies no one should commit to paper in case their children one day have to sift through them. Smutty, bushy Greek porn. Tax returns from fifteen years earlier. Almost a thousand empty trash bags on the metal shelves. Burned-out light bulbs. Receipts of donations to the church. Evidence of bad spelling everywhere. No will. No suicide note.

Tacked to a corkboard hung a paper I'd written for Greek school on what Easter meant to me that I could no longer translate in its entirety. I remembered my teacher's fury when I'd gushed about candy and a bunny instead of penitence and Jesus. Next to that hung two blue-and-white-striped international envelopes—letters from my aunts in Greece—and I stuffed them into my back pocket. It seemed smart to have their addresses, just in case. Under a mound of files, I discovered a stained manila folder with my name on it and tore it open—unguarded, unprepared. My father had thirty-two pictures—I counted—of me as a child that I'd never seen, and I flipped through the happy, smiling stack. It was evidence of a childhood I simply didn't and don't remember. Abuse does that, you know. Closes the door on hours, days, months at a time. These could've been fakes—like the fish photo—but maybe not. I ran another count; he only had fourteen pictures of Mike. The man who'd made his inequitable love for my brother clear, the man who'd named his business after his son, the man who'd violated me again and again kept an envelope stuffed with my glee. Did he sneak down to his basement when his conscience screamed to remind himself that it wasn't all bad? That he hadn't ruined me? I pressed my forehead to his desk and, for the first time since I'd gotten the news, wept.

My moment was interrupted by a soft scratching sound coming from somewhere behind me. Spinning around in the chair, I stared into the musty darkness but saw no signs of life. I'm embarrassed to admit that my mind immediately turned to ghosts, but before I could go wild thinking about what I'd do in the face of my father's specter, I heard it again, a much clearer scrape coming from a place close to the ground. I dropped to my knees, scanning the cracks between shelves until I caught two yellow eyes peering at me from beneath the water heater. I crawled across the concrete floor to get a closer look, afraid it might be an oversize rat or raccoon, when I realized I was nearly face-to-face with my father's cat, Joshua.

Imagine how scared Joshua must've been when the night escalated, when the shouting grew louder, when the gunshots rang throughout the house, when he remained alone and trapped. I wept harder than when I'd found the pictures. I'd felt that terror before, and here it was again, filling my body like a special-effects spirit entering a medium.

I whispered his name, and he bellowed—a low, guttural noise, a mewl of distress. I inched my arm under the heater, tried to grab hold of a leg, but he clawed me and I drew back. I called his name again, barely choking it out through my sobs, and again he clawed me, each sharp swipe of his paw drawing a clean line of blood. For ten minutes, I reached for him, only to earn another lash, and when eventually I got ahold of him, I cradled and rocked his wriggling body. *Everything will be all right, everything will be all right, everything will be all right,* I whispered, until Mike shouted my name from the top of the stairs. Perhaps he sensed it wasn't okay to descend. I stood with Joshua in my bloody arms and wiped my cheeks against my shoulders, cleared my throat.

"I'm done," I shouted.

And I was.

～9～

Upstairs, I dumped a hill of food into Joshua's bowl and let him leap from my arms to run off and hide. Mike held a faded cigar box in one hand; my father's coin collection was all he'd unearthed. No will. No suicide note. We stood in the living room, staring at it. A lifetime with my father and what? Half a dozen rolls of wheat pennies and a loose pile of Eisenhower silver dollars.

"You ready to drink?" I asked.

We drove to the closest bar, a dive my father had likely frequented, and ordered mugs of happy-hour beer, cheap and yellow. When we opened the box to pay for them, the young bartender turned the coins over in her hand.

"What even is this?" she asked.

I sighed and assured her silver dollars are like regular ones—only bigger—and we drank until the collection was gone.

I wish I remember what we talked about, and I'd like to write we discussed feelings—our vulnerability, our anger—but I know us well enough to know that's not true. More than likely, we sank into our stools while classic rock beamed out of shitty speakers. More than likely, we talked about everything but our father. Just like we always had.

◦—◦

A few days later—maybe even a week later—we were slated to meet some members of the surviving family at the house, including the son, the boy who no longer had a sister, a mother. I don't remember how this plan came about. Did our attorney arrange it? Did I speak to them? That information is gone. What remains is dread. The idea of stepping back into that space was awful, but meeting the family of the people my father killed was unbearable.

What would they say, these people, these strangers? I convinced myself they would be cutting and cold, brimming with hatred for us because our father had destroyed their lives. I thought they'd be right to feel that too. Displaced anger doesn't care where it lands; it needs only a soft target, and in the wake of my father's crimes, I was softer than anyone alive. I called a friend I used to tend bar with, a man who'd moved from slinging drinks to the police academy, and asked if he'd stand guard. *You won't have to go in*, I assured him.

Mike and I arrived an hour early to make sure we'd gotten everything we wanted the first time around. The thought disgusted me and conjured images of village lootings, like in *Zorba the Greek* when the shriveled *yiayias* wait for a woman to die so they can claim her luxurious things, wrapping their wrinkled bodies in her expensive clothing and jewelry before she's even dead.

We didn't loot anything, and I suppose that word is too harsh, but a dirty opportunistic feeling kept creeping up on me, so I spent most of the time before the family arrived standing in the living room, staring at the painting of Crete that hung above the sofa—the one that once hung in my parents' bedroom. The sea was the bluest blue, a blue so deep it seemed you could sink into it, and so I did.

The single thing pacifying my anxiety was the certainty that I'd never have to come back to the house. This was it. It would be awful, but it was already upon us, nearly over.

They were late, and we listened for an approaching U-Haul, something large enough to collect the possessions of everyone who'd lived there. When the family pulled up—grandmother, uncle, and surviving son—in a Honda Civic hatchback, Mike and I exchanged an exhausted look, and I bent over. They could have squeezed a grand total of two small boxes in their car. I knew instantly we'd have to come back.

Again.

Standing in the doorway, I felt dizzy, and my heart slammed in my torso as three people approached—two I'd never met, one I'd met only once. A grandmother took small steps, a lightweight windbreaker pulled over her tight shoulders, and an uncle lagged behind, sporting a stained, too-short T-shirt tossed on over sweatpants. He looked as though he'd woken up from a decade's long nap and been asked to pick up a pizza.

The son. It hurt to look at him. In baggy jeans and an oversize Eminem shirt, his gaze remained fixed on the ground. Not even a teenager and his family was gone.

The grandmother paused on the steps and looked at us, her eyes watery.

"You poor kids," she said. "I'm so sorry."

Her reaction still surprises me. I don't know if I'd have been as generous.

I opened the screen door, and she touched my shoulder as she went by. That touch, her kindness, was too much. I leaned over the railing and vomited.

❧

After looking around the house as Mike and I had on the first day, the grandmother and uncle sat on the couch, my brother on a chair next to them while I stood by the door. I needed to be close to the exit.

We watched the son walk between rooms, disappearing and reappearing to announce his observations. Looking at the space where the wall was missing, he said, "That looks weird." A few moments later, he said, "It smells different in here." I studied his face, the stiff line of his mouth, the stillness of his eyes; his flat affect suggested he hadn't yet processed what had happened. Of all the things I'd seen and thought about, his disconnect in that space was the one that split my heart open. I mean, we were in *his* home. Did he understand his family wasn't coming back? Was he as shocked as the rest of us, or had he seen it coming? Had he known a different man than we had? I wanted to tell them to take whatever they wanted, please, I couldn't bear the thought of coming back. Instead, the grandmother wanted to talk.

"We always knew he wasn't right," she said and drummed her fingers on her knee. The uncle nodded in agreement. Finally, I thought. Someone had seen him for who he was: a man not right. The grandmother took a breath and said the next line so plainly it had the cadence of talking about the weather.

"My granddaughter told us he used to sneak into her room and masturbate on her feet while she pretended to sleep." She shook her head. "Can you imagine?"

Yes.

~⊙~

My entire life I'd wanted someone to recognize my father's menace. Finally, I was face-to-face with validation, and all at once, I sat down but also left.

I retreated to someplace where the thought of my father's abuse seemed far off, like a movie reel of someone else's life that I didn't have to watch. The grandmother's mouth moved, the uncle's, too, but I was high above them, at once anchored to the living room and floating like dust above them all. I may have nodded occasionally, may have even spoken, but I have only blankness. Whatever happened, whatever we might have exchanged, my mind immediately redacted. It's as though my nervous system blasted the shrill test of the Emergency Broadcast System and came up with danger. After that sentence, there is nothing but five people sitting in a crime scene, one of them so far away you could have lit her on fire and she wouldn't have realized she needed to put herself out.

⌒◦

When they stood to leave, I crashed back to earth. I suggested they bring a truck next time. The grandmother paused on her way out and asked me to get her daughter's gold cross back from the police. "She always wore it," she whispered, tears in her eyes. I promised her I would try, and Mike and I stood on the steps and looked on as their Honda disappeared into suburbia.

In the weeks to come, I called the police half a dozen times before finally getting the cross back. Every time I phoned the grandmother, my hands shook and a warbled answering machine clicked on. I left messages. So many messages.

She never called me back.

⌒◦

Back inside, Mike and I stood in the living room and scanned the panorama of violence. This was the last time either of us would set foot indoors. At the same time, our gazes halted on the painting of Crete.

"We should smash that piece of shit," I said.

"Oh yeah," Mike agreed. "Absolutely."

He hoisted it off the wall and held it between us so the painting faced up and the narrow end of the frame rested against the floor.

"Ready?" he asked.

We each lifted a leg and one, two, three: stomp. To our surprise, our feet returned with a bouncing jerk.

That painting, the embodiment of everything my father stood for, was nothing but a framed beach towel.

"What the fuck?" Mike asked. "Who frames a towel?"

I laughed. It seemed absurdly funny, a great practical joke from beyond the grave. We fell into contagious, ridiculous laughter, cackling until our muscles seized and tears crept down our faces. Our laughter brimmed with anger—laughter on the edge of mania—but if we didn't laugh, we'd crumble.

As quickly as that episode came, it left. We quieted. Our business wasn't finished.

Turn after turn, we furiously stomped the cloth, our legs springing back to us repeatedly in failure. We retaliated with a flurry of stomping, with determination to drive a hole straight through that impossible goddamned towel, but the towel kept winning, and every time it did, it was as though my father claimed another point.

Breathless, we paused and stared at one another. Finally, Mike said, "I got it," and opened the Swiss Army knife on his key ring. He looked at me as though for approval, so I nodded quickly, and he jabbed his stubby knife clean through the towel.

"Oh, you gotta try this," he said.

And so we stood in that house, the scent of decomposing bodies still hanging in the air, and took turns stabbing the beach towel my father had often pointed to when recalling tales of his home. I pierced the Minotaur's forehead, slicing from the tip of one horn down to the center of its dark and broad torso. Mike took to the lettering, slashing through the words "Crete" and "Greece," splitting the Hellenic alphabet in two. Had anyone looked in the front door, I'm sure they'd have thought our focus on destruction and violence was some depraved family tradition, but we passed the knife back and forth, not speaking a word, carving the blue, blue fabric of the Aegean Sea into foamy white shreds until there was no decipherable picture left.

∽

I wouldn't see anything so blue again until the cloudless sky of the perfectly crisp September day we buried my father. We drove together—my mother, brother, and I—to a cemetery, where we walked beneath a massive stone archway that opened to a field of meticulous grass and aging headstones. For obvious reasons, we hadn't advertised the funeral in the paper, but there were more people gathered at the gravesite than I'd expected—five men and a woman, none of them family. I do not know who they all were, but I gathered they were connected to the Greek Orthodox Church.

As the priest read from his Bible, I made eye contact with one of the men who nodded politely in return. The day had been surreal enough, as funerals are, but there nodding at me was one of my Greek bar regulars, a man I didn't know particularly well beyond his Dewar's rocks. I found out later he had contributed a hefty donation to the funeral tab, which made me feel at once awkward and unbelievably grateful. How do you accept that kind of tip?

The service was in Greek, so none of us understood much of it, and the casket was unlike any I'd previously seen: powder blue as the '70s leisure suit my father wore to his wedding. Standing before the casket, knowing that box contained the decaying remains of my father, I felt like a dumb animal, an empty thing. Shouldn't I have reminisced or cursed or wailed? Something? Anything? Instead, I couldn't get over how small the casket looked. It was impossible to reconcile the cognitive dissonance: how could someone so terrifying, so much larger than life, fit into a box so small? When I picture my father, he towers over me like a tsunami, but the truth is he was five foot eight. In memories of my father, I am forever a child.

When we piled back into my mother's car, we were quiet for a bit, stunned.

My mother gripped the steering wheel and turned to us. "Where do you guys wanna go? I'm up for anything."

I suggested a drive to New Hope, Pennsylvania, a quaint town full of shops and bars a couple of hours away. I don't remember what music we listened to or who broke the proverbial ice with a joke. I don't remember speaking a word. Instead, I remember only that stupidly blue sky and feeling comforted and safe by my mother's willingness to drive us wherever we needed to go.

In New Hope we sat at a wrought iron table on the dark wooden slats of a patio, drank goblet after goblet of Chimay on draft, and did not talk about my father. Though my mother and I would discuss him later many times, conversations that often ended with her crying and apologizing, silence on the topic would remain between Mike and I for a long time. They'd lowered our father into the ground, but for my brother and me, he was the ghost that pushed more and more space between us.

At that table, my body roared with emptiness. Colonies of men on Harleys periodically revved by our table, and it was only in the loud reverb of their hogs that I felt my insides silenced. I suspected that for my mother and Mike, the funeral marked something final. Closure. A chapter completed. I don't mean to suggest they were suddenly over what had happened, but the worst day of it was now behind them. That's how my family operates: put it in the past and keep it there. But I wouldn't be able to stop scenes from replaying in my head: my father large as Goliath, still powerful in his death. Trauma is a string plucked in the body, the mind. For my family, this might have been over. For me, its resonance was only beginning.

I wanted to run away—from the table, from my family, from New Jersey and my father and my brain. But you can't outrun your central nervous system, the thing that floods your blood with adrenaline and cortisol, the thing that tells you to run, man, fucking run. No matter how much you limber up, no matter how cute your workout gear or how often you train, you cannot outrun yourself.

CHAPTER 10

NERVOUS SYSTEM

Every legal document that needed signing—every single piece of paper—required both of our signatures, and it was slowing the process down. One thing remained certain: Mike and I wanted to get past this, to get through it and beyond it as fast as possible. I went to the courthouse with my attorney, signed lord only knows what, and bam: I was named *executrix* of the estate. That's Latin for She Who Rules All That Sucks.

The instant I signed the paperwork, Mike disappeared, and with him, our relationship. Since the phone call, we'd been in this together, talking about logistics and next steps and everything but grief, but now he was gone. I want to write that I appreciated how he protected himself, but I felt abandoned, and the rage that had been growing inside me calcified further.

I should have cared about that—should have felt the loss of my brother's friendship acutely—but I didn't. *Fucking coward*, I thought without a shred of generosity. But of course I had none to dole out; I barely cared about my own life. What I cared about instead was pain: How much of it could I get? Without it, I wouldn't have known who I was.

"A violent emotion, such as rage, may immediately affect the organs of the body," *Britannica Junior* warns. My stomach has always been first to sacrifice itself in times of stress, a spiky fist, and instead of listening to the pain, I blamed it on the booze. Clearly my stomach hurt so often because I drank too much. How quickly I forgot the cramps and hives and ice-pick migraines of my sober childhood. How unable I was to connect emotional to physical pain, to understand how the brain and body anchor one another.

One of my new duties was to maximize my father's estate, and our lawyer cautioned me it might be sued for wrongful death. Even with that futility in sight, I was determined to get the house ready for market and sell off his possessions. In retrospect, someone else might have been better suited for the task. Drunk, I sold his boat at a bar for $500; the look in the eyes of the man who bought it told me it was worth far more. I gave the cars away to a mechanic I'd known for years—told him they were his if he could get them off the property. I passed TVs and audio equipment out to friends, though I kept a CD player for myself. When I found it enjoyed making songs skip during my favorite parts—more thoughts of ghosts—I carried the machine down to the street and smashed it against the blacktop as the neighbors looked on. The surviving son took Joshua, the cat, and I adopted the most useless witnesses to crime: my father's fish. I monitored them with disdain and periodically changed their water.

Every time I talked to my mother, she offered help. *You shouldn't have to do this alone*, she'd say, and I'd respond, *Why drag someone else into this misery?*

My hand is on fire? Cool. I'll put it out.

I've got alcohol poisoning? Nah, I don't need a ride.

I'm in charge of a crime scene of an estate? No worries, bro. I'm good. I'll handle it myself.

Thank you for offering, but I'm fine.

I'm fine.

Fine, fine, fiiiiiiiine.

Clearly I'd been absent the day they taught how to ask for help.

I wouldn't learn how until my midthirties, and even then—hell, even still—it takes everything I have to rely on someone else, no matter the size of the trouble. You're in this alone. That had been the fundamental lesson of my life. You can only rely on yourself. It's you, just you. American individualism + trauma = I'm fucking fine, man.

But I'm not fine. Not all the time. No one is. Sometimes I'm messy, a genuine wreck, bruised and broken and bonkers, and I worry that letting others see that will make them run. Perfectionism is self-loathing in a cheap mask.

I wish I'd understood sooner that sharing my struggles honestly with someone—really connecting with another person—wasn't shameful or useless or weak. I wish I'd understood that being "not okay" with someone grants far more reward than being "fine" alone. I wish I'd understood it was time to ask.

⁓

A perk of tending bar is knowing every manner of tradesman, so I collected men for the jobs I didn't know how to do. A fellow bartender's husband was a professional painter. After suffering the missed appointments of a drunken real estate agent who made her own wine, an odd but reliable man with a Realtor's license came to my rescue. A guy who worked in the liquor store with Matt had the skinny on cheap carpet. And a man with an indecipherable mumble offered his services as an electrician. Rumor had it that he'd developed his speech impediment from getting zapped so many times, but help was help. These people were willing to work for free, a kindness I repaid in twelve-ounce mugs of beer.

Despite Mike's desire not to be involved, I had two small things that needed doing, so I called and asked him to turn the water off before the start of winter and later, come spring, mow the lawn.

"I don't want to," he said.

"I don't want to do ninety percent of what I have to these days, but someone has to," I said. "The least you could do is help."

"I won't go back there."

I heard the stubbornness of *won't* when I should've heard the weight of *can't*.

"Just do it, man," I said and hung up.

A couple of months later, in winter, the painter came to my bar, his face sunken.

"Lis," he said. "Did you have trouble opening the door?"

"What do you mean?" We'd used the key without problems.

"I had to jam it with my shoulder."

"That's weird," I said and thought nothing of it until he removed his hat and pressed it to his chest.

"The pipes burst," he said and shook his head. "The ceiling fan, it was like a limp sunflower. It points at the ground now."

I don't know why—maybe it's the writer in me—but the painter's image was so vivid, I held out my hand for the key and slipped it into my apron. I asked an off-duty employee to watch the bar and went to the bathroom, where I stood in a stall, shaking, weeping. That was it; I couldn't subject anyone else to that house.

Once the house swelled, so too did my fury. I spent every day steeped in phone calls with the attorney and the real estate agent, and my brother couldn't turn a fucking valve?

Looking back, it would have been so easy to hire someone—a land-scaper, a neighborhood kid, anyone—to turn off the water, to mow that lawn. Why was I hell-bent on Mike doing it? Maybe I wanted him to feel my pain, to have a partner in mutual hurt the way I'd had the day we heard the news. Or maybe I was envious of his ability to walk away from it all. I couldn't walk. Not for the life of me. I felt driven to be near the grief and shroud myself in suffering, as though feeling like total shit was the only thing that affirmed I was still alive.

From the bar's jukebox, 50 Cent's "In da Club" shook the bath-room walls—the fourth time I'd heard it that hour. *What kind of life is this?* I thought. *It has to get better.*

I checked the mirror, wiped my streaky mascara off with a rough paper towel, and went back behind the bar, where I poured two shots of Jameson. I set one in front of the painter and held on to the other.

"Thank you for trying," I said. Then a clink of glass and the sweet, sweet burn. Things were already looking up.

∽

By day I dealt with the estate, but at night, when I wasn't behind the bar, I spent every moment drinking and trying to solve the riddle of what happened in that house. "A clever question, that answer of which is to be guessed, is a riddle," notes *Britannica Junior*. This was my father's favorite kind of humor, and he loved nothing more than the one time he really stumped me: *A man and his son are in a car crash and rushed to the hospital. They're about to die, but in the operating room, the doctor looks at the boy and says, "I can't operate on this boy; he's my son!" How could this be?*

If you've been around the riddle block, you know the answer: the doctor is his mother. Oh, how my father laughed when I couldn't untangle that one in my youth. Of course I couldn't; he'd raised me to believe women couldn't be anything of value.

Though his death was, for a time, a terrible puzzle, his last riddle, I couldn't help but think of my own jokes:

What blows and sucks at the same time? MY DAD.

What threat is present but invisible to all who meet it? MY DAD.

What's mean and dead? MY DAD.

I know. They're not very good and in terrible taste, but the brain performs twisted gymnastics when the unthinkable happens.

But as with all good riddles, the one about my father misdirected me. It had me asking the wrong questions. I still wanted to know why— and it is the first question people most often ask. Why did he snap? What, precisely, had happened that day? What drove him to pull the trigger? How had things escalated? Who did he kill first? How much had they had to drink? What other drugs were in his system, in their systems? Why did he kill himself? Why, why, why? Had he planned it for days, weeks? Or did someone press an invisible button that set his spree into motion? I spent a year turning those questions over because I needed a narrative to latch on to, some sort of order to impose upon his chaos, but the questions that should have gripped me from the start are: *How do I survive this intact? How do I protect myself?* I slipped into the journalistic who/what/when/where/why of it all like using a side door to avoid dealing with a crowd; what lay beneath those logical narrative queries—what stood behind the front door—was how close I'd come to death. When my father had pulled out a rifle years earlier and threatened me and my mother, had I stood a millimeter away? What kept him from doing to us what he'd done to this new family? Why had I been spared?

I begged my lawyer to get me the autopsy and police reports, as well as the crime-scene photos. Tough girl. *You don't want those*, he said, and I said, *Yes, I do*, without considering he might be right. The answers I searched for would be in those pages—I was sure of it. When I went to pick them up from his office, he handed me thirty-nine pages of reports but no pictures.

I may have thought myself the Toughest Girl in All the Land, but thank you, dear attorney, for never showing me those photographs. Words were enough.

I studied the pages, the descriptions of gunshot wounds, of the holes in skulls, in occipital bones, in chests. It never once occurred to me to stop. And the images came without photos: they appeared when I closed my eyes, when I stared blankly into traffic, when I least expected them. I filled myself daily with the unwanted, the violent.

This is not how you survive intact. It is not how you protect yourself.

I researched the anatomical parts in the postmortem reports—the pinna, the zygoma, the alveolar ridge—and reenacted the scenes. I got on my knees on my bed and held my hands up like I imagined the daughter did, my father towering before her. From that, I knew the gunshot through her palm was a defensive wound. How human the impulse to shield the head from a bullet with the hand. But as soon as I thought I'd figured something out, I'd regroup and start again. I know that's me—some younger, wounded self—on her bed enacting her father's murder, but I also don't recognize her. I want to fly through time and pull her into a hug she would resist. I want to tell her that she doesn't have to do this. I want to tell her to stop. She isn't in danger.

I want to whisper to her words that aren't yet in the cultural lexicon: mental health days, mindfulness, self-care. I want to tell her that loving others so fiercely means she has the capacity to love herself. I want to tell her she will survive.

No matter how hard I tried, most things couldn't be known. Most.

Here's what I do know: the house had evidence of ongoing domestic abuse—walls scarred with holes and dents. There was alcohol in all three of their systems. His gun held eight bullets, and six casings were spent. He shot the girlfriend once in the jaw, her body supine in the hallway. In the master bedroom, he rested on his side of the bed, the left, pressed a Smith & Wesson .357 Magnum to his right temple, and pulled the trigger. He wore denim shorts.

But before that, he shot the daughter multiple times.

He shot the daughter multiple times.

He shot. The daughter. Multiple times.

When I read that—when I read that she was fifteen, her hymen still intact—the animal sound I'd made when I first heard the news leapt from me again.

I've written of rage as a rock, a stone, something hard and growing within, but that's oversimplification. Rage has the feet of a spider: tactile, able to grip whatever more complex feelings circle round and suck their blood. Grief, sadness, betrayal, disappointment: all of them can so easily be renamed *rage*. It is a holy wonder how simple our emotions seem when we refuse to look at them closely.

Yes, I raged. I seethed and bristled, blew up and boiled over, rampaged and roared. I made all of that angry noise because I couldn't bear to tease apart what was going on inside me.

The adults in my life had failed me—no question—but they'd failed that teenage girl too. The police report states that her brother knew what my father did to her. At one point, he and his sister had plotted to slip him rat poison but thought better of it. The grandmother confirmed the abuse and told an officer it was her daughter who told her. Two women, mother and grandmother, knew my father crept into her room at night, not a boundary in place, and neither did anything. They didn't leave. They didn't call the police. They didn't insist on sleeping in her room to stand guard. Instead, they let her go on living there in a room of her own, where anything could happen.

Perhaps I'm being too hard on them. Maybe the mother did confront him. Maybe *that* is what set everything in motion on that awful September evening. But even if it's not, I know why women stay; I'd watched one do it for the bulk of my childhood. Self-esteem slowly scraped away, financial dependence, an unceasing belief that maybe, just maybe, he'll change—or worse, that they deserve it.

The hardest truth to wrestle was that I'd failed the daughter too. I know now I didn't have the tools to help her the last time I'd seen her, that pitiful Christmas when I recognized her unspoken pain. But at twenty-seven, I felt as complicit and guilty as the rest of them. If only *I'd* told on my father. If only *I'd* called the police. If only I hadn't tucked that little girl away, far away, out of sight. If only.

Of course I couldn't tell. My father had made it clear—with words, with fists, with a rifle—that if I ever ratted him out, I'd be dead. My mother? Dead. The cost for telling was death.

It's human nature to minimize trauma. *I don't have it that bad. He's just scaring me. He'd never actually do that. He loves me too much to kill me.* The logic of a young girl caught in a trap. If as a child I'd faced the full horror of my house, I'd have killed myself. That is not hyperbole. I'd written half a dozen suicide notes in my youth. Once, in my preteen years, I swallowed every pill in a new bottle of Advil. When I awoke sixteen hours later, I sighed. *Still here*, I thought.

To survive my father I had to believe he would never make good on his threats. And the oblivious adults in my orbit didn't see it either—or wouldn't see it, refused to see it. To admit what was happening would mean they'd have to face their own guilt. So I was gaslit from all sides. What danger? What menace? What an imagination on this young girl!

But then he did it. He killed the mother and the girl—the girl he shot multiple times—and I knew in an instant it could just as easily have been me. That it almost was. That I was lucky it wasn't. The danger I'd felt around him in every inch of my body had been right all along. I howled the day we got the news because of that truth. It could've been me, and when he shot that little girl, I took the shrapnel. And no matter what anyone tells you, shrapnel feels like guilt.

∽

"Certain substances are harmful to nerve tissue," *Britannica Junior* observes. "Among these are nicotine, alcohol, and certain drugs." I knew only one way to pacify the guilt, and yup, you guessed it: alcohol. Rivers of beer and booze, seven days a week. On days I was so hungover the thought of another drink made me green. On days I had bronchitis or the flu. Three-sixty-five. I wasn't worried about my body; years of dissociating had disconnected me from it. What worried me was the brain that would not let me sleep, an organ I foolishly thought of as separate from the rest of me.

"The best hours for sleep are at night when it is dark and quiet . . . Young people should sleep alone when possible. This prevents their rest from being disturbed by someone else who uses the same room." *Britannica Junior* assumes that people are safe in their bedrooms; my learned habit of staying awake and alert in darkness only worsened after my father's death. I could not sleep. I hadn't slept right for years, but now, unless I drank until I passed out, I'd remain up all night, eyes wide, brain spinning and spinning and spinning.

Usually any tip other than money stinks when you're a bartender. Someone once left me three tins of cat food for my services, even though I had a dog. Others left coupons for stores I didn't shop at, pennies shrouded in pocket lint, and—the worst—fake twenty-dollar bills that when opened told you about the good lord.

But one day someone left me a pamphlet titled "101 Ways to Fight Insomnia." I wonder if that happened to be what the customer had on hand, or if they saw the circles beneath my under-eye concealer, if they watched me yawn and yawn while making Jack and Cokes, unable to catch a satisfying breath.

In the top ten of that pamphlet, I found a repeat of my encyclopedia's advice: "Some people who habitually have trouble in getting to sleep may have less difficulty if they drink a glass of warm milk before bed." I was lactose intolerant. A spritz of lavender on my pillow did nothing, and "get your worries out of your system before bed" was laughable.

But one suggestion did work: alphabetizing the States. If I got one wrong—I missed Idaho, say—I started back at Alabama. It helped because it didn't let in the roar of my guilt. Eventually, I got too good at it—could cruise through all fifty—so I made up my own things to order: one-word movie titles (*Amélie, Bullet, Chinatown*), two-word movie titles (*American Beauty*, *Bottle Rocket*, *Chasing Amy*), exciting ways to die (Avalanche, Bellhop Incident, Camel Attack).

For most of my young life, I survived on three to five hours of sleep a night, and I was back to that schedule, perpetually deprived. When I did sleep, I awoke sweating, crying, occasionally laughing, with a jolt, my heart slamming. I began keeping my nails cut short. If they were long, I scratched my skin open and in the morning found lines of blood on my chest, legs, arms, face. My father appeared in nearly every dream, and the terror that disturbed my meager sleep lingered throughout the days. I barely ate, and I could not breathe—I was starved for breath. My chest rose and fell within the span of a shallow inch throughout the day and night. I never breathed from my belly—did not know that was possible. It wasn't until I was forty that a doctor pointed out I breathed backward, essentially hyperventilating all the time.

The panic attacks that had been with me since I was fifteen grew worse, and everything set me off: going to work, driving over a bridge, driving anywhere, being in a store, taking a walk, going to the gym, sitting in class, a room too warm, no exit. The rest of the world seemed to do these things with ease, but no matter my task, a crest of adrenaline hustled through my blood and made my body hot, my breathing worse, my heart clop. I thought of it all as the cost of being me, a young woman broken beyond repair, her only salve the bottle. With the first drink came a slight calm, a light breeze on the brain. By the bottom of the second, I stopped ruminating, my anxiety only a mumble. By the fifth, the seventh, the tenth: What anxiety? Now outta my way so I can sleep.

∽

Despite working two jobs, Matt was perpetually broke, and at the time of my dad's death, he owed me a few thousand dollars. We fought, of course, but money wasn't the only topic.

AVERAGE BRAWL:

A Seventeen-Second Play

Setting: a kitchen, suburban New Jersey

LISA, twenty-seven, stands against the counter, arms folded beneath chest.

MATT, thirty-two, paces, wide eyed with false incredulity.

LISA

Stop following me and pretending to show up like it's an accident. I'm not stupid.

MATT

(doesn't make eye contact)

I don't follow you.

LISA

For fuck's sake. You didn't happen to show up in Atlantic City at three a.m.! You're just like him. Always watching.

MATT

STOP COMPARING ME TO YOUR DEAD FATHER! I LOVE YOU!

Fin.

Matt had done a lot over the years. There was endless stalking. One time, when we were broken up for a couple of months, he banged on the window of a man's apartment while we slept together inside. He spied and listened to my conversations, his feet secretly planted in my mother's garden while I yammered on the phone to Mike, back when Mike and I were still friends. If a man looked at me wrong or hit on me, he wouldn't hesitate to follow him to the bathroom of a bar and threaten him or throw a punch. Once, he started a bar fight in front of my mother. Another time, angry with me for lord knows what, he hung my stuffed animals by nooses from the ceiling of our bedroom; later he apologized by making cartoon speech bubbles out of construction paper and taping them to the wall above each animal's mouth. On vacation in New Orleans, he erupted in rage so frightening, I sat on the floor in the corner of our hotel room, knees to chest, while he paced and yelled. Eventually he passed out, and I, for once, regretted drinking. Had I been sober, I'd have stolen his car and driven the twelve hundred miles back to New Jersey alone. But the next day, I needed a ride, and he apologized—they always apologize—and there we drove, across Lake Pontchartrain while clouds began to funnel in the sky. At our next stop, Savannah, he got food poisoning, and I had the joy of exploring the city on my own, of feeling like, for once, the universe delivered a swift comeuppance.

I was no angel, by the way. Matt brought out the worst in me, but I didn't do anything violent. I never made him cower with fear. I also didn't know how to love wholly, to trust a man enough to give him my affection and not withhold it when I wanted something. Over the years, I'd break up with Matt but keep him on the hook, certain I could pull him back to me with one phone call. I hadn't yet learned that love doesn't have to be transactional. I hadn't yet learned that it's okay to be alone.

We who've been chronically abused can take a lot. So much. So much more than a person with a normative brain and a normative nervous system could or would. Of course we can; our baseline for "normal" is less of a line and more of a lightning bolt. But when we're through taking shit, we are *done*. I think of it like a stretchy trash bag, and, yes, in this metaphor I am the trash bag. You can stuff me full of garbage that no one wants; for years, I might think, *I should take myself out to the bin*, and instead I push it all down with my foot. Eventually, the bag breaks, and it could be something as small as an apple rind that splits it open.

With my father, it was his not recognizing my voice on the phone. With Matt, it was a purchase. He owed me all that money, and though we talked about repayment, he never followed through. One day, he came home grinning. *Come see*, he said, and there in our driveway sat a fucking motorcycle. Instead of paying me back, he had bought a bike, and they say you can't feel your blood pressure rise, but I assure you, you can. As he beamed at it, I stood there, a dormant volcano starting to rumble.

A week or so later I ended it, and god I wish I were making this next part up. We stood in the foyer during the breakup, the front door open, the long glass of the storm door beaten furiously by rain. In the middle of that final fight—why could nothing be simple?—a sound interrupted us, and we looked down to find an albino ferret scratching at the door. Some old David Lynch shit right there. I wasn't much for signs, but I loved symbols, and though I couldn't pinpoint what that meant exactly, I was sure it wasn't good. Matt left the house that night, and the next morning, every fish in the tank I'd inherited from my father went belly up.

I immediately started dating someone new, someone I for years referred to as the Best Man I'd Ever Known. Was I ready to date? Of course not. He'd have been smart to run the moment I told him what was happening in my life.

The Best Man I'd Ever Known worked and supported himself. A blue-collar gig, but he rarely complained. His work ethic was solid. He was the funniest man I'd dated, and even when I'd get angry at him—when I'd verbally launch at him as though he were Matt—he'd tilt his head and say, "You're so pretty," and I'd laugh and apologize for being a jackass. He kept me even like that, and while it would take time to feel it, his consistency is precisely what made me love him.

Even with Matt gone, even with the Best Man I'd Ever Known by my side, I had to remain on alert. Matt had shown up wherever I was when we were dating; he wasn't about to stop following me now. A couple of months after we split, he stopped by my bar to take off his shirt and show me something: across his heart, he'd tattooed my signature, a gesture he thought grand enough to win me back. It wasn't, and I looked for his car wherever I drove.

All this time, there was a word I avoided, which too often means that's the very thing at the heart of the matter. Fear. I'd been terrified of my father in life, and after his death, I feared what he'd done to me, the ways he'd bruised and fractured something so essential that I was certain I would remain broken forever. With Matt, I feared never being loved again; forget that his love was toxic. Someone had finally told me how much they loved me, and that was all I'd ever wanted. But I'd wanted that because behind it all—the curtain of survival swiped stage left—I was terrified of my brain, of its thoughts and feelings and needs. I did not know how to be alone without the solace of booze or sex or some distraction big enough to pull me out of myself, albeit temporarily. The worst sentence I could imagine was a life spent alone with my own mind.

So when my father's first birthday after his death rolled around, I decided to mark it with a new tattoo. Above those old Ginsberg fish, I had the phrase "I refuse to fear life" seared in Greek into my flesh. It wasn't true yet, but goodness did I want it to be. I hoped that every time I caught sight of it in a mirror, it might remind me to be a little braver. It might remind me that my father hadn't won.

∽

One night, I arrived at my house after my shift around 3:00 a.m. When I opened the front door, I froze: the tile floor was coated in blood, the walls stained with bloody handprints. Yellow crime-scene tape blocked off the living room and wound around the railing of the steps like a morbid plant. Unable to move or make a sound, I stood there and quaked and thought I was about to be murdered, but it wasn't Matt. Michelle, my oldest and best friend in the universe, had without a second thought decorated our house for Halloween.

I grabbed a beer and locked myself in my room. On my computer, I typed "Craigslist Philadelphia" and clicked on apartments for rent. A month later, I moved to my own apartment—a place where no one, not even my family, could find me. The Best Man I'd Ever Known spent some nights, but most of the time, I was alone, drunk, staring, and weeping while I waited for my father's house to sell. That fall, mercifully, it did.

The house should've been a final hurdle, an ordeal over. Instead, I suddenly had an abundance of time and nowhere to put the energy. I didn't know what to do, so I applied to a handful of MFA programs in writing, expecting to get into none. I could barely focus on the applications. I didn't revise my writing samples. I can't begin to imagine what my personal essay looked like. So I drank. I drank when I learned the estate was, indeed, being sued for wrongful death. I drank when the acceptance letter from the University of Pittsburgh arrived. *They must pity me*, I thought, unable to give myself credit for anything. I drank when I called Pitt and told them I couldn't come, that I was embroiled in legal issues in New Jersey and couldn't guess how long it would take to settle the case. I enrolled in the master's program for English at Rutgers, the place where I'd completed my bachelor's, the return to it feeling like another failure to move forward.

Wrongful death: no contest. The surviving son got every cent of my father's pitiful savings, and I received $9,000 for being the executrix. Nine thousand dollars for the blowflies and the smell and those goddamned ears of corn. Nine thousand dollars for a life still haunted by him.

I stopped by my mother's house to give half of it to Mike. It was the first time I'd seen him in months. On my way out, my mom said, "I can't believe you did that. You did all the work." I told her that for $4,500, I was buying my peace of mind. Whatever fractures existed in our relationship, money would never be one of them.

I was also unsure why Mike and I weren't considered victims of wrongful death, too, but that isn't the way the law is set up. Since our father was the perpetrator, my brother and I were, by proxy, defendants. There are no pain-and-suffering payouts to those who clean up the mess of a criminal, to those left knowing that for the rest of their lives, when they think of the word *father*, *murderer* will shortly follow.

I attempted to pour myself into graduate school, but do you know how difficult it is to care about writing a twenty-five-page critical essay of *Their Eyes Were Watching God* when you're half convinced the ghost of your father still watches you? I did it, but even Zora Neale Hurston couldn't distract me for long.

One evening I sat in a twentieth-century literature class and burrowed into the bottom of my backpack to find a pen. In there, beneath my notebooks and novels, I felt a thick ream of folded paper and lifted it out. The autopsy reports. I'd been physically carrying them strapped to my back for a year and hadn't even noticed. The metaphor wasn't wasted on me; what kind of martyr to misery had I become? I spent the rest of class shifting, fidgeting, spacing out for stretches so long that when I tuned back in, I was lost. I walked down a stairwell after class with my professor, and he asked if I was okay, asked what was going on. Without any warning I said, *It's the one-year anniversary of my father murdering two people, then killing himself.* My professor stopped walking and cemented his ass to the steps, but I kept climbing down because, really, what is there to say to that?

So there I was, one year past my father's crimes, filterless and barely functioning. A friend said, *Dude, I'll be here to listen, but maybe you should see a therapist.* One day on campus, convinced my panic was giving me a heart attack, I climbed four flights of stairs to our university's clinic to make a psych appointment. In tears, I stood in line at the plexiglass, and when it was my turn, I choked out my words to a student receptionist.

"I need help," I said. She looked at her computer, and I interrupted. "Not a student in training. I need someone with an actual PhD. This isn't test anxiety."

She continued searching and asked flatly, "Is this an emergency?"

Still crying, I answered, "What does that mean?"

"It means are you thinking of self-harm."

I considered it. I wasn't actively suicidal, but sometimes I cut lines into my left forearm until it released my pain. I often thought it would be fine if a bus hit me, if my car careened off the Ben Franklin Bridge.

"I guess not?"

"Well, there's a wait. But we'll call you when a slot opens up."

It took every inch of my courage to climb those stairs and ask for help. I waited for the call. Three months later, it came.

When I told Dr. Dan all that had been going on, his jaw literally swung open. No poker face. But I didn't want to talk about my father. I wasn't ready. I wanted to know why, despite knowing he was awful for me, despite having the Best Man I'd Ever Known as my partner, every bit of me wanted to run back to Matt. How could I crave something I knew was bad?

He walked to his filing cabinet and retrieved a sheet of paper. On it, the cycle of abuse, a wheel with four distinct phases: (1) tensions build, (2) incident, (3) reconciliation, (4) calm. Somehow, I'd never seen that graph physically depicted, and in it I saw my relationship with my father, of course, but also Matt. Until that moment, I hadn't thought of him as abusive, but it was plain as yogurt on the sheet. I'd been stuck in that cycle my entire life, and now, dating someone reliable as rain, I missed the fireworks. But fireworks singe and burn. They take off fingers. I fought hard to keep away from Matt, and as time passed, I loved the Best Man I'd Ever Known more and more. He gave me the gift of safety. Until him, I hadn't known I could feel safe with a man.

I adored my Philadelphia apartment—the cathedral ceilings, the line of exposed brick, the Sunday sounds of gospel that flooded my windows—but I had never lived alone. When the Best Man I'd Ever Known stayed at his place, I remained on my own. Instead of having roommates to distract me, I circled the living room and told my story aloud to no one. Again and again, I paced the hardwood floors and whispered to the air what had happened to me, to my father, to his girlfriend, to that fifteen-year-old girl. When trying to organize a story, I still pace, a tiger walking the length of a garage, a living room, a yard. I know now this is how I climb over metaphorical roadblocks, the mountains that form, sometimes over years and sometimes overnight. In this case, I paced and told my story to empty rooms because I'd gathered and held a vast collection of fragments, the shards of trauma, and I needed to glue the vase back together. In telling and retelling the story, my brain made the smallest space for the largest truth: my father was dead, and he wasn't coming for me. He could never come for me again. But I didn't know then what I was doing. It simply felt like a compulsory odyssey. I only knew that through narrative, I might make some sense of my life. I knew I had a story to tell.

PART III

Homecoming

CHAPTER 11

ODYSSEY

In my undergraduate years, I read two editions of Dostoevsky's *Crime and Punishment*. One contained a pickle; the other did not. It was my first lesson in how varied translations could be. An object as concrete and specific as a pickle was there; then it was gone. I called this conundrum the Inexplicable Pickle.

There are at least seventy-five English translations of the *Odyssey*, and because I am a Greek woman, its story is part of my own. That is unavoidable. You can try your best to stick with Judith Butler and bell hooks, but Homer comes for you.

Depending on whom you read, the *Odyssey* begins:

> "Sing in me, Muse, and through me tell the story
> / of that man skilled in all the ways of con-
> tending . . ." —Robert Fitzgerald

> "Sing to me of the man, Muse, the man of twists
> and turns . . ." —Robert Fagles

"Tell me, Muse, of the man of many ways . . ."
—Richmond Lattimore

So for fifty years or so in the twentieth century, it seems only men whose names began with *R* translated the *Odyssey* into English, and none of them gripped me. I worry about committing that to paper. It is nearly as much a sin to find Homer boring as it is to hate lamb. I am a terrible Greek.

But in 2018, Emily Wilson showed up with her searing and simple, "Tell me about a complicated man."

Yes, Emily. I will.

This is what I did for years—what, in fact, I've done again here. I have tried and tried to tell the story of a complicated man, my father, my deeply flawed (and not heroic) Odysseus. But in doing that—in trying to figure out the story of what happened after the crimes, his ship long sailed for the River Styx—I failed to deal with myself.

If, instead, I centered myself as Odysseus, I should have found myself blown by the wind home to Ithaca the moment the estate settled. But I was rudderless, my companions the complicated grief and exhaustion I'd confronted with booze, which is to say, I hadn't confronted at all.

Britannica Junior describes the *Odyssey* as "an ancient collection of story-songs of the sea," which, sure, maybe, but whoo-boy does that weaken the sauce. For those who don't remember their Homer, Odysseus leaves Ithaca to fight in the Trojan War and upon killing the son of Troy's ace hero (Hector), the dead boy's grandmother begs the gods to curse Odysseus, and they're like, *Sure thing. We ain't busy.* Odysseus spends the next decade trying to get home, and the story of the trouble he gets into on that quest is what we know as the *Odyssey*.[4]

But what if you're out at sea and have no home to return to? What if your actual home has never felt like where you belong? What if when you set foot on the stomping grounds of your childhood, you feel despair, your insides hollow with the youth that was taken from you? What if you, too, want revenge, but the gods have already cursed the man who broke you? Where does your quest take you then?

Tallahassee, Florida, of course.

When I got into Florida State University's creative writing program—at first for an MFA, then for a PhD—three of my professors at Rutgers said the same thing: "You're going to get a serious education." In the *Odyssey*, Tiresias warns Odysseus about what awaits him when he eventually finds his way home (spoiler: a bunch of bros trying to sleep with his relentlessly chaste wife), but Odysseus has the good sense to ask follow-up questions. I stood silent as each member of my committee said those words—*a serious education*—and took their warning to my apartment, where I imagined what it might mean. Was it a shot? Did they not think me smart enough? Hadn't Rutgers given me a serious education? In the end, I decided it meant, *Sober up, young lady*, and I planned to. *As soon as I get to FSU*, I thought, *I'll get serious about my scholarship by getting seriously sober.*

Had I bothered to google it, I'd have learned quickly the currency at FSU is drinking. Lucky for me, that was the one area of my life in which I was rich.

---

4   *SparkNotes* should pay me.

The (Former) Best Man I'd Ever Known helped move me to Florida, even though he was staying in Philadelphia. Up until the end, I'd been a good girlfriend, but I regret those last months. First, I signed a lease with him, then backed out. Next, fearful that my self-destruction would lead me back to Matt, I backslid all the way to Chad, the teenage boy who'd once stuffed my vagina full of miscellany. He was the worst person I'd ever dated, so of course I dated him twice. It should surprise no one but my twenty-nine-year-old self that he was still an insufferable asshole.

I thought I'd grown up a lot. After all, I'd been in a mostly healthy—albeit drunk—relationship for a handful of years. Filled with a harrowing fear of being alone—of being unlovable—I couldn't let the Best Man I'd Ever Known go, but I also couldn't commit to him. I hadn't learned that loving someone isn't enough, and despite my behavior toward the end of our relationship, I had loved him deeply. So he waited in Philadelphia, waited for me to wave the green flag that meant "join me," and though I was racked with self-doubt, I knew it would never come. What a selfish and unfair thing to do to someone. If you know you can't be with someone—whatever the reason—respect them enough to say so, no matter how scared you are.

Jason, I am sorry. And I know that's not enough.

I rented what turned out to be the darkest apartment in the Sunshine State, and I sat in it on the first night listening to the new sounds it made, the quiet scritches and creaks. Something wasn't right, and I found out what it was when a roach the size of a Volvo flew at my face. The apartment was infested with palmetto bugs, and the exterminator tried to console me by explaining their quest: *They search for water, not food*, he said. *How do they feel about gasoline?* I asked. A couple of months later, a Florida panther ran out in front of my car on the interstate. I'm talking belongs-in-a-zoo big cat. *Where the hell am I?* I wondered. Perhaps I'd made a grievous mistake in moving. Or perhaps I was being tested.

Back in New Jersey, Mike got engaged and had a baby. The life we're conditioned to strive toward. But I couldn't make sense of it. How could he stay there? How could my mother? Come holidays, I'd fly home from grad school and sleep in the same house I'd grown up in, dread climbing my veins, though everyone else seemed to move on with ease. *HOW?* I wanted to scream. *DON'T YOU FEEL HIM STILL?* The turkey was carved, the presents handed out. Not a word about him, the Greek elephant in every familial room I entered.

People sometimes ask why I got a PhD, and my answer is always the same: spite. It's an answer that gets laughs, like so many jokes that are rooted in truth. Of course, I'd wanted to escape the Northeast—I'd long hungered to be away from home—but I also needed to prove that my father hadn't set the limitations of my life. I needed, more than anything, to prove he hadn't broken me.

With a move comes reinvention, and I was thrilled to go someplace where no one knew me or my father—a thrill I'd spoil almost immediately by writing about him in my nonfiction workshop. So much for anonymity. Still, I was determined to be a new woman. Sure, I'd keep drinking, but I wouldn't tend bar anymore or sleep around. I'd find a good, smart partner, and together we'd build an intellectual life. I had only one rule, the same rule I'd had my entire life: no Greek men.

One Sunday afternoon, I sat at a dive bar grading freshmen papers while the strangers next to me worked on a crossword puzzle. One of them read the clues aloud. *Zeus's mother, four letters*, he said. *Hera?*

"Rhea," I answered without looking up.

"How do you know?"

My posture straightened. He had an accent.

"I know my myths."

He was handsome, especially in profile: wavy black hair, designer stubble, a hand-rolled cigarette between his stained fingertips, an anarchy symbol pinned to the lapel of his army-green jacket.

"What's your name?" I asked.

"Perseus."

"That's not your name," I said and laughed. "Let me see your ID."

He handed me his license and there it was: Perseus, the Greekest name I could think of. Perseus, a man whose accent sounded like my father's.

"Way to murder Medusa," I said, and he slid over and bought me a Guinness. Then he bought me three more.

One rule. I had one fucking rule.

We dated for the better part of my first year in Tallahassee, and we were drunk for all of it, but his drinking scared me. Even if he stopped by at breakfast, he'd nip the whiskey on the way out. We took blankets to the park and spread out our *mezedes*, a bottle of wine and olive oil always on hand, and made out while the sun baked our skin. We sat on washing machines at the laundromat while he helped me work on my language skills from the very textbooks I'd used in Greek school. Sure, he'd shown up for our first date on acid, but he'd also awoken a part of me I'd long tried to keep hidden: I was Greek. And maybe that was okay.

But things went sideways one Fourth of July weekend when our condom broke. I swallowed Plan B almost immediately. A few weeks later, I called him and told him I'd missed my period. So much for reinvention. One year after I'd arrived in Florida, I was still drunk and anxious and couldn't breathe or sleep. Now I was pregnant.

When I told him, he ghosted me. After a year: poof. What boyfriend, where?

Some will hate me for my decision, but I couldn't take care of myself—emotionally or financially. I made $12,000 a year as a teaching assistant. The cells that grew in my uterus had been daily steeped in cortisol and adrenaline and booze. I have never—not for a moment—regretted my choice.

Afterward, I swore off sex altogether, but how short the fall from Perseus to worse men was. Within a year, my old habits slid back into place with a soft click. I got behind the bar—a job I swore I'd never do again—which made remaining drunk and finding terrible partners easy. Blitzed and broken, I slept with men I kinda-sorta liked, men I didn't like, men I actively disliked, men who actively disliked me, men who stalked me. Had I learned nothing? Would I never learn? I was growing academically smarter by the semester, but I remained a dimwit on the subject of myself.

⌒⁹

In the *Odyssey*, most of our hero's trials take place on varied islands. *Britannica Junior* explains, "In the land of the Lotus-eaters some of his men eat the lotus flower and completely forget their homes. Odysseus has to drag them to the ship by force." Gobs of intoxicating fruit and home, the object of their quest, disappeared. I still felt like a stranger in Tallahassee, in the land of live oaks and strip malls. I wasn't sure I'd ever belong, but I didn't belong in New Jersey, in my mother's home, either. Still, I visited her each December for six years in a row. Odysseus didn't drag me back there, but guilt sure as hell did. Had you offered me a lotus, I'd have eaten it with glee.

When I flew home for the first set of winter holidays, my mother placed my things in her new guest room, a space redone in a theme best called Sand & Surf. But you can't paint over trauma. She led me to my father's old bedroom, a daybed placed against the wall beneath where the framed beach towel used to hang.

Why are you so angry? she asked at breakfast the next morning, and I didn't know how to articulate the venom that seeped out of me. *Triggered* was not a word I possessed. And though my mom got the brunt of my wrath—I had yet to unpack my anger over her bringing my father into our life—Mike was no better off. Mike the Deserter.

Once, for Mother's Day, we gathered at her house. Mike barked an order at my mother—flashes of my father if ever there were some—and in a blink, I pressed him to the wall by his throat. *You don't talk to her like that*, I growled. She begged us to get along long enough to sit for a photo, and we spun toward the camera—*one, two, three, cheese!*—then back to fighting. She keeps that one tacked to the side of her fridge: a reminder that if we tried, we could be civil, and after the photo was taken, I slunk back to my haunted guest room to cry.

I wanted to be better than that. I had to be. I could fake politeness with the rudest customer, but in the face of my mother showing me love, a bitchy, wounded girl flew from my throat. The meaner I was to my family, the more I reminded myself of my father, and the more that happened, the more I hated myself.

When I returned to Tallahassee, I found a therapist. She repeatedly suggested I quit drinking, and I laughed and laughed.

"Just for six months," she said.

And I laughed and laughed.

"That's not the problem," I said, my hangover still bowling through me. And she stared at me hard.

"Six months isn't a long time," she said.

"In drinking time? It's an eternity."

"Then you have a problem," she said flatly. "I can only take you so far. You have to start making healthier choices."

I agreed, but I didn't know how. I could not see the connection between my past and the bottle. I did not see—despite it being obvious—that I was self-medicating. I thought I was simply surviving.

But something needed to change.

∽

In May 2009, five and a half years after my father's death, I sat alone in my Tallahassee apartment—a new one, sans palmetto bugs—and drank whiskey by the amber light of my desk lamp. A thought possessed me: *I should go to Greece and find my father's sisters.* The notion was absurd—like a lifelong vegetarian looking forward to a T-bone steak. Moreover, I hadn't thought about those women in years. Why were they resurfacing now?

For kicks, I searched for deals on flights. Between student loans and bar shifts, I could afford it, but there was a much bigger problem: I still feared everything. My panic was under control(ish) when drunk, but it was a fight to do everyday tasks. Sometimes when I taught, I excused myself to the restroom and locked myself in a stall, shaking. The flight from Atlanta to Athens is eleven hours. The longest I'd ever sat on a plane was under four, and I'd clawed the underside of my seat for those last two. I'd never make it.

Perhaps the more relevant, eloquent question is, *What the fuck?* What was I thinking? I'd never wanted anything to do with Greece. I'd stopped speaking Greek when I was a kid to spite my father, and I'd long boycotted feta cheese, octopus, and oregano. When I graduated from Rutgers, my grandmother bought me a ticket for a cruise to Greece. I gave it to Mike and made up an excuse. For me, my father was Greece, and he was the last person I wanted to be connected to.

Maybe dating Perseus had opened the door on my own Greekness. Maybe it was walking alone through the fall festival at the Greek church in Tallahassee, the one with so few Greeks, the one that served potatoes dusted with incredibly Italian Parmesan cheese. Maybe, like so many people, I needed to know more about where I'd come from.

For a couple of nights in a row, I sat at my desk and stared at a discount airline's website. I chose flights to Athens, got to the "Purchase Now" square, and chickened out every single time. On the third night, I cried. Fear had ruled my life, and even though I panicked everywhere— the grocery store, the park, the classroom—I still got through most days intact. I realized I had a choice: I could accept my overwhelming fear as my life's limitation, or I could fight it. I downed a shot of Jameson and bought the ticket. That was May 27; my plane left on June 21. I had less than a month to figure out what the hell I was doing, but one thing was certain: I was going to Greece.

☙

I had sixteen days in Greece to spend however I saw fit, and I'd never traveled alone, so I joined Couchsurfing.com and created a profile that made me look like someone you might want to hang out with and let sleep in your home for free. Part of the organization's aim is for people to share their cultures. And yes, I wanted to be immersed in Greece, to live like a local and skip the tourist traps, but I also couldn't afford to stay in a hotel for sixteen days.

A brief glimpse of what I sent into cyberspace in preparation for Greece:

CURRENT MISSION

See the world. Meet interesting people. Write the books. Survive zombie attacks.[5]

ABOUT ME

Well . . . I'm a bright, quick-witted, down-to-earth, creative lass[6] who is a writer, first and foremost, but also an amateur photographer, trained sculptress, painter, bad singer, etc. I hate to be idle, so I am always working on projects—both goofy and serious. I want nothing more than to see this world, meet cool people, and drink good drinks with them.

PHILOSOPHY

I try to remind myself of that Oscar Wilde quote, "Life is too important to be taken seriously," whenever I feel like I haven't laughed enough.

INTERESTS

Writing, literature, good drinks w/great food, languages, conversation, music, film, laughter, people, debate, art, cooking, philosophy, Modernism, meat sculptures,

---

5   Zombies were big in '09.
6   I'm head-hung-in-shame embarrassed that I referred to myself as a "lass."

critical theory, conversations, dancing dancing dancing, exercise, dirty limericks, physics, time travel, the
ocean, animals, and great stories.

I worried that this, like everything else, was a dating site in disguise,
and though I looked for women to stay with, more men responded. I
wrote long personal letters explaining to them what I was doing as best
as I understood it myself: *I am on a quest to find my father's family.*

Since I wanted to avoid getting killed or assaulted, I talked with
everyone I'd stay with over lengthy instant messages. The man I would
stay with in Athens wrote, "It's the trip that counts, said the poet, on
your way to Ithaca." Of course he invoked the *Odyssey*. And with that
message, like so many things that were to happen in Greece, it felt like
I'd stumbled directly into my fate.

CHAPTER 12

ATHENS

At its core, a quest narrative—like a sentence—needs an object. Some tangible thing or experience or discovery drives the tale home. The object of a quest—Odysseus's family, the Tin Man's heart, Indy's Ark of the Covenant—is what makes the story feel important to the reader. But what happens when one feels the call but doesn't know why? What if the quest is driven by unexplainable compulsion, the questee unsure of everything? What happens if one day you hate Greece and the next you're on board Delta Flight 138 to Athens in search of a family you never missed?

The night before the trip, I got home from work at 4:00 a.m., buzzing with booze, and shoved my belongings into what was technically a backpack but looked more like a body bag with straps. I did not yet know how to travel light. As the sun rose, I decided to pull an all-nighter so I might sleep away my anxiety on the plane. At the Atlanta airport, I double-fisted Guinness and Jameson, my throat tight, my heartbeat quick, sweat stretching down the snake of my spine. When boarding began, I called my mother, but she didn't hear the fear in my voice. While she talked at me, I stood at the gate, tears falling onto the receiver.

In my seat, I closed my eyes and repeated my most frequent mantra: *This is discomfort, not danger; this is discomfort, not danger; this is discomfort, not danger.* I worried that at any second I would jump up and scream until they opened the cabin door and released me into the terminal. I pictured doing that—LET ME OOOOOOOUT!—when a man said, "Happy Father's Day." I opened my eyes, and a guy in a Hawaiian shirt shook another man's hand. "Happy Father's Day to you," the other replied, and laughter erupted from my belly, laughter too loud for a plane. The people in my row squirmed. I had unknowingly chosen Father's Day to fly to Greece. Of course I had.

But I couldn't sleep. I chose the longest movies—I watched *Gangs of New York* twice—and none of them knocked me out. Instead, I journaled, sketched the people sitting next to me while they slept, and, once an hour, looked up a Greek word I didn't know in my travel dictionary. My language had grown so rusty over the years. I would've been better off studying conversational basics, but I chose instead to learn fun words. *Coincidence. Fight. Swordfish.*

By the time the wheels dropped for landing, I'd gone staccato: my thoughts scrambled, my body an exhausted sack of weight. I'd been awake for forty-eight hours, but ready to be moved by the Athenian scenery, I perked up, each rung of my lower back cracking, and peered over the well-rested folks to my left. I expected to see ruins, the Parthenon, maybe even the specter of my father in the clouds, but my first glimpse of Greece revealed the brilliant-blue rooftop of an IKEA. I quickly sketched Homer in a toga, a Grecian urn balanced nicely on a DIY end table by his side.

Mitsos, my first Couchsurfing host, had emailed me directions on how to meet him that didn't inspire faith:

> It's very simple. Get into the suburban from the air-port and get off at Neratziotissa (the mall is there). Enter the green line from there towards Piraeus (different ticket). Get off at Ano Patisia. I hope the gods of Olympus will help you. I'll be there waiting.

Somehow, I found my way—though I stood before the closed door of a train for way too long before realizing I had to push a button to gain entry. At every stop I felt like I was still moving, an imperceptible, internal sway I hadn't felt since the last time I'd been fishing with my father, a day that ended with me being convinced my bed was beating against the ocean waves.

Upon arrival on the green line, I called Mitsos, and he assured me he'd be right there. Slumped on top of my oversize bag, I waited for forty-five minutes on the corner of a busy street, craning my neck at every passing male stranger. A terribly obvious thought occurred to me: if he didn't show up, I had no backup plan. *Were the maps in my travel book from Barnes & Noble accurate? Where would I stay? Where, precisely, was I presently?*

At the end of that fear spiral—when my pulse was really picking up pace—Mitsos showed up, all swarth and smirk, driving a green Suzuki Sidekick and sporting a messy ponytail. His small, round-framed, and badly smudged glasses made him look more hippie than city dweller. That impression turned out to be true; while composting in his back-yard, he would frequently go on tirades about the necessity of preserving the Athenian mountains that annually caught fire. He would also regularly refer to himself as Pan during my stay. He looked to me about one evolutionary chromosome away from hooves.

"*Yiassou,* Lisa," he said and came in for a sweaty hug and kisses on both cheeks. I'd expected him to be taller, based on the single photo I'd seen of him. I had a good four inches on him—and I'm five foot nine when my posture's worth a damn.

"Welcome to Athens," he said. I must have looked annoyed because he added, "You will get used to Greek time." Without asking, he took my backpack. He raised an eyebrow but said nothing about its weight and put it on his passenger's seat. My laptop and documents stayed strapped to me, already digging a pair of parallel trenches into my shoulders.

"You bring the heat from Florida with you," he said and wiped his brow. "This is the most hot it is so far."

I nodded. Heat: my primary trigger.

"You have plans for the day?" he asked, and before I could respond, a Ford Fiesta clipped the curb where we stood and drove onto the sidewalk. Before my flight, I'd read that more pedestrians are killed by cars in Greece than in any other country in Europe, though I'm not sure if that's true. I suspect it's something like the many places I've visited in the US that claim to be the lightning capital of the States.

"*Ella!*" Mitsos yelled, shaking his right fist in the direction of the car. To me he added, "You must be careful here."

Suddenly the time on the plane, all that time awake, seemed a terrific waste. I should have been planning what to do—something, *anything*. I'd bothered to stuff a tourist guide into my carry-on but hadn't once opened it. I'd assumed Mitsos would hang with me and help me navigate the city.

"Today is for the Acropolis," he said, ruffling the hair loose from his ponytail and pulling it back tighter. "You go be the tourist. Then you will live like a real Greek."

"What are you going to do?" I asked. Though we'd messaged a handful of times before I'd arrived, I felt awkward, like I should have known more about him. Eventually, I'd learn he ran the family business selling screws. My future in Athens depended on a man who sold screws for a living.

"I return to work, but when I finish, I will call, and we meet near Monastiraki," he said. *"Entaxei?"* He started walking back to the car. I stopped him. *What if my phone died? What if he lost his? What was Monastiraki? Where the hell was the Acropolis?*

"Maybe you could give me directions. Your address?" Though I'm thankful I had the wherewithal to ask, I love that it didn't occur to him; if we were supposed to meet again later, the universe would handle things. The map he sketched is laughable—a Greek hieroglyph meant to explain how to travel to Monastiraki (the part of the city where the Acropolis is located), a military time notation of 17:00 marking the spot closest to where and when we'd reconvene. He might as well have handed me a child's drawing.

As he pulled away into the Athenian traffic with my belongings riding shotgun, I thought, *That could be the last time I see my stuff.* A thought immediately followed by, *So what?* I had the necessities—laptop and passport, notebook and phone. I felt physically lighter somehow, and it wasn't the loss of my backpack. At the mouth of the green line, I'd handed my fate over to a virtual stranger—to a Greek man—and it seemed okay. For a woman who'd spent most of her life drowning in anxiety, that shift was a mercy.

The Monastiraki stop of the metro dropped me in the nucleus of Athens—the ancient area known as the Plaka—where tourists converge in the main square, cameras swinging from their sunburned necks, to explore the cobblestone streets with their hive of fruit vendors and places to pay too much for plastic busts of Zeus. I filed out of the train station and looked up; there towered the Acropolis above it all, the ruins so perfect they looked more Hollywood than history.

I made it a block from the train station, so hungry from traveling that I'd considered eating my pencil on the metro, before following a bald man with a menu who had put on the pressure with his, *Pretty lady! Pretty lady! You sit here!*—a sure sign I'd chosen the wrong restaurant. Before long I had an oversize Stella Artois (another bad sign that not one local beer graced the menu) and a Greek salad—a real one topped with a brick of feta so smooth and dense it went down like bitter, salted butter. I sketched the host who was working the crowd in an attempt to fill the tables. Stopping to peer over my shoulder, he lamented I hadn't given him more hair. Not once did he blink, his mouth a dash of seriousness, so I blasted the top of his head with a fury of curls, and his face surged into a smile. "That is how the women will love me," he sang.

Britannica Junior states that modern Athens "has broad boulevards with flowering oleander trees. The streets are crowded with people, streetcars, and taxis. Donkeys, loaded with goods or pulling carts, are still a common sight in the older parts of Athens." There were people, so many people, but the oleander trees seemed replaced by jewelry stores and bridal shops, lavish places often flanked by discount clothing and cheap tourist wares. After lunch, I had six hours until Mitsos and I would meet again, so I ambled through the marketplace for a bit, slipping into the nicer stores to feel a whisper of air-conditioning. With little idea of what else to do with my time, I decided to heed Mitsos's advice and make the trek to the Acropolis.

If you haven't slept in a couple of days and it's 98 degrees outside, I don't recommend tackling the Greek ruins. If you do, learn what I did not know: there is an easy way and a hard way. You can guess which one I took. I was fit enough for the climb—and it's not Everest—but I'm no hiker. Heat plus no sleep equals woozy, and I started my ascent when the afternoon sun achieved smoldering. I had to pause in the shade a few times to shake off the dizziness that kept taking over, my legs wobbling beneath me. Folks smarter than me climbed slowly with umbrellas clutched overhead. While I rested on a thin stone wall, a priest who looked as old as the ruins, bearded and clad in a thick black robe, paused, sat next to me, and began to text someone.

By definition, an acropolis sits high up, but that prefix, *acro-*, comes from the Greek word for "extreme," which seemed fitting. Portions of the climb are slick with mixed marble and broken gravel, much of it without a railing. Visions of myself as an unidentifiable corpse kept my gaze fixed on the path. I'd be damned if I'd be found unconscious wearing a sweat-soaked T-shirt that read STAND BACK: I'M ABOUT TO TRY SCIENCE. When I finally did look up, directly in front of me sat the Parthenon, a structure I'd seen countless times in my textbooks from Greek school, at every Greek restaurant in existence, in my encyclopedias.

But there it was. Real and under construction, the Parthenon loomed as magnificent and ancient as anything I'd ever seen. The moment my foot touched that sleek pink bedrock, my right foot whipped behind me, and I landed in a pose of involuntary genuflection. Though I didn't want to, I cried. I realize how dramatic that sounds, how befitting a Greek tragedy, but situated before that building, the temple constructed for Athena, goddess of wisdom and courage and justice—goddess of everything that seemed absent in myself—I shrunk, humble. With the carved gods hovering above me, I wondered if my father had ever stood before the Parthenon and felt so small.

For nearly two hours, I perched high above the sprawling Athenian landscape beneath an enormous Greek flag—one that in 1941 had been removed by German soldiers and replaced with their symbol of hate. A plaque next to me commemorated two men—Santas and Glezos—who at eighteen years old tore the Nazi flag down in an act of resistance. Glezos's first name was the same as my father's, and there he was, by my side, from nearly the start of the trip. Maybe he'd been on the plane with me too. Maybe our biological others are with us always.

I stared at the city beneath. Before my arrival, everyone warned me to expect a place brimming with litter and smog and graffiti, but looking down on it from the Acropolis, Athens glittered like a glass mosaic. I opened my sketchbook and outlined the Parthenon's Doric columns, knowing they draw in on themselves in curves designed to hide their dirty secret: they aren't straight lines. The human eye, the mind, yearns to be fooled and sees only what it craves. A young boy with dark, close-set eyes and gelled hair looked over my shoulder. I tilted the sketch toward him, and he nodded in approval before placing a small gold euro next to my feet. He waved goodbye and grinned while his mother dragged him away by the sleeve of his shirt.

A feeling began in my knees and slowly spread throughout my body. Not a tingle, exactly, but something like a low hum, a throb of bass. I'd long felt rootless in my life, but in front of the Parthenon my body listened as the ruins themselves murmured, *It's going to be okay. Everything will be okay. Welcome home.* Somehow I'd traveled all the way to Greece, the single place I'd never wanted to go, the space that connected me more than any other to my father and my grief, and much to my surprise, what I'd found was home.

By the time Mitsos finished work and we met in one of Monastiraki's many squares, delirium had proudly staked its claim on me. Anyone who travels regularly will tell you the trick to fighting jet lag is to stay awake the first full day you arrive—*put yourself on their schedule*—then sink hard into sleep that night. When Mitsos found me in Monastiraki around 6:00 p.m., an oversize drum slung across his back, I'd been awake for fifty-six hours. I kept at my sketchbook to try to stay conscious, but even those drawings devolved into pitiful self-portraits, the bags under my eyes scribbled in dark, dispirited half-moons.

"Now we go become musicians, then dinner," he said. "Should we get you a drum?" He'd already sweated through a gauzy shirt, which, in the States, would quickly be called a blouse.

"Can I bang my head against it?" I asked.

He laughed at first but straightened to grim quickly. "You do not enjoy the day?"

"Oh no. It was unbelievable. So beautiful." I hate having to explain a joke. "I'm just exhausted. I promise, tomorrow I'll be more normal."

He laughed. "No, you won't."

Mitsos fights to keep ancient traditions alive, and his Greek band had close to a dozen members, the instruments, mostly drums, found only in museums nowadays—even in Athens.

"We play Icarian dance music," Mitsos said. "To me it is more than perfect." At least that sounded upbeat.

In a blink of international time travel to my fifteen-year-old self, I landed at band practice: bored, feigning interest with occasional nods and half-hearted smiles. I slumped down on a curb and rested my back against a peeling wooden fence while the band discussed their set list. I'd like more than anything to write that the music was charming or stirring, but truthfully, the repetition of a single drum that began most songs—or was it all the same song?—droned in unrelenting, soporific rhythm while I wished I, like Icarus, would be granted waxen wings, especially if it meant falling quickly to my death.

Occasionally I leaned my head against the fence, my eyes closing, but Mitsos pounded his drum and shouted, "No, no, no. No sleep for you, American girl!" And then more drumming.

A thin violinist with a smile twice the size of her other features was also Couchsurfing his place. She studied traditional Greek *rembetika* music—the mournful ballads of outcasts, songs akin to the blues—and played along with the group. During my stay in Athens, she repeatedly did her best in my presence to prove she was close with Mitsos. Violin Girl would loop her arm through his on the metro, or over drinks she'd lean her forehead into his shoulder and laugh too hard at things that weren't exactly funny. Message received. If she'd known that I would never fall for another Greek man, she could have saved herself some energy. And if she'd realized that Mitsos was missing every neon-lit clue she threw at him, she might have aimed her courtship at a more receptive man. I was astonished that he could be surprised when, weeks later, she finally proclaimed her love aloud. "How could I miss this?" he'd ask me, and I'd laugh, shake my head, and say, "I don't know, man. It's kind of like not knowing you're on fire."

Anyone who has ever written about Greece has obsessed about the food, but that first full dinner in Athens—the sight and smell of dishes I hadn't had since my father had cooked them years ago—was among the few moments I've encountered the sublime. At an outdoor *taverna* in Thissio, on the outskirts of the Plaka, we sat—Mitsos, Violin Girl, and I—with a rare breeze offering some relief from the day's merciless heat. Dining out is an ordeal typically lasting hours, so the focus is more on the conversation than the food, but I spoke little at first, my concentration entirely on the feast Mitsos had ordered. There was barely enough room on the table for the spread: a trough of mussels *saganaki* floating in a broth of ripe tomatoes, olive oil, and feta cheese; *horta*, a simple dish of bitter dandelion greens saturated in lemon and olive oil; a plate of eggplant stuffed with fresh herbs and feta; skewers of charred chicken; fried zucchini and squash blossoms; baskets of tiny, whole fried smelt—bones and all.

For a while, Violin Girl and Mitsos talked to one another, and I was happy to have time to stuff myself with every single thing on the table, but then, as it so often does in Greece, the conversation moved quickly into Relationship Land.

Violin Girl asked, "You have a boyfriend in the States? Maybe a husband?"

I took my time chewing my fish, never eager to answer this question, very aware of the eyes locked on me.

"No, neither. I mean, I had a boyfriend, but he kind of sucked. So now I don't." Next fish in.

Violin Girl giggled and inched her chair closer to Mitsos.

"What this means, 'he kind of sucked'?" Mitsos asked.

"He was Greek," I said, "but I'm not in a hurry for a husband. I know this seems weird, but I'm more focused on writing than marriage right now." Another fish.

"This is not so weird. I mean, look at me," Mitsos said and pounded his fist against his chest. "I am here in my late thirties and not married."

Another inch closer for Violin Girl.

"How late?" I asked.

"What how late?" he asked.

"Into your thirties are you?"

"Oh. Forty-one," he said and winked.

When things fell quiet, I apologized and assured my company that typically I'm lively—sometimes even funny—but my brain had given up working a good fifteen hours back. They were kind enough to talk among themselves, a happy chance for Violin Girl to twirl her hair and giggle more. If I would have had the capacity to keep the conversation going, I'd have told them that the skewered chicken we were eating, which had been doused in the traditional Greek trifecta—lemon, olive oil, and oregano—tasted exactly like my childhood.

The rest of the first night in Athens is hazy, even though I documented it, because my notes constantly turned to one primary thought: sleep. The margins of my notebook are lined with a steady trail of *Z*s and sketches of four-poster beds, plush pillows, and smiling stick figures with *X*s for eyes. I walked with Mitsos and the musicians that caught up with us after dinner through the uneven streets of the Plaka, the lot of them playing songs as we strolled. I lagged behind, smiling in an attempt to be good-natured despite being certain that at any moment I'd collapse onto the cobblestone.

Finally, around 2:00 a.m., we went back to Mitsos's flat, and I saw my living quarters, a space I'd share with Violin Girl for the next five days. By European standards, the room was large and looked like an opium den: tapestries and rugs in rich violets and burgundy lined the walls and covered the floor, every speck of furniture low to the ground. It was blazingly hot—almost no one has air-conditioning in Greece and many, I swear, believe that fans cause disease—but I was too tired to care. As soon as Violin Girl sat on her bed, I quickly turned my focus to the other mattress and crumpled, face-first, in a matter of seconds. I'd been awake for sixty-two hours.

As I lay there on the verge of finally passing out, Mitsos sat on the floor between us and read from a comic book his sister had written. Had I been in my own apartment, I'd have barked at him to get out. I didn't need a fucking bedtime story, but he had given me a free place to sleep—even if he seemed determined to keep me from doing that. The Greek was dense, and I fell in and out of the story—something about an old man selling things and repeatedly turning violent.

"Your sister," I said without opening my eyes, "she likes men?"

"Of course," Mitsos said. "Why?"

"The story seems kind of anti-man," I said and yawned.

"No, you misunderstand. It is anti-fat, middle-aged, Russian merchant," Mitsos said. "Maybe you miss this because you are tired."

I do not think this was the case.

Thankfully, he and Violin Girl left to share wine in the garden, and before he finished sliding the door closed behind them, I fell into a sleep so thick and inky, I do not remember dreaming of the flight or Greece or my father. Just a long, quiet, and welcome darkness.

In Athens, the language wriggled back to me in snippets, and although I could grasp the gist of some conversations, others were utterly foreign to me. Participating in them—speaking fluidly—seemed impossible. Frequently, I'd find myself at dinner with a table full of cackling Greeks, and I'd smile along and toss my head back in laughter at the right times, but mostly I felt like someone was sucker punching my kidney. Though I never asked him to, Mitsos was kind enough to speak English often, but after a few days of roaming the trains, streets, and markets alone with my limited vocabulary, isolation surged through me. *Britannica Junior* reports, "Although its history was said to date back to mythical kings, Athens probably began as a fortress." I understood that deeply. Part of me, indeed, felt intensely at home, but the rest of me was as much an outsider as I'd ever been. My face passed for Greek, but my tattoos and lack of language betrayed that I didn't belong. The Greek word for this, *xenos*, was as bad as a curse word when I was growing up; more than "outsider," it implies that one is a stranger everywhere one goes.

By my third day in Athens, it felt as though a fat finger jabbed the center of my chest and wouldn't quit. Wandering around the city,

I often walked into people or lampposts, sputtering apologies to both. Twice I nearly stepped into traffic only to jump at the reprimand of a car's horn and a torrent of colorful phrases. I'm nearly certain someone yelled, "Fuck your little spinach," though maybe my translation was off. Despite wanting to be present, to engage fully with this new environment and soak in all the details—like the smell of the market, which was at once fishy, sweaty, and sweet from baked confections—my thoughts turned again and again to my father. A man in a shop might say hello, and I'd spin around wide eyed, expecting to see him. Everyone I met and everything I saw reminded me of him. This was different than feeling haunted, as I had in New Jersey and Philly. This was like taking a vacation inside him.

Britannica Junior maintains, "To Athens we owe an immense debt in art, in literature, in some of the sciences, and in philosophy, the science of thinking." I intended to test that last one out. After the Father's Day incident on the plane—after the day I'd turned on the TV to find a support group for children of murderers—I'd become obsessed with coincidence. Part of me wondered if the universe was sending me signs, but more of me believed it was another way to avoid thinking directly about my life with my father while bouncing around a land that at every turn smacked of him. Still, it's a subject that allows conversation to move beyond small talk—I am a hater of chitchat—particularly in a place like Greece, where damned near every person is an amateur philosopher.

At a *psarotaverna* (fish tavern) in the middle of a busy market district, I sat with Mitsos, his brother and sister, and many of their friends, sharing beer, wine, *rakomelo* (a warm, spiced, and honeyed raki), and more food than eight people have any right ordering. After answering some (and shrewdly avoiding other) questions about President Bush and American foreign policy, I asked about coincidence.

"This is not the Greek way," Mitsos said and took a long sip of wine. Hairs had fallen from his ponytail and clung to his cheek. He looked around the table and back at me. "I do not speak for everyone, but I am not so sure I am a puppet, the strings pulled all from above."

His brother, Vasilis, a pale Greek who read comic books and excelled at wordplay—traits that instantly endeared him to me—interjected. "I believe many think the show is set in place before we show up."

Mitsos smacked his hand against the table, and I jumped. "Ah, the fools, they are everyplace you look here. But this is not how it works." He leaned across the table toward me and paused, thoughtful. At certain angles, he was unbelievably handsome. "Why have you come here?"

A deceptively easy question. "Because I'm Greek."

"No, no, no," he said and laughed. "You are Cretan, like we are Cretan." He motioned to his family. "This is something different. You are a part of the land, whether you wish to be or not. The feeling is different from the rest of Greece. It is in the blood." His family nodded as Mitsos launched into a winding speech, a trait I'd come to recognize as his trademark. In that moment, he could have been my father, spouting the rhetoric of Crete's splendor, and just like when I was a child, I unintentionally spaced out. When I snapped to, he was saying, "You are here because you are asking questions of the universe. And if you listen close, it will answer to you."

Surely I'd have to listen more closely than that.

Lost in the Greek logic that led us to asking the universe questions, I tried to get back on point. "But wait. What does that mean for coincidence?"

"Bah," Mitsos said. "This is only a word."

I must have looked confused because Vasilis said, "I think what my brother means is what is meant to happen will." His voice was almost too gentle to hear above the restaurant clatter. "But you have to be, how do you say, open for business? So is this coincidence? No. Not the same."

Mitsos smiled from across the table and addressed me again. "You must be careful what you ask the universe to show you. Sometimes the picture is too bright to look at with human eyes." He paused. "So let us be robots!" He moved his arms stiffly in a quick pantomime, and with that, everyone fell into a spasm of laughter. Mitsos refilled my wineglass and raised his, still giggling a bit. *"Yeia mas."* To your health.

See what I mean? Philosophers.

The next night, we climbed to the rooftop of Mitsos's flat so he could grill various meats beneath the setting Athenian sun.

"You are pretty," he said. "You just need to lose some weight."

Adrenaline settled on my cheeks in splotches. I was twelve years old again. I wanted to tell him to fuck off, but he'd done so much for me that I quickly rationalized his rudeness as a cultural difference. While he flipped the meat with tongs, he sang The Smiths' "Some Girls Are Bigger Than Others."

It was time to leave Athens.

Over the next week, I wandered through the Cyclades—Mykonos, Naxos, Paros, Santorini. By day, I made up for a lifetime of lost sleep; by night, I drank in the hope I might pass out.

At a lounge in Mykonos, a man named Tommy—tanned to burnt umber in a white, mostly unbuttoned shirt that revealed a triangle of tangled chest hair—asked, "You are Greek?"

I answered him with my most fluid Greek sentence, one I'd uttered a hundred times over the course of my life: "Yes, I am Greek and American. My father was born in Crete."

"Ah, you are Cretan!" he said and wagged his finger. "This is a most special thing, you know. The greatest beauties of Greece come from Crete."

"It is true," added his friend Stavros, whose name means "cross"—religious, not angry. "Crete is best of Greece. A bit crazy, maybe, but the best."

After a long sip of wine, Tommy continued. "You will see your family in Crete, yes? Is your father there?"

My father was everywhere in Greece; surely he'd be hyper-present in Crete. But I knew that wasn't what Tommy meant. Instead, I told them of the vague search for family, of my mission to find them there so many years after my father's death. I wasn't sure it could be done, but I was hopeful. That might have been a lie. I'm not sure that I was hopeful or, honestly, that I actually wanted to find them. Until that point, my plan had sounded like a cool thing to do when uttered aloud, but it was more a theoretical venture, something I intended to do when I got around to it.

I deflected. "Allow me to ask if you believe in coincidence."

Tommy spoke up immediately, the inner rim of his lips stained purple. "You ask this question because of what you do, you look for family, but there is no such thing. The universe, it knows everything about you, and nothing is left to chance. It is all planned to make you bigger, stronger."

Oh, I liked Tommy.

"What if the universe has the wrong information?" I asked. A half joke, but Tommy looked very serious. Stavros glanced at him and then at me with an eye roll, as if to say, *He gets like this sometimes.*

"It cannot be wrong," Tommy said. "Look, this life, this world, everything around you—it is a dream. This is all a dream. And what is the point?" He looked around the bar and then back at me. "Happiness. It is only what matters. You must visualize your life, visualize your happiness, and you will see it come."

In Santorini—the last island I visited before mustering the courage to take the six-hour ferry ride to Crete—I stayed one night with Anna, a woman with a plume of dense curls and terrible taste in men. I loved her immediately.

We dined on a rooftop and drank colorful shots with the kitchen staff before heading back to her studio apartment, where I inflated an air mattress and Anna declared she would read my cards. She said they were named after Katina, a woman from Smyrna who had used witchcraft to take over the city and, among other things, worked her powers to marry a handful of wealthy husbands.

We faced one another, sitting cross-legged on her tie-dyed bedspread. "The way this works," Anna said, "is it will tell of your past, your present, and your future."

"Okay," I said, trying to mask my skepticism.

She laid out three columns and read from the left. "This card here is the further past only, and I see much darkness. One figure darker than the rest. Hardships."

"That sounds about right." I hadn't told her the details of my father's death.

"In the present, which is this card here," she said and motioned to the center, "is to say there is still some dark but things—they look better. I do not see the same figure."

I wanted to say something eloquent and encouraging. I landed on, "Hmm," and smacked a mosquito sucking on my knee, the size of the insect so large, the bite left a bruise.

Anna focused on the final card. "In your future you must be a fox: cunning," she advised. Her lips pursed as she stared at the cards, and she erupted into raucous laughter, leaning back against the wall. "Do you see this card here?" she asked, pointing to one in the corner. On it, a young woman in a disheveled bed—hair loose, clearly naked beneath the sheets. "This means you will have much sex soon."

I laughed at this too. Over dinner, I'd told Anna I had absolutely no interest in Greek men—in dating or sleeping with them.

"I don't think so, dear, but wouldn't that be nice?" I said. She hadn't given me the answer I really wanted, so I asked, "Will I find my family in Crete?"

"How should I know?" she said. "I am not a witch."

I chuckled.

"But the cards suggest you will not unlock any of life's mysteries this week." She put her hand on my itchy knee. "For this, I am sorry."

The next morning, terrified of the ride, I boarded the ferry from Santorini to Heraklion. It had been easy to stay distracted by the food and beaches of the islands, by generous new people and tumbling ruins everywhere. But sitting on the upper deck, I found myself surrounded by a different breed of Greek, the Cretans, and the accents—the soft / sh/ instead of /h/, the chewy /ch/ instead of /k/—threw me. Of course it had been easy so far; no one had sounded quite like my father. All I had to do was pick up my sketchbook or drink a couple of beers and I made him disappear again. But suddenly I was surrounded by him on the Blue Star ferry, by men in fishing hats with rooted grooves in their faces, everyone dressed in drab navy and black despite the July heat, the sound on that ship like sitting with an army of ghost fathers. In Crete, my father would be omnipresent, and I had six hours to prepare for him. I slipped my earbuds in to drown out the platoon of surrogate fathers, hugged my backpack to my chest, and surrendered myself to the plain truth: there had never been a way to prepare for my father, and there was no way to prepare for Crete. I closed my eyes and waited for the hitch of the ship that meant we'd arrived.

I promise you: it was the longest ride of my goddamned life.

CHAPTER 13

CRETE

As I stood in the queue to exit the ferry, the top of my back itched fiercely. When I scratched it, I found that the tattoo I'd gotten on my father's birthday—the Greek one that reads "I refuse to fear life"—was raised, the lettering puffed up as though on high alert. Minutes later, I raised my foot to cross the metal ramp of the ship onto Cretan soil for the first time, and the moment my foot touched ground, every hair on my body stood on end.

I'd thought I was home in Athens, but I'd been wrong.

From the Heraklion port, I called my final Couchsurfing host, Stelios, a man who told me he'd pick me up in ten minutes. By that point, I understood Greek time and didn't worry as I waited for thirty while the wind whipped my dress up around my waist. In the darkness, the buildings that surrounded the port sparkled, and every car that approached raised my hope; maybe my ride had finally arrived. When Stelios did pull up, he smiled and waved with one arm while he steered the world's smallest scooter with the other. I laughed and lifted my backpack with a groan.

"*Yiassou*, Lisa," he said and grinned. In a striped rugby shirt, khaki cargo shorts, and ratty Chuck Taylors, he was so tan that he looked to me more Middle Eastern than Greek. Everything about him screamed twenty-five years old—seven years younger than me; a silly grin seemed at odds with the black unibrow that hung on his face like a strip of electrical tape. To this day, I have never met anyone with thicker eyebrows.

I hoisted my bag onto my back and hopped on behind him. He had only one dented helmet, which he wore. I hadn't been on a motorcycle since I was a child, but nearly everyone in Crete travels this way. Over the next days, I would see men on scooters maneuvering with one hand while smoking, while eating, while children piled on, while talking loudly on the phone, barely gripped to anything, as though they were simply sitting on a stool. I held on tighter than necessary to Stelios's waist and clenched my eyes shut when my hair lashed into my contact lenses. He assured me he lived one kilometer from the port, but we rode for three while the bike lilted slowly, weighed down by my bag at its rear. It was so heavy that when we arrived at his flat, the instant I let go of him I fell off the back of the scooter and into a chain-link fence.

Stelios's place was large and airy with gauzy white curtains that blew into the living room from a balcony running the length of the apartment. It looked like the music video set for an '80s hair band.

"This is your bed," Stelios said and pointed to the couch. I put my bags down and surveyed the room while he retrieved a bottle of raki and two shot glasses from the freezer, then sat across from me.

We'd chatted online at least a dozen times before I'd arrived, exchanges that had taken on flirty enough tones to worry me, so one night I typed something like, *I'm looking for a place to sleep—not someone to sleep with.* Despite his protestations, I'd been around long enough to know when I was being hit on, and prior to traveling halfway across the world to stay with a virtual stranger seemed like the right time to make my boundaries clear.

Stelios poured us each a shot and pushed mine toward me across the wooden coffee table, past an ashtray overflowing with butts. He assured me that after one, we'd go out for dinner.

"Thanks."

He crinkled his magnificent brow. God, I wanted to pluck it.

"What is it with you Americans always thanking people?"

"It's considered polite. You know, manners."

He snorted. "When I give you my organs in the street, then you say thank you to me, yes?"

Stelios stared at me intently, like maybe I'd offended him, then broke into a giant smile. Goofy bastard. That ability to go from one extreme to the other usually raised red flags for me, but he was so comical it didn't register as threatening. His cheeks were soft, full as a chipmunk's, but his brow was so strong that one look from him when he wasn't smiling was intimidating.

"We will leave after this," he said and pushed another shot toward me. "You like raki?"

"Of course," I said and picked up the moonshine. My gaze moved up and over his shoulder to the kitchen, where a handgun rested on top of the corner cabinet. Probably loaded.

"*Yeia mas,*" I said, sure to look him in the eye. "Thank you so much for hosting me." Then I smiled.

He drank his in one fluid motion and swirled it through his puffy cheeks, then laughed. "You tease, yes?"

"Yes."

"I do not mean to sound angry, but I speak from here," he said and hit his fist against his diaphragm twice. "So. Tell me everything." He lit a cigarette and rested his chin in his palm, as though he expected a real answer.

"That's a tall order." I laughed.

"What does this mean, 'tall order'?"

"It means it's a lot to ask for."

"Bah. I do not ask for much. I only want to hear how Greece has been so far. The order is not so tall." He smiled at his use of a new phrase.

There would be wide enough misses in our senses of humor to drive a Greyhound through.

"I'm in love with Greece," I said.

He beamed. "You are?"

"Hell yes! What's not to love? It's beautiful, and the people have been so nice."

"They are nice because you are a woman alone, and to be truthful, not an ugly one." He smiled and poured us two more shots, his knee bouncing. "Is it too early to talk about art now?"

Three rounds of raki later, we were still on the couch, and our plan to *leave right after this* seemed thwarted. I learned he was an actor with a local theater troupe that performed a handful of plays a year, but his real passion was photography. I zoned out a little during the geeky lens talk and tried my best to look engaged while hiding how quickly I was getting drunk on an empty stomach. As Stelios talked about his various projects, I thought about how comfortable I was. He felt like an old friend whom I happened to know almost nothing about.

He paced in front of the open balcony door, smoking his fifth cigarette since we'd been there. "My problem is with people. I don't know how to express this. Onstage, I am lucky to become something else, but talking to people is a worry for me. It comes easy with you, which is nice, so very, very nice, but many people, I think they do not understand me." He sat again and looked at me hard. "Do you understand?"

"I'm not sure. Like you have problems communicating?"

"No. It's not that I cannot speak, but I feel like maybe no one knows who I am." He poured us another round. "After this one, for sure, or we will never go."

"Maybe the trouble is you don't know yourself." Oh, I could be a philosopher too. "Ever been in love?"

I worried he might get defensive again, but his face relaxed, as if he'd managed to unwind for the first time since I'd met him. "I do not think so," he said quietly.

"Darling, if you're not sure, you haven't. I might not know a hell of a lot, but I'm sure of this." I raised my glass, and we threw back the last of the raki. "Now let's get some food."

"I hear of a place," Stelios said and tossed me a puke-green tie-dyed sweatshirt, "where tonight the music is the old Greek style. I am not sure where it is, somewhere in the mountain a bit, but we will find it."

I climbed aboard the back of the scooter and pushed my body against his. It had been a long time since I'd been pressed against a man, maybe a year, and I closed my eyes as I rested my head against his back, which smelled like spring. We wound farther up the narrow mountain roads, the air noticeably colder as we climbed, and though we had to ask for directions a couple of times, we eventually found the small *taverna*, clearly a place that didn't want to be spotted by tourists.

People sat outside at iron tables shrouded in trees so low and weepy, it seemed as though we'd stumbled into a secret garden. Large tiles, some of them cracked, paved the ground from street to stage, which was framed by a carved wooden arch. Soft amber lights lined the floor, illuminating the musicians, the entire restaurant a faint glow in the middle of that wooded darkness. I took dim, blurry photos of the men—the lyra player looked like a Greek Michael McDonald circa 1978—and he played the most mournful notes, each one longer and sadder than the one before it. Stelios ordered a bottle of wine and too much food—warm *dolmades* in lemon sauce, fava, fried potatoes, chicken, *dakos*. That was my first experience with *dakos*, the Cretan salad made of barley rusks, tomatoes, feta, and herbs. After coming back to the States, I would eat it nearly every day for a year.

The conversation was pure ease and almost entirely about relationships. The only time we ceased talking was when Stelios had to sing, his loud vibrato accompanied by a smile at songs he knew as effortlessly as his alphabet. He asked me to dance, practically begged me to, and embarrassed, I said no and planted myself more firmly in my seat. I wished I'd remembered the dances I'd learned in Greek school.

Stelios danced alone, a cigarette hanging loosely from his lips, his movements graceful and confident, while I tapped my foot to the beat, moved by songs that sounded like the very epitome of Greece and my father. Though almost everyplace else I'd go in Crete played pop, that first night tucked up in the mountain, with all that food and wine and song, with the canopy of trees and fiery stars like holes poked in a canvas above us, was exactly what I'd hoped to find in Crete.

On the cold scooter ride home, I hugged Stelios hard and breathed in his scent. I whispered, "You smell so good," and right then I knew I was in trouble. We continued to talk, not a pause in the forty-five-minute ride, and he tapped the back of my palm to reassure his agreement, my safety. That night I slept easily on the couch, certain I'd found the right guide.

Before I'd left for my trip, my Tallahassee therapist said I was caught between two personalities: one utterly responsible, the other self-destructive. She wasn't wrong. Many times over the years, I have crawled into party mode and had trouble slinking out of it when confronting something difficult. It's no surprise that once I got to Crete, well, I got drunk. A lot. Stelios was a perfect partner in crime: still young enough to be committed to partying without worrying about the excess. My years spent slinging drinks behind the bar had only helped make my boozing seem all the more ordinary. I'd relied on the justification that at least I wasn't like the regulars I'd served over the years, the ones who'd lost their licenses, jobs, children. I told myself that I might drink, but I wasn't a drunk. And sure, there was some truth to it, but the bigger truth is I drank too much, especially when facing anxiety, and

Crete—despite my instant love for it—presented a Trojan horse full of problems.

On my second day in Heraklion, a city tattooed with beautiful graffiti and rushing people and street performers, I took a bus to the palace at Knossos, the ancient Minoan capital where the Minotaur supposedly roamed the labyrinth until Theseus finally killed him. As a child, I'd seen that creature repeatedly on the beach towel of my father's wall, had been obsessed with the outline of a man's torso topped with an enormous bull's head.

Upon arriving at the ruined palace, I'd expected to see something large and towering, my idea of palaces sadly taken mostly from Disney films, but Knossos is flat with stonework, surrounded by a smattering of columns and holes cut out in the cracked and collapsing floors. It was difficult to imagine this place as a labyrinth, a space so tricky a beast as great as the Minotaur couldn't escape it. It was impossible not to be moved by the sheer age of the ruins—I mean, Homer mentions Knossos in the (freaking) *Odyssey*. I'd just gotten lost in that thought—Homer might have been here—when I heard a sound unlike anything I'd heard before. *Some kind of animal*, I thought, so I followed the noise through the other tourists, who seemed not to notice it. High in a tree above the entrance to the palace sat a peacock with plumage spread about it, the dozens of eyes on its tail staring at me as it yawped. Stelios would later tell me that this is a rare thing to witness, a lucky thing, as a peacock at Knossos is considered to be the reincarnation of a king. At the time, it was a stolen moment in which I again felt alone in a crowd.

When I returned to the flat, Stelios was on the couch in front of his laptop, sporting his usual daytime outfit when he wasn't at work: boxer shorts. He said it was too hot to wear much else, and it was, but I couldn't imagine being comfortable enough with anyone to lounge about in my bra and panties. Yet there he was, farmer tanned from scooter rides, a forest of black chest hair faded above his stomach until continuing again beneath it and disappearing into the band of his boxers. I told him I wanted to cook dinner to show my gratitude for his hospitality, so he put on shorts, and we walked to the local grocery, where we scored the supplies I needed to make pasta sauce from scratch to go with the wine I'd brought as a gift from Santorini. While I stunk up the apartment with garlic and onions, he moved the kitchen table onto the balcony so we could eat with a warm breeze sweeping over us.

"We must toast," Stelios said, raising his wineglass.

"To?"

"Ah! I have a favorite toast!" He lowered his voice an octave and said seriously, *"Sta kalitera erhontai."* Then he held his glass out for me to tap it.

"Um . . . care to translate for me?" I asked and held my drink back.

He laughed. "Yes, yes. It is something like, *To better things to come.* This is okay?"

"This is perfect," I said and tapped his glass with mine.

After cleaning up, we headed to a bar, where we slouched into the same side of a booth, leaning toward one another and sharing strong beers with great, dangerous names—Belzebuth, Judas, Cobra—and after deciding it cost too much to keep drinking like that, we left and stopped at a kiosk, where we purchased two large bottles of Amstel—the real deal, not the American light—and walked out to the Venetian fort on the harbor. We climbed the enormous stone wall, waiting at passes for the waves to cease crashing so we could press on. Stelios held my hand as we moved through darkness over the rocks and debris until we came to a flat pass, where we sat under the stars and cracked open our beers. Stelios asked again about love, and I wasn't very good at explaining what love was like, what it felt like.

"But *how* do you know?" he asked with urgency.

I told him it was something intuitive that you don't think about, like your kidneys working, and he didn't buy it.

"It's like your whole body feels at home," I said, and he dropped the subject.

A peaceful silence fell between us as we sat on the wall of that fifteenth-century fort, the hum of the city drowned out by the waves slapping the great walls.

"You know, my girlfriend is not so happy with me," Stelios said.

I sat up. "You have a girlfriend?" I wish I'd asked this in a cooler tone of voice, but after two days of talk about love and relationships, it seemed a suspicious thing to leave out.

"Yes, but I do not call her while you are here."

"Do you think that's smart? I mean, won't she be angry?"

"I do not care so much about this. We fight a lot. She is, how do you say, annoying."

"Then why is she your girlfriend?" I asked and tossed a pebble toward the water.

Stelios laughed. "I don't know. We used to get along, but now it is always a problem with something."

"How old is she?"

"Nineteen."

This time I laughed. "Well, there's your problem. You date a child, she'll act childlike."

"You think maybe I need an older woman?"

I heard the smile in his voice.

"I think we need more beer," I said.

We closed the night at one last bar, a place owned so shockingly by a woman, the fact was relayed to me five times. The bartender bought us a shot of our choice—my call, Jameson—and when he went to add ice to it, I said no. He asked if I wanted Coke instead, and I shook my head. "Straight?" he asked, and when I nodded, he put down the bottle, wiped his hands on a bar towel, and shook my hand.

Stelios put money in the jukebox—some kind of dark trip-hop—and when he returned, we leaned toward each other while we spoke, the music too loud to keep conversation at a normal distance.

"What was your father like?" he asked.

I sighed. "I spent most of my life thinking he was an asshole, but it wasn't until a while after he died I thought maybe he was sick," I said.

"How do you mean sick?" All eye contact, no breathing room. A long pull of beer.

"In the head. He wasn't right."

Stelios thought for a bit. "But many people are this way, yes?"

No. By then I'd learned it is easier for me to say what happened than it is for most to hear it.

"He didn't die in an honorable way. And the things he did while he was alive . . . they were bad."

"Why do you not speak here? We have been talking so truthful these days, but in this matter you say nothing," he said and reached over to tuck a loose strand of hair behind my ear.

I ran my thumbnail through a groove in the bar top. "People usually don't want to hear such things, but my father killed his girlfriend and her daughter, then committed suicide. Almost six years ago."

His face remained unchanged, as though what I'd said didn't shock him in the least. "Why did he do that?"

I am amazed by how often this is the first question people ask.

"It's impossible to know," I said. "And trying to figure it out drove me crazy for a long time."

Stelios ordered us two more beers by snapping his fingers, a motion that made me cringe, then turned back to me and lit a cigarette. "Does your Greek family know?"

"I'm not sure. Maybe? A few days after it all happened, I was at my mother's, arguing about the funeral when we got a call from Greece. My aunt, I think. She still thought he lived at that house. Probably didn't even know he was divorced. But my Greek was so bad then. Hadn't spoken it in years. I got out the words for 'father' and 'died,' but other than that, I don't know. Nothing I wanted to say came out right. They said something about Greek radio, so maybe it was announced. But that seems kind of crazy."

He nodded. "This does not make sense, but if they called, they must know something," he said and paused. "You do not look happy now. Do you wish to talk of something else? Maybe go home?"

"Please."

We went from kissing to naked in under a minute.

I'll spare you my thoughts on chemistry and body parts that fit so well they seem engineered for one another and move right into the stuff that leaves me unsettled: dirty talk in English followed by the same in Greek that, when it flipped back to English, I demanded be in Greek again. Domination in every corner of the flat, against every wall and piece of furniture. Biting. Smacking. Choking gone so far, I almost blacked out. And a moment in that drunken fuck, the light almost absent, in which Stelios looked so much like my father, I had to look away and shove the idea out of my mind with force.

At 7:00 a.m., Stelios snored while I lay awake, still naked, still quite drunk, and on the phone with the airline. I told the man on the other end I wasn't ready to leave, that I needed more time, and in some miracle of airline service, he allowed me to extend my trip for a measly fifty dollars. Every other time I've tried something like that, the cost of the change was more than the original round-trip ticket. I shook Stelios until he looked at me.

"I'm not leaving."

He smiled and rolled over, back asleep in seconds. Despite the morning heat and balcony birds incessantly doing their best to keep me up, I slept peacefully.

My original plan in Heraklion had been to board a bus headed for my father's village on a Sunday, since I figured no one would be at work—only at church in the morning—but it was clear I couldn't look for them yet. Some part of me still wasn't ready for what finding my aunts would mean. Then, the first Saturday night there, things got out of control, even for me. Earlier that evening while walking through the downtown markets, Stelios pointed to a small red dot in the mountains.

"Do you see that?" he asked. "This is where we go tonight."

"What is it?"

He smiled. "A surprise."

Later, I pulled his hideous sweatshirt over my dress, thankful I did when the air cooled the higher we rose. His scooter wanted no part of the struggle against the mountain's incline. Stelios made me close my eyes for the last stretch and wouldn't let me open them until we were indoors. He held my hand, leading me over the gravelly terrain, and once inside, he told me to open my eyes. The first thing I saw was him, beaming, but directly behind him was the inside of a restaurant the size of a banquet hall. Hunkered in the corner sat a live band playing traditional Greek music, and dozens of people danced while others chilled at their tables, shouting and eating and laughing. But the surprise was the long back wall of the place: entirely open, it offered anyone who sat there a panoramic view of the glowing city and sea beneath it. Stelios watched only my reaction, smiling like a kid who'd gotten the present he most wanted.

We ate everything—snails, potatoes, tzatziki, *dolmades*, octopus, prawns, bread, and more and more wine, of course, followed by raki. We took photos of ourselves, some serious, most goofy, and spent the night on the same side of the table, laughing and making out more voraciously in public than I'm comfortable with. When we left, before getting back on the scooter, he leaned against a crumbling stone wall, pulled me toward him, and kissed me hard, the night around us nearly silent, the city so far away, it seemed like a dream or a postcard or a scene from a romantic movie I'd likely hate.

On the way back to Heraklion, the traffic slowed, barely moving as we crawled through a village.

"A wedding," Stelios said over his shoulder. "A small one. Maybe only six hundred people."

I'd heard tales of Cretan weddings: the fireworks, the bride and groom arriving on horses, guns fired, sprawling tables of food, so many people dancing in unison that chandeliers fell to the ground in explosions of glass. I asked if we could crash it.

Had my tattoos been covered, we wouldn't have looked so conspicuous, him obviously Greek, me passing without a problem, but I'd left his sweatshirt at the restaurant, warmed as we were with booze and lust. We walked around the reception for all of five minutes, and I was transfixed by a table of fish, glorious and whole and gleaming bright pink under the lights, the size of them unlike anything I'd ever seen in a supermarket or restaurant. We got such looks, people pausing and staring hard, that Stelios grabbed my hand and whispered, "I think we leave now if we want to live," and though I followed him, I was lost in a memory of my father in the kitchen of our house, his attention on me while I stood on a footstool beside him at the counter. He snapped his fingers.

"Lisa, hey," my father said, and his voice made my eyes dart from the fish to his face. "With some fishes like this, you have to make sure to get all of the guts out or else they can be a poison." He lifted half of the fish wide, its slit body a slimy smile. "Put them in a bag so the cat can't get 'em. You got that?"

"Yup. Guts in the bag."

"Good. You know, you'll need to know how to do this for your husband someday."

I rolled my eyes and groaned, then looked back at the split-open fish.

"You not getting married?" he asked.

I shook my head and lifted onto my toes like we did in dance class.

My father laughed. "You will change your mind. Someday you find nice Greek boy and you marry."

"What if he's not Greek?" I asked, thinking of the short Italian boy in my class whom I had an i's-dotted-with-hearts crush on.

"Of course he will be Greek."

"Dad," I said, "not everyone in my school is Greek."

"Trust me when I am talking. Marry a nice Greek boy," he said and removed the spine of the fish in one slick motion.

∽

Stelios and I left the wedding and dove into another night of barhopping and conversations about love and our futures—where we were going and what we wanted out of life and all of the drunk talk that happens when two people have fallen into some kind of traveling flash love. We drank so much that I don't recall how we ended up at a strip club or why we got kicked out. I don't know how many bars we went to afterward or how much more booze we poured down our throats.

The next morning, I awoke wearing only a bra into which I'd apparently shoved five lighters. The thick stink of cigarettes poured out of my mouth. I struggled to sit up, dizzy with hangover, and discovered I'd rearranged the living room furniture. While getting dressed, I found that, incomprehensibly, I'd lost a single shoe.

I plopped onto the edge of the mattress and wept, my pulse throbbing in my temples. I hadn't come to Greece to get blackout drunk and sleep or fuck the endless pain away. Lord knows, I could do that in Florida. On the edge of that bed, an old word crept through my mind: *broken*. I'd come to Greece with a plan, half-cocked, and there I sat, spinning at rock bottom. I was blowing it. If I wanted to find my family, they weren't going to come to me.

Tomorrow, I thought. *Tomorrow I will go*. And the next day, I walked to the bus stop in the blazing 100-degree heat and purchased a ticket to Vori. While I sat on a bench and waited, a man walked by whistling "You Are So Beautiful," and my heart galloped. The universe's quick reminder that there was no escaping my father. I stood up and began to pace. For six euros, I was headed to my father's village, and it appeared he was invisibly riding shotgun. From here on out, there would be no avoiding him.

CHAPTER 14

NOSTOS

On the bus, I watched the craggy landscape flicker by. The dusty, orange earth swirled occasionally in a light breeze, and spotty patches of green poked through the soil where olive trees somehow found enough water to sprout. In the background, mountains stood tall and wide, obscured by clouds and the haze of heat. Small white buildings, crosses jutting out from their ridged roofs, overlooked various hills. At one point, the passengers crossed themselves in unison; I do not know what the trigger was.

I assumed the bus would take me straight to Vori, but we made a dozen stops, the bus grown crowded with each pickup. *Where is everyone going?* I wondered. How would I know when to exit? Eventually, we pulled into a village, and the driver made eye contact with me in his long mirror. *You get off here*, his face said, so I did. A handful of people stepped off with me, and I hadn't thought Vori was a tourist destination, but it's the home of the Museum of Cretan Ethnology.

Before disappearing down a small road, the bus let us off in the center of town, a cluster of empty cafés flanking the square. Immediately, I saw a sign that confirmed I was in the right place: a coffee shop with a name that ended in *–akis*.

These had to be my people.

To say it was hot seems obvious, but Crete in July is nearly unbear-able if you're unaccustomed to the heat. I was told it's so close to Africa that clouds of Saharan dust periodically make their way across the sea and coat everything in a fine red powder. Vori was the smallest village I'd visited at that point—fewer than eight hundred people live there—and at two o'clock on a 100-degree Monday afternoon, it appeared nearly deserted. I swiped my forehead with my forearm and surveyed my sur-roundings. A couple of men sat outside a café. One patted his neck with a handkerchief and turned the page of his newspaper; the other stared blankly into a demitasse. Both wore dark colors—a royal-purple shirt unbuttoned to the sternum, a gray-checkered one fastened a bit more. I looked down. Almost any day of the week, you will find me in black, but my travel clothes had the stink of overuse on them—an odor I could no longer hide with a spritz of Febreze. The only clean item left in my bag that morning was a fuchsia V-neck dress. Pink: like my mother's world, like lipstick, like the center of a wound. Without realizing it, I'd announced myself as a stranger because I hadn't bothered to do laundry in ten days.

Before me stretched two paved but worn paths I could follow, and as one looked a bit more traveled than the other, I chose it, deter-mined to find someone who seemed friendly enough to approach. I walked for maybe half a kilometer from where the bus had dropped me off and saw a single pack of men sitting in the shade, playing cards, sipping frappés. I'd noticed them from a distance and had every inten-tion of speaking to them, but as I approached, they stopped talking and turned from their game to glare. The village was mostly silent, only the call of an occasional bird swooping by to break the stillness open, as though I were in the middle of a forest instead of a town. My pulse banged in my temples as I neared the card men, but under their watch, my courage disappeared, and I breezed past them like I had an actual destination, still feeling their stares on my skin when they were long behind me.

I saw no one else on my walk. After maybe fifteen minutes, I paused, sweat slicked on every inch of me—even my knees—and took a sip of water as I looked around. I'd made it to a residential area, whitewashed homes on all sides. The one to my right looked split by time—half of it two stories tall and remodeled with bright stucco, the other half squat and swallowed by grapevines. Laundry hung still on a makeshift line, and a deep-pink petal from an enormous bougainvillea sat shining by my foot. I would find no coffee shops or *tavernas* in that direction, so I turned back for the museum and hoped someone there would seem friendlier than the men I had to walk past once more, their repeated gawking making me so self-conscious, I pretended to talk on my phone.

The museum cost three euros to get into and didn't have much to look at (a couple of darkly lit rooms that contained old farming equipment, tools, and photographs), though it was refreshingly cool. Next to a glass case boasting twenty-five different types of woven baskets stood a woman with a clipboard and no makeup who eyed me, so I walked past her quickly, feigning a sudden and deep inter-est in Byzantine ironwork. I moved on and paused before a wall of black-and-white pictures—women with their hair yanked back in tight buns, kerchiefs over their foreheads as they squatted in a field. I thought of my deceased *yiayia* and wondered if she were in any of the photos.

I was stalling, and I knew it.

Finally, I inhaled deeply and approached the curator. Between her bits of English and my meager Greek, we forged a conversation. I explained I was looking for my family, and she asked what my last name was. When I told her, she laughed.

"You come to the right place. Everyone here is Nikolidakis."

After years of my name being butchered by teachers, telemarketers—everyone—it hadn't occurred to me there were more of us.

"I do not know how I help," she said. Her face apologetically revealed she thought my cause was hopeless. I wondered when the bus would be back.

"Well, if you were me, where would you start?" I asked.

She drummed her fingers on the counter, a reflex so familiar it set me at ease. Then she reached behind her and riffled through a plastic filing box.

"Maybe go to this *taverna*," she said and handed me a business card. At the bottom, in fat green Greek letters, was my own last name. She gave me shaky directions, and I thanked her before shuffling back out into the heat.

The *taverna* was uphill and in the middle of a field of scratchy overgrown weeds. I'd thought for sure I'd lost my way or misunderstood the directions, but eventually I stumbled upon an empty café. I expected a building as decrepit as everything else in the village—shabby paint, cracks in the ancient stonework—but the tavern looked modern, like a stack of nested boxes. A woman stood out front watering flowers.

"*Yeia sas,*" I said, and the woman jumped. She looked surprised to see anyone, let alone a very tan girl in a hot-pink dress with pit stains.

"*Signomi,*" I apologized. "I didn't mean to scare you."

"Is okay," she said. Her name was Angelina, a stunning woman from Spain. How she wound up in that village I do not know, but I was thankful to have found her.

"I'm from the States and am looking for my family. My father was born here. They moved to Athens many years ago, but I'm hoping to find someone who knows where they went." It was the first time I'd said any of this aloud, and while she processed what I said, I really thought about what I was doing. *I have come for my family. My father's family.*

"What is your father's name?"

"Manoli Nikolidakis." My accent was flawless. Though my command of the language had faded, what I could speak sounded as authentic as anyone who lived there.

"And his father?"

As far as I knew, my grandfather had abandoned his family when my father was a boy.

"I'm not sure, but my *yiayia* was Garifalia, and my father had two sisters, Georgia and Despina."

"Hmm." Angelina continued watering her flowers, seemingly unfazed by our exchange.

There is a saying in Crete: *siga, siga.* It means "slowly, slowly." But it's more than a saying; it's a mantra, a fully embraced philosophy, a deep-rooted worldview. Maybe it's the heat. Or village life. Either way, nothing moves quickly.

"I do not know those names," Angelina said, and we both stood there, stupid and silent, cicadas singing their chorus in the fields around us, a song broken when a few children playing with a stick and a ratty dog ran between us laughing.

Where would I go from here? Back to Heraklion?

"Let me get my husband," Angelina said, as if the thought of asking someone else had just occurred to her. "He is Nikolidakis too."

And so I waited. Between the heat and hunger, my hands shook. At a large, empty table covered with a waxy checkered cloth, the corners weighed down by rocks, I traced the squares in the pattern and guzzled my water. A few minutes later, a man with a white short-sleeved shirt fully unbuttoned came around the corner. He did not smile. Instead, he looked at me as if I were a curiosity escaped from the museum or some creature he'd heard about as a child but dismissed as adults pulling one over on him. His name was Gus.

Gus asked me each of the questions his wife had, in almost the same order, while she translated for both of us. *Who is your father? His mother? His father? His sisters?* The two of them looked at each other every time

I answered, as if to confirm that I did not know enough. And they were right. I didn't know much. By the time he finished questioning me, I had been at the *taverna* for forty minutes. I was certain we'd reached a dead end. I wanted to eat, and was in a place to do so, but thought it would be rude to ask them to cook for me when they were already trying to help. Plus, how serious could I be about this mission if I ordered it with a side salad?

The children—three of them—flanked Gus's legs, and as he patted their heads, I thought of my father, of myself running around the backyard while he sprayed me with the garden hose, both of us laughing until we collapsed on the grass, kicking our feet into the air and choking for breath.

"I know," Gus said and held one finger up, like a cartoon character with an idea. "I will get my mother." He walked into the kitchen, children trailing, and when he emerged, a thin woman in black with oversize eyeglasses followed him. She moved slowly, taking each step like a member of the bridal procession walking down the aisle. One foot, together, pause. One foot, together, pause. She could have been the thin ghost of my own *yiayia*.

We exchanged hellos in Greek, and she told me her name: Adelpha. Again we worked through the same questions at the same rate.

Who is your father?

His mother?

His sisters?

His father?

I felt trapped, stuck in some fluke in the space-time continuum, and wondered how and if I would ever leave. When we got to the question of my grandfather's name, Angelina explained what the trouble was.

"The names of the girls are common here, and they change when they marry," she said. "You are sure you do not know your grandfather?"

I was sure I didn't. But maybe my mother did. So I called.

I once saw my mother answer the remote control instead of her phone, so when I asked if she knew who my grandfather was and she ran the gamut of Greek male names—*Giorgos? Yiannis? Kostas? Nikos?*—I had little faith and was long-distance-prices short: "I need you to pick one, Mom."

"I think it's Kostas," she said, so that's what I repeated to the three strangers staring at me.

Again, more silence. *Siga, siga.* Crete is an exercise in patience.

But then Adelpha sat back an inch and seemed to stop breathing as she studied my features. A new depth appeared in her giant eyes. She inhaled deeply.

"Was your father killed?" she asked softly.

I did not need this translated.

My eyes watered against my will, and though I didn't cry, I couldn't even cough out the word *yes*. I simply nodded.

With that small motion from me, Adelpha removed her glasses, reached forward, and grabbed both of my forearms. She held me for a moment and said quietly, *"Paidi mou."* My child. The same thing my *yiayia* had called me. Then she stood and walked back to the kitchen. I knew something had happened but wasn't sure what.

Angelina looked at me, smiled fully for the first time, and said, "You are not alone anymore."

~

There is no *Britannica Junior* entry on *nostos*, but it is the word that belongs here. In literature classes, we use it to mean "homecoming" or "return by sea." The nostos in the *Odyssey* is Odysseus's return to Ithaca. But it's more complex than that. Stelios told me it comes from the ancient Greek verb νέομαι (*naomai*), which means "to return home." It's also half the root for *nostalgia*, a word born by adding the Greek *nostos* to *algos* (pain). A return home to pain. A painful return to home. The pain of missing home.

I did not understand what it was that had drawn me to Greece, but now, right now, it is clear: I needed to return to the home I never had, to the home that I'd been missing. My Greek family waited—they did not give up hope—and I arrived. I'd spent so much of my life making bad and dangerous decisions. Finally, I'd made a good one. I chose to find my home.

∽

The bare table before me was quickly covered in food, and the three of us—me, Gus, and Angelina—relaxed in one another's presence. I picked at a salad and potatoes, but despite my hunger, I was too excited to eat, my leg involuntarily bouncing and shaking the table.

Ten minutes later, Adelpha came back and placed before me a wallet-size black-and-white photo of my father, a boy I barely recognized at first, a boy maybe seventeen or eighteen, his face round, so soft. In that picture was a person I'd never known, but still, his straight mouth and broad brow—his dark, dark eyes—did it show? Was the man he'd become visible even then? I wished he were smiling, something to separate him completely from the man I'd grown up with, but there it was: my father, this stranger.

Without warning, I began to cry. Adelpha nodded, stroked my hair once, and said, "I will call your aunt." After flipping through a black leather address book, she made a call I didn't understand because the Greek was too fast, but she smiled as she spoke.

"Okay. She comes," Adelpha said after she hung up the phone.

"She comes from Athens?" I asked, confused.

"No, child. She lives close. A few roads away."

"But—but I thought they moved. To Athens." I had the envelopes from my father's basement. I had time before going back to the city to get ready, to print pictures, to know what to say to them. In that moment I understood I hadn't really expected to find them. I would never have shown up empty-handed if I had. A few roads away? I had nothing.

"Yes, they leave. But they come back," Adelpha said.

My father never went back, even when his mother fell ill and died. It hadn't occurred to me that others did.

~

I continued to glance at the entrance to the *taverna*, waiting for my family to burst through the doorway. Instead, they came slowly over the hill between the trees and houses at the back of the place, their silhouettes a small, slow-moving fleet on the horizon. My aunt Georgia; her husband, Dimitri; and a close family friend: they knew this village, its shortcuts and nuances. And as they came closer still, I could hear nothing but the swirling blood in my ears.

My aunt Georgia hobbled toward the table with a cane and hugged me so hard I almost fell. I hadn't known how much I'd needed that hug until it nearly swallowed me. She pulled out a chair and slowly lowered herself into it. Facing one another, we sat so close, I could feel the heat from her knees against my own. The folks who'd helped us reunite looked on, grinning, and said the same word a few times: *thavma*. I tried to memorize it so I could look it up later.

Georgia crossed herself three times and spoke.

"Garifalitsa."

I nearly choked at the sound of my Greek name. The name given to me by my father, the name of my *yiayia*. Until that moment, I'd genuinely forgotten it existed—no one had called me that in two decades. Hearing it unlatched some long-closed door. Not only was I Greek, I was and had to be my father's daughter. And despite the twenty-five-year gap in our having seen one another, I immediately remembered Georgia as the body remembers. I knew her in my bones.

I do not know how long my aunt and I stared at one another and cried, but we filled the café—maybe the whole village—with quiet reverence as tears rolled down our cheeks, silent. We didn't need to speak. Instead, we sat quietly in disbelief and the deepest joy I have ever known.

The second thing Georgia said was that one day earlier at church, she'd prayed to find me—had lit candles and crossed herself three times before the *Theotokos*, the Virgin Mary, for that very purpose. It was the day I'd originally intended to visit them too. And then there I was, sitting with my estranged family in the middle of my father's village, a prayer answered.

The third thing Georgia said was, "You are not leaving." And I knew that was true—there was no way around it—but as a woman who has experienced panic her whole life, I've always needed to know where the exits are. The lie I told myself was I'd be imposing on them, but when I looked more closely at my reluctance, I found the truth: I wasn't prepared for what might happen. Still, I agreed with a smile and called Stelios so he would know not to worry when I didn't return.

"I found my family," I said, and my voice crackled. It was the first time I'd said it aloud.

"I cannot wait to hear about this, but I knew you would. Go. Be with them," he said and smiled. I heard him smile all the way from Heraklion.

When we left the *taverna*—my aunt, her husband, and I—we walked slowly along the dirt paths that connected the village, the trenches between the houses like the veins of a body. For hours afterward, not a word of English was spoken. My aunt didn't speak even conversational English, and though we managed to communicate a bit, me frantically looking up words in my portable dictionary, there were many moments of concession, both of us shaking our heads and smiling. "I'm sorry," I said repeatedly. "I don't understand." What else could I do? Sure, I could spit out some basics—order food, talk lightly on a number of subjects—but with these fast-talking, heavily accented family members, I deeply regretted not having studied harder before I'd come. I could sense them thinking, *What kind of Greek doesn't speak the language?* I'd probably been more fluent the last time they'd seen me, when I was a scabby-kneed child. It felt like deep failure, a betrayal of self. And though there was something beautiful in our pantomime, in our repeated attempts to communicate, there was so much more I wanted to know. I simply didn't have the language to do it.

As we trudged through the narrow paths between the houses, most of them with trellises wrapped thoroughly in grapevines, I had the distinct feeling of being shown off. We stopped at the home of a first cousin of my grandfather, and the woman there, whose name means "freedom," smiled and hugged me four times. Plates of watermelon and honeydew were laid out, a bottle of raki and five glasses produced, an air-conditioning unit that did nothing to cool the room turned on for the occasion. As in many cultures, the hosts will pour your glass each time it's empty. They will also encourage you to drink up at every turn. People assume it's ouzo all the time in Greece, but not once in my entire trip did anyone offer me anything other than homemade raki, straight from the backyard stills, its toxicity unknown, poured most often from a recycled two-liter water bottle. I found myself thankful that my many years of bartending and drinking suddenly seemed like training.

Freedom told us she'd seen me walking earlier, and though she hadn't known who I was, she'd been certain I wasn't a tourist. Pointing to her own lips and eyes, she said, "It is here. You look like you live here." She and my aunt repeated the word *thavma*, the one I'd heard at Taverna Nikolidakis, so I scribbled it down to look it up later. Behind them on a side table sat a framed photo of my father—the same one Adelpha had shown me at the café. I stared at it while they smiled. *Who was he?*

Before we left, Freedom went into the other room and came back with a crocheted white scarf that she tied around my head. The lacework was so stunning and delicate that if I'd had the language, I'd have joked that she'd just promised me to her son for marriage. She kissed me on both cheeks and held me in a long hug. When we pulled away from one another, she wiped the damp lines on her cheeks. It was as though she'd made the scarf years ago in case such a day arrived.

I wished I had something to give her in return.

Back on the streets, Georgia introduced me to every person we walked by—*my brother's daughter, Garifalitsa*, she told them all as she held my hand tightly, pride in her voice, a signal to the people that something enormous had happened. We stopped briefly at a pharmacy in the hope that I could find contact lens solution, which I did for nearly twenty euros, and while I tried to decipher the label, my aunt told the pharmacist about the day's events. Then I was introduced to another first cousin, Georgia's neighbor, who lifted her arm and pointed at her skin, spiked with gooseflesh. She was shrunken and draped in black, like almost every woman in the village, and her smile betrayed a lack of dentistry. In fact, the entire village had bad teeth and fungal feet, yellowed toenails a quarter of an inch thick, the teeth and feet of meager means and hard lives.

I didn't know where we were going, but when Georgia opened the door to her house, I stopped moving. To my left, the tangle of pink bougainvillea; to my right, the line-hung laundry, the home split by time. I'd seen all of this hours earlier. She lived in the very house I'd walked to when I'd first gotten off the bus. I did my best to explain that to her, but my Greek failed me again. I wanted to say, *Of all the homes to stop in front of, I chose yours.* Had she been out front collecting the laundry, had she walked outside to stretch her arthritic legs, our reunion would've unfolded like a surrealist's dream. It was as though my body instinctively knew where to take me. Had I let the notion of fate grab me for just a second, I might have trusted myself to knock upon her door.

At Georgia's home, it took me some time to understand the setup of the place. Where the now removed laundry once hung, a table and chairs were set in its place. The patio, the table, and I were in front of what looked like a new townhome—a two-story cream-colored stucco facade with an expensive door. But this attached to a rundown single-level dwelling, the lot of it surrounded by thick grapevines. This is where Georgia and her husband, Dimitri, slept and lived; her son, a man now in his forties, had claimed the newer, remodeled section. Though it is often the custom for Greek children to remain with their parents past the age when American teenagers feel the itch to flee, it seemed to me he had long passed his expiration date. And more than that, it was utterly peculiar that he had what amounted to a swanky bachelor pad while his parents slept in a dilapidated alcove.

Georgia wiped down the table—I offered help that was denied—and she set out another plate of watermelon. Her husband joined with the raki. Always the raki. While she prepared the table, I called my mother again and told her the news.

"You give them my love," she said. "I mean it. Hugs and kisses." She exhaled. "I'm so happy for you, sweetie."

When I went back to the table to drink and eat more, the severity of our language barrier propped between us like plexiglass. Georgia asked me questions, her accent thick as concrete, so most of them were impossible for me to translate. Instead, we were left chatting about the weather.

"It's hot out, eh?" Georgia asked.

"Yes. It is hot. Very, very hot," I said because I knew how to say that.

Silence. A bird. A flash of fading breeze.

"Ach, it's hot," Georgia said.

"Yes. It is hot. Very, very hot."

Ugh.

When she asked about the family, I used my phone to show her photos of my mother and brother, astounded by the miracle of 3G in the village (I'd gotten no signal in far more populated Santorini). Georgia asked after Mike, if he had a wife, and when I said, "Yes, in May," she said, disappointed, "So no children." I told her that his daughter was nearly two, which made her shake with laughter, slapping her husband's knee with her hand. "Married in May, but the daughter is two!" she exclaimed. "Like the Cretan style!" I found a couple of photos buried in an old email, grateful that sometimes my family thought to send me pics. When Georgia saw my brother's daughter, she snatched the phone and kissed the screen, wiped a tear from the corner of her eye, and said over and over, "Beautiful. So, so beautiful."

Soon, a dark-blue sports car with Greek pop music blaring sped toward the house and abruptly stopped, a tan cloud of road dust rising from its tires. Out of the driver's side exited a tall, intense-looking man, and I knew instantly we'd met before. It was Theodoros, one of the terrible cousins who'd visited us so many years ago, but he stood now at six foot four, a thin stack of bones topped with clothes too baggy for him, a full beard despite the July heat. I later learned he'd grown it in mourning—an old Cretan custom—for a friend who'd passed away, but at first glance I took him to be an ex-communicated Orthodox priest. I smiled as he leaned in for the kind of half hug siblings are forced to give when they apologize.

Georgia asked what I like to eat, and I said anything was fine, but she looked at me as though she might crack me one if I didn't give her a more specific answer, so I said, "Seafood, vegetables. No beef or lamb." She sent Theodoros back out to fetch ingredients for our celebration, and he came back with seafood, all seafood. I couldn't have been happier at the prospect of eating the real deal, the cooking one can't get in a restaurant. A home-cooked meal with my family.

Then people really started showing up.

When I'd walked the streets earlier, it had been empty, but once the sun started setting and people heard the news, the foot traffic grew, some stopping to say hello, others walking by and craning their necks to get a glimpse of the stranger who'd come to town. For a fat stack of cash, I couldn't have wiped the dopey grin from my face. Soon enough, another car pulled up and parked behind Theodoros's, and though it looked too small for it, six people poured out—a woman, a man, and an army of children. The woman wore a slim black tank top that clung to her torso, her brown hair tossed back in a messy ponytail. She had the busy, distracted air of a mother, answering questions and organizing her clan at once. Georgia introduced her as Irene, one of her daughters, and when she said in English, "Hello! I never think I would meet you," I could've kissed her sandaled feet. It would become clear she hadn't spoken English in some time—her eyes searching for words, the wheels grinding—but her presence immediately alleviated the language embargo that had hung over our reunion.

Irene's husband, like so many Greek men I'd met, wore a white shirt mostly unbuttoned and looked very serious at first—a wrinkled forehead, penetrating eyes—but he laughed quickly, faster than the rest of my family, and had an ease about him that made him a pleasure to be around. Over the evening, he'd check in on me—nod and ask, "Okay?"—and that small kindness seemed so generous, I quickly thought of him as one of the kindest men I'd ever met.

I'm a sucker for kids in general, and all four of theirs were undeniably adorable, but their oldest daughter, Chloe, a fiery eight-year-old with a handbag the size of her torso, was my instant buddy. Every time I looked at her, she was watching me, astounded I'd come from America. She'd learned some English in school, and her mother encouraged her to talk to me, but she spent the first hour parked in a chair a mere inch from my own, staring and looking away quickly when I looked back. When she finally gathered enough bravado to talk to me, every syllable was elongated and interrupted by bursts of embarrassed giggles.

"Yoooooooou are (giggle) veeeeeery beeeeeeautiful (giggle)."

"Efharisto," I answered, smiling.

"No, no," she said. "You speak Eeeeenglish."

"Ohi," I said and clicked my tongue, raising my eyebrows. Suddenly I was caught in the reverse; she wanted me to speak English, and I refused for a playful bit, answering her in Greek. A different power in that choice. When I'd denied my father the sound of his language, it was spiteful. Now, I wanted to be included. I wanted more than ever to really be Greek.

Irene stood to pour me more wine—they are forever pouring more *something*—and asked, pointing to her brother Theodoros, "Do you remember him?"

I smiled. Tortured Barbies and smashed vinyl and that damned Thriller jacket. "Yes," I said and paused. "He was *bad*," I added in Greek.

They laughed, all but Theodoros, who forced a crooked half smirk. I never once saw him smile in my time there. Maybe that's not his way.

And then a topic so regular I could have been sitting at Thanksgiving dinner in New Jersey.

"Are you married?" Georgia asked loudly—more accusation than question. Everyone joined her to look at me. It is no wonder I only remember her visiting and not her sister, Despina; Georgia is a bull, wide and solid, her temper flaring regularly. I found it nearly impossible to tell when she was mad, emphatic, or loud. Dozens of times, I thought she was angry at someone, but then she'd burst into laughter, her torso shaking. You'd think I'd expect this genetic quirk after years of standing by my father's side as he chatted up other Greek adults the same way, all raised voices capped off with back-slapping fun.

If I were fluent, I might have said something like, "I've chosen to focus on my writing and graduate school; plus, every guy I've dated was flawed in ways that made us too incompatible for the long term." Some long-winded justification, the bullshit I'd gotten so used to uttering, I didn't even have to think it through. Instead, I smiled and gave them one of the few Greek punch lines I had memorized.

"I don't have a husband. I have a cat. I am free."

When they laughed, it felt good to know I could be funny in another language, but I know they worried. By Cretan standards, a gal in her early thirties should not only be married but also have at least two kids by her side. I am certain they were as happy to see me as I was them, but I sensed them sizing me up, trying to figure out if it was too late for me.

Neighbors continued popping by throughout the night, and about every thirty minutes or so, someone handed me a phone. I took notes on whom I spoke to, feeling the heavy anachronism of cell phones in a village that was still very much married to an old way of life. The stand-out of those conversations was my cousin George, my aunt Despina's son, who was in Athens.

His voice squeaked when he said, "I cannot believe this, that I speak with you now."

"Yes," I said.

"It is a *thavma*." That word again. I asked him what it meant.

"It is a miracle," he said, and I smiled.

We made plans to meet when I returned to Athens, and I scribbled his number along with the rest of my notes under a shaky-looking family tree. In truth, without looking at my notes, he is the only person I remember talking to. Something about his voice: so light and young and genuinely sweet. He told me he remembered my father and had always wanted to meet me, and I looked forward to a different experience upon my return to Athens.

Almost immediately upon my arrival, Georgia began cooking, and here's the lot of it: fresh *spanakopita* (not flaky or greasy); prawns the size of my forearms (no exaggeration); *horta* (stewed greens with lemon); feta and olives; small fried fish called *gavros* that one eats whole—head, bones, every bit of it; grilled octopus; snails; *dolmades*; gorgeous bread; a never-ending stream of freshly fried potato wedges; and platters of fruit. There was barely room enough on the table for the carafes of wine and raki, neither of which stopped flowing, though I couldn't bring myself to add Coke to my red wine, as the others did. The ten of us seemed to eat all night long, but the supply never dwindled.

I'm no fool in at least one regard: they don't eat like that every day. The feast was for me, for family.

There was a magic to that evening I'm afraid I'll never accurately capture. Something about sitting under the darkening Cretan sky in that village, miles and miles from light pollution, the night sky speckled with stars so bright it seemed lit by bulbs. Despite the language barriers, we shared food and looked at one another in disbelief and smiled. Some kind of pure joy was there, something rare and beautiful I have never felt anyplace else, even in other truly happy moments. More than anything, I felt full: full of food, full of gratitude, full of love.

After we'd mostly stopped eating (you never *really* stop), Theodoros went inside and returned with a lyra. He'd barely said a word during dinner, but he played with such intensity and force, he seemed in a trance, channeling himself through the instrument, as though by taking the bow to those three strings, he could communicate what words wouldn't allow.

Chloe latched on to my hand. "Come, Garifaliiiiiiiitsa," she said. "We dance." She grinned, her plump cheeks flushed from the heat that still hung over the evening.

"I'm sorry," I said. "I don't know how, sweetie." The days of the lessons in the Greek-school gymnasium were long gone, and besides, none of them had been Cretan.

"Come, I teach," she said and grabbed my hand. "I am gooooooooood teacher. Pleeeeease?"

How could I say no?

At a speed typically reserved for the side effects of medication, Chloe explained and demonstrated the dance moves. There's not much I like more than to dance—it's fundamental to my philosophy of enjoying life—but I couldn't get the hang of it. The folks at the table clapped and laughed and encouraged us both, but the photos of our exhibition feature my lips twisted in concentration, arms held incorrectly in front of me instead of by my sides, one leg in the air, my face plagued with deep confusion. I am sure I brought some shame on the village, but I tried. Maybe not all things are in the blood. Or maybe they'd plied me with too much raki and wine to pick up anything new. Either way, it didn't matter. I was with my family.

CHAPTER 15

PHILOSOPHY

Despite the joy of the evening in Vori, I'd begun planning an exit almost immediately upon arrival. I couldn't stay there. I was on the verge of tears the entire time and couldn't fully process what was happening, what it meant. *Healing* was the word that quickly and repeatedly sprung to mind—I knew this all had something to do with moving forward, moving beyond the pain and grief my father had left me steeped in—but at the same time, I was so much closer to him there than I'd ever been, and there was no quick fix for my wounds. Healing was a simple concept: easy to say, so hard to come by.

My family had good memories of my father. When anyone spoke his name, Georgia crossed herself and said he was such a good man. Over and over, that simple line was repeated. Neighbors, second and third cousins, strangers all said: *he was such a good man.* My Greek family was lucky to have known a version of my father worth celebrating. I envied them that. But a good man?

Britannica Junior states, "The word 'philosophy' is formed from two Greek words, one meaning 'love,' the other 'wisdom.'" I had over the years built up some wisdom about my father. I knew he was unwell;

I knew what he was capable of. I knew he drank too much, and I'd eventually learn that he'd used both cocaine and crack. I also knew he sometimes collapsed in a heap of self-loathing and regret—like a man incapable of controlling his urges, his body, his brain.

When my family told me what a good man he was, I thought about how easy it is to say you hate someone—to make them a caricature clad in malice. I'd done that for years. The truth is that my father was sometimes kind and generous and he, like his sister, laughed with his entire body. I thought of the New Year's Eves of my childhood, when he dealt blackjack into the morning, throwing hands with a wink so Mike and I could hoard our bounty. But other times he was, indeed, a monster. That complication is impossibly difficult to reconcile—to hold those two opposing truths in my cupped hands.

In Vori, being flanked by family who loved him so deeply didn't undo his crimes or abuses. It didn't magically heal me or even make the nightmares go away. The complex PTSD I'd be diagnosed with a decade or so later would remain active for years, maybe forever. But this new family forced me to recognize something I'd long denied: part of me had loved him, too, and that is as close as I've ever stood to a philosophy of father.

The bad is easier to remember than the good. I wish I thought regularly of the times when my father and I made up and the world seemed to boil over with hope—those times when I believed, again, that things would be different, that my father would be good, would stay good, like a real father. And I wish all those innocuous spaces in between—the breakfasts and gardening and watching TV—were real memories, not moments that have been eclipsed by the shadow of trauma. Instead, I think of the heartache, the damage. I picture him looming over me—yelling, imposing, terrifying. I see him watching me through my bedroom window. And from now until I die, I will imagine him holding a gun to a fifteen-year-old's head, precisely as he'd done to me years earlier, only now he pulls the trigger every single time. Being surrounded by folks who spoke and thought well of him in Vori—even if what they believed in was mythology—felt like a step toward healing, but I wasn't ready to be fully immersed in that. When asked when I was leaving Greece, I told my first lie.

"I leave from Athens in three days," I told them. "First, I go to Chania to see friends, then back to Athens for the States." Never mind that I had extended my ticket.

"How long have you been here?" they asked.

"Two weeks. I started in Athens, then Mykonos, Naxos, Santorini, Heraklion."

Throughout the evening, my lie was parroted back to me. "Can you believe it? Here for two weeks and she only finds us now before she leaves." In unison, their heads shook while they clicked their tongues. "This is too bad. Too, too bad."

I learned I would stay the night in the remodeled section with Theodoros. My bed was downstairs, his up, and once he said good night, I didn't see him again until later the next afternoon. Notebook in hand, I climbed into bed; my body and mind had been wrung through with fatigue by the day's events, but I had to get it all down. I lay on my stomach scribbling snippets of dialogue, what people looked like, the basic order of events, my handwriting loose from speed and exhaustion. Finally, when I could write no more, I turned the light off, and fully dressed—I'd brought no change of clothes—I slipped into the easiest sleep of my adult life.

The next morning in Vori, I awoke from a dream in which I'd been onstage performing "Simon Zealotes," a song from *Jesus Christ Superstar*, and as I slipped back into consciousness, in that strange half sleep, I literally mouthed the lyrics, "Christ, you know I love you." As soon as I snapped to, I laughed at how ridiculous it was to be feeling so, well, groovy. Before walking next door to Georgia's place, I wrote a little, trying to fill in the gaps of the previous day's notes. Stepping out into the beaming sunlight, I felt the oppression of the morning's heat already falling on the land. I'd yet to see the inside of my aunt's side of the house, so I knocked lightly before entering. When Georgia saw me, she smiled and handed me a crocheted cross. I wondered briefly if she'd somehow had access to my dream.

"For you," she said. "To take."

I thanked her, touched by the gesture, but then she yelled, "Sit, sit! You are hungry, yes," and shoved a chair at me. It was not a question.

While she prepared breakfast, I took in her small space. It was per- haps half the size of my one-bedroom apartment, and the room was a step back in time: a refrigerator with a small rabbit-eared television atop it; a musty, earth-toned couch with center cushions that sagged so much it seemed to smile; a flimsy two-person folding table; a kitchen sink deep enough for laundry needs; and a small stove with only two burn- ers. The floors were exposed, and the mossy concrete slab was partially covered by a rug so worn down, the print was no longer discernible. It may have been purple once, but I couldn't be sure. I caught a glimpse of a bed behind a thin hanging tapestry. When my gaze drifted to the ceiling, I realized it was made of what looked like intricately intertwined twigs, something that might pop up on Pinterest in the impossible DIY section. I learned my *yiayia* had made it when she was pregnant with her second child. There'd been no roof when Georgia was born.

I tried to memorize the room. Above the couch on the wall hung a smattering of icons with a candle burning beneath them—in Greece, most homes have this eternally lit flame—a large photo of my cousin

Dimitri, the one who'd visited the States with Theodoros and had died young of leukemia, beneath it. Next to him hung an enormous photo of my father, the same black-and-white one everyone in the village somehow owned. There was also a calendar for the wrong year.

"You sleep good?" Georgia asked.

"Yes, thank you," I said, stuck on my father. I rocked in my seat to test his eyes, to see if they followed me the way Jesus's had from the iconostasis of our church. They did. The entire village appeared to have fixed my father in time, at seventeen, right before he left for Athens and then, quickly, the States. Maybe they thought of him so well because when he was a teenager, he was still good. Just a handsome young sailor looking to make his way in the world, ready to work and help out his sisters and mother, because that's what good Greek boys do. Maybe. Though he'd left Vori nearly thirty-five years ago, my father remained omnipresent, a myth, so different from the man I'd come to know that when people spoke of him, it was as though they were sharing stories about a stranger.

Breakfast: a carbonated orange drink, two over-medium eggs drowning in olive oil, and half a loaf of crusty bread. That amount of oil would've daunted me any other time, but it's all about being grateful, and I ate every last delicious bit.

Georgia told me the bus would come in one hour, and a flash of immeasurable relief surged through me. Fight or flight—I was through fighting.

My aunt and I, the only two in the house, looked at one another for a bit, my father above her shoulder on the wall.

"Can I ask you a question?" I asked.

"Yes, yes. What is it?" She fanned herself with a folded newspaper.

"Is this the house my father grew up in?"

She said yes, and I'd suspected as much, but learning I'd spent the night in my father's home, in his actual house, seemed as preposterous as sleeping in Dracula's castle. I can never picture my father as anything but a man; in my faulty imagination, he cannot be a boy, but in that very room, of course, there was once an infant who cried when hungry and took first steps and seemed like the greatest blessing; how can one look at a baby and envision an end like my father's?

"I ask a question," Georgia said and paused. "How did he die?"

It was the single question I should have been prepared for. I should have practiced the answer over and over. I should have thought about it the entire time we ate dinner, when I failed at dancing, while I slept. But I hadn't. Even though almost six years had passed, even after traveling halfway across the globe to find these people, I had no idea what the right thing to say was. Fortunately, because of the language barrier, there were fantastic gaps in our conversation, so I had a few seconds of silence. In English, that pause and what I said next would've been telling.

"What do you know?"

Georgia smashed her fists together and said "car."

"Yes," I agreed. "A car accident."

"Yes?" she asked.

"Yes."

She released a sigh, a breath trapped for years, and crossed herself three times, looked toward the ceiling. She repeated, "Thank you, God. Thank you, God. Thank you, God."

I looked at the photo of my father on the wall, a wall his hands had touched hundreds of times, and stared at his mouth. One side of it now looked curled into a barely perceptible smile.

The size of that lie will weigh on me forever. Was it the right thing to do? Didn't his sister have a right to know the truth? Isn't the truth always the best option? Like so many kids, I'd been taught that honesty was the best policy, but we all know that's bullshit. Sometimes your friend looks awful in her new yellow dress, but you can tell she feels fabulous, so when she asks if she can pull it off, you toss her a thumbs-up. But, of course, this wasn't that kind of lie.

The bigger question it raised—and continues to raise—is: Who was I protecting? Was I trying to spare my aunt the same grief and pain and mourning I'd gone through? Or was I protecting my father? Worse still, had I become one of the adults I resented—an adult who couldn't bear to speak the truth of him aloud? Had I made myself his accomplice?

I'd come to the one place in the world where people still thought well of him; I didn't want to take that away from them. How could I thrust these people into facing a truth about their beloved hero—a truth I was barely able to reconcile? I couldn't. I didn't. I still don't know if what I did was good or right. Of course, the intention was kind, but people with good intentions can still cause harm. I told a lie. A big one.

The bus would come by the same café I'd been dropped off at the day before, and we walked there in the heat—*siga, siga*—passing again by the museum, where things had really started to go right for me. In the shade of the café's umbrellas, we rested and ordered drinks while people joined our surrounding tables and took photos of the occasion. Three bottles of raki were given to me, and smiles all around, despite a noticeable sadness about my leaving. "It is too soon," someone said. He was right, but I had to go.

At one point, Georgia hobbled off, was gone maybe ten minutes, and returned with Anastasia, at ninety-six years old the only surviving sibling of the grandfather I'd never met. Slowly, she took a seat before me and held on to my hands firmly. Over and over she said, "I cannot believe it." She, too, told me my father was a good man, maybe the best man, and we sat there holding hands. She is the oldest person I've ever spoken to or touched, the deep lines in her face and hands tracing a lifetime of hardship. My throat grew so tight, I began silently counting the seconds until the bus arrived.

Twenty minutes later it did, and I hugged everyone, kisses on all cheeks.

Georgia said only, *"Garifalitsa, agapi mou."* Lisa, my love. I hugged her as though I meant to take a piece of her with me. Aboard the bus for Heraklion, I smiled and waved, mustered as chipper a final image as I could for them, but as soon as my family was out of sight, I wept so hard I choked.

On the bus, the parched Cretan landscape whipped by once more, the beautiful mountains looming again in the background, but this time it felt more familiar, as though a part of me had been there forever. And in that space more than any other, it was impossible not to imagine what my father had felt the first time he left the village—the first and last time.

I pictured him at seventeen years old in khakis and a short-sleeved button-down shirt, his suitcase and a duffel bag stowed beneath the bus. He'd have leaned his head against the bus's window as he stared at the locals lounging at the café, sipping frappés, reading newspapers. Both of his sisters and his mother had already fled to Athens, where there was work, and he had been living for more than a year with an uncle he couldn't wait to get away from. I bet he'd have thought about missing the people who stared at him through the tinted glass, but the farther the bus got from Vori, the faster the weight of village life would have lifted, his chest suddenly feeling open, loose. No more sharing a space cramped with so many people, with so little food. No more knowing every single stinking person's name and them knowing every lick of your business in return.

And maybe best, there'd be no more working for an uncle who'd beat him for not tending to the fields and animals correctly. He'd have wondered what Athens was really like. Sure, his sisters would have sent him letters talking it up, both of them now making good money with Olympic Airways, and they would've told him there would be work for him at the port of Piraeus. But he'd also have heard about it from some of the men in the village on nights when he'd snuck out to watch them play cards at the *tavernas*, the lot of them perpetually shrouded in a pall of smoke from their never-ending cigarettes. *The women in Athens*, one man could have said, *poutanas. Nothing like the girls here.* And another, *I didn't hear you complaining so loud when they suck your dick!* Then laughter all around. By the time my father boarded the ship at Heraklion, he'd have been swimming in visions of women, gambling, money—everything big-city life has to offer.

But after a year and a half in Athens, his daydreams would have turned to America. Until he'd hit the city, he hadn't met anyone who'd actually made it to the States and back, but in Athens, more men would've filled his head with talk of opportunity, even more money to be made, more women to be had. A handful of odd jobs later—mostly dishwashing in the pits of sweaty Athenian kitchens—he'd have met the right people to get the job he needed as a crew member on a freighter headed straight for the States, the only way he could afford a ticket. Once the ship set sail and he heard the foghorn wail, he would have rested his elbows against the railing of the deck and watched his country recede until every stitch of mountain and beauty faded into an indecipherable blip on the horizon. Of course, he had to work lifting heavy crates in the bowels of the ship, but he would be sure to stand on the deck again three weeks later as the Statue of Liberty and the lights of New York City slowly came into view.

Yes, in America, he could make his dreams come true, they'd have told him.

In America, a man could be whoever he wanted to be.

Back in Heraklion, I wrote emails, first to my mother and then to Mike, to tell them all that had happened. I wept on my keyboard and didn't bother to correct my typos. I told them both the story of Vori, the story of family, and couldn't wait to see them again in the States. Mike wrote back:

> I am shocked, stunned, and amazed at your email and all you experienced in Vori. I got so emotional (which is an anagram for "no to email," as my brain just processed) reading your email . . . I can't believe you found so many relatives and stayed in Dad's house. Holy shit. Thank you for sharing in such detail.
>
> Love, Mike

The instant I read his email, I knew our fighting days were over. They would end because the fight came from me—had always come from me—and the part of me that once buzzed with rage had settled. Maybe that's what healing is: the body gone quiet.

Once I arrived in Athens, I called my cousin George, and we decided to meet for coffee before driving to see my aunt Despina. I expected him to be eighteen or twenty because his voice had sounded so high and sweet, but he turned out to be a few years older than me, with thick black hair and eyes so kind that I have trouble imagining anyone disliking him.

While driving and after a bit of small talk, George surprised me.

"Did you like your father?" he asked.

I looked over at him in the driver's seat. That's not a Greek question. In Greece the answer is understood: *Yes, of course. He is my father.* The logic is as simple as that. Liking isn't optional.

But I took a shot. "I think he was a bit of an asshole."

George looked at me for a second, then turned his eyes to the road again. "Yeah, mine too," he said.

And right then I knew we had something special. We didn't touch the subject again for a while; in fact, we quickly moved on to horror films, which turned out to be an obsession for both of us. By the time we reached my aunt's apartment twenty minutes later, I'd decided George and I would've been friends even if we weren't related.

My aunt's apartment had air-conditioning in the living room (woohoo!), icons in every corner, and the same picture of my father I'd seen all over Crete resting next to the sofa.

Despina stood short as a middle schooler, a mound of soft speech, wiry hair, and a bruised and bumpy arm that recorded the wreckage of dialysis. She was also instantly likable; George had inherited his kindness from her. It's no wonder I didn't remember her visiting when I was a child; she's so quiet, she would have been swallowed by Georgia's intense shadow. Smiles, tears, more coffee, poor attempts at Greek by me, and thankful translations by George filled the evening.

After an hour or two of smiles and caffeine, Despina asked the big question and, again, I told the big lie.

"A car accident," I said.

"Alithia, einai?" she asked. *It's the truth?*

I couldn't very well tell one sister a lie and the other the truth.

"Yes," I said.

"Oh, thank God, thank God," she said and cried, crossed herself, and grabbed the photo of my father from the table to kiss it. Almost the identical steps her sister had taken. I smiled, but my side cramped like a runner's stitch. I thought, *Maybe this is what you get for running from the truth.*

George knew a *psarotaverna* (fish restaurant) by the docks in a lovely open square illuminated with amber rope lights—a good forty-five minutes outside Athens—but he assured me it was the proper place to get seafood, so we drove out there and walked around for a bit before finally settling on a place with immense fresh fish mounted in hunks of ice out front. No menu to peruse—just rows and rows of glorious fish. George ordered for us—as always in Greece, enough food for a large family—and we took a picnic table, where he proceeded to chain-smoke and we shared oversize Amstels. For a while, we talked about my travels through Greece—where I'd been, what the village was like. I told him how the family and I had danced all night, how it was the happiest I'd been in a long, long time.

He lit another cigarette, his third in the half hour we'd been there, and said, "I am surprised by what you tell my mother today."

My heart pumped one loud beat, then seemed to stop. "Why?" I asked and kicked the leg of the table.

"Because what you say is not what I hear."

Hear? How could he hear anything? Could he have learned something different than Georgia? Wouldn't the whole family think the same thing?

"What did you hear?" I asked.

George paused. "What I hear was bad. Very, very bad." He exhaled and looked from the ashtray to me and back again, then shook his head.

"I can handle it," I assured him. I added in Greek, "Tell me. Please."

"Okay," he said and leaned toward me, elbows on the table. "I hear that he kills a woman and child and himself with a gun."

Involuntarily, I held my breath for a beat. *Fuck it*, I thought.

"Can I have one of those?" I asked, motioning to his Winstons.

"Of course. Take, take. Do not ask."

"Yes," I said and inhaled the smoke deeply. "That's what happened." I prayed he wouldn't leave me there at the docks, a ten-pound fish on its way, fifty kilometers from where I needed to be.

"Motherfucker. How could he do that?" he asked.

I wasn't sure what to say next, so I kept quiet and savored the light-headedness from my first smoke in ages.

"What you tell my mother"—he paused to exhale—"this was a good thing. Thank you for saying this."

"Really?" I asked and settled into a regular heartbeat again. "I didn't want to lie, George, I really didn't. But I couldn't tell them. And when Georgia brought it up in the morning, she told me she thought it was a car accident, so I agreed. It's the only reason I said that to begin with."

"She did?" he asked, eyebrows raised. "I do not know why she would say this. We all hear the truth."

I should have known my aunts' excessive thankfulness and praise to god meant they'd heard the truth. Looking back, it is clear they were relieved by my news. I'd assumed they were glad to know it had been a quick death. Turns out, they were glad to know their baby brother wasn't a murderer.

"But how?" I asked.

"Someone from the church in the States call and tell us."

"Then why would she say 'car accident'?" I asked.

He shook his head. "I do not know. This does not make sense."

"But you think I did the right thing?"

"Yes. Yes," he said. "You bring them peace, and I will never tell." He poured some beer into my glass. Then he smiled. "They should have asked you at night, after the drinks. They say here, children and wine speak the truth."

"Yeah, 'they' are pretty smart," I said. Would I have answered differently after all the raki and wine? I'm not sure.

"Let me ask," George said. "Why did he do this?"

"I don't know why. We'll never know why. And that's the hardest thing. So many questions, no answers."

"Jesus Christ," he said and whistled.

"Yeah."

Our food arrived, piles of it, and as delicious as it was, my mind was focused on the relief of being able to tell a member of the family the truth, to have him tell me in return that the lie I'd told was a good thing. I still wasn't sold on that—still am not sold—but it helped. For hours, we shared food and beer and cigarettes, never returning to the topic of my father, and with every passing minute of conversation, I felt lucky to have gained a friend and ally.

On the way back to the city, George pulled over in the middle of nowhere and said, "Come. I show you something."

I followed him in the dark through a gravel lot until we stood before a small lake, the circumference of the water lit low by lights, a mound of caves rising above it. The reflection was a perfect optical illusion, making it impossible to tell where the water ended and the caves began, all of it multiplying in a way that made the caves appear infinite. After some time, George said quietly, "It is like this—if you point to the water and say it is a cave, you are not wrong, yes?"

"Sure," I said.

"This is what you give to my mother, my aunt. They need to believe the cave never ends."

I said nothing, thinking about that idea, and he added, "The good way they think of your father, this is the cave for them. The good goes on forever. And you choose not to throw a stone into the water, to let them believe. This is what they need."

I'd already liked George, but in that moment, I loved him. In the dark, I slipped my arm around his shoulders and squeezed, and together we stood reverent before the infinite cave of belief.

On my last night in Greece, George and I met for a beer at an outdoor café in Monastiraki beneath the Acropolis, where I'd started one month earlier, the Parthenon glowing radiant purple above its spotlights. We were exchanging stories, mostly funny ones from our childhoods, laughing easily but both clearly sad that I was leaving.

"There was a time, I am told," George said, "when your father was a boy, very small, playing in some dirt. He was with other children after church, still in his good clothes, going down the dirt hill. So many times he did this that when he comes home, the back of his pants is missing." He whistled. "*Yiayia* was angry. The one good pair of pants, ruined." George laughed, his body heaving, a twinkle in his eyes.

I stared at him.

"You do not see this is funny?" he asked.

"Let me ask this first: What happened? Did he get in trouble?"

"Yes, of course. They say he was yelled at much, but maybe too he was hit a little."

I shook my head. "This is why I'm not laughing, though it's funny in a different way. When I was ten or so, my family was at my grandmother's place for dinner. Mike and I got bored, so we wandered around her neighborhood, and do you know what we found?"

George cocked his head and smiled. "No."

"A huge pile of dirt. Right away we started climbing and sliding down, king of the mountain stuff, over and over climbing and sliding. By the time we went back inside, Mike had lost one of his shoes to the mud, and the back of my pants was totally gone." I paused to light a smoke. "It's the same goddamned story! And I got in so much trouble with my father."

"You think maybe he would see this and laugh," George said and waved his arm at the waiter. "Two more beers."

"That's what I mean! It's like this is all genetic. I bet if I have a kid, it'll rip the ass out of its pants too."

George, a father himself, smiled. "If this is the only wrong he does, you are lucky in this world. *Yeia mas.*"

"*Yeia mas,*" I said and tapped my beer against his.

"You know, I have never been there," George said and pointed to the Acropolis.

"What? That's totally crazy. It's so beautiful! You have to go—take your son. It's, like, the Greekest thing ever." My disbelief rendered me half Valley girl.

George smiled. "Maybe someday I will go. I should, you are right. But this is always the way: the thing that is in front of you, you do not notice it so much."

"Jesus. Every one of you Greeks. You're all philosophers!"

Leaning forward, George put one hand on my shoulder and made the *tsk-tsk* sound folks all over Greece use to punctuate sentences. "You are no different, my friend."

The goodbye with George: embraces and sweat on the street in front of my aunt's apartment, a couple of final photographs taken, the two of us beaming big, toothy smiles, arm in arm like old partners in crime. For the first time in a long time, I didn't cry; I knew I'd see George, my cousin and friend, again. He'd arranged for a taxi to take me to the airport, and while the driver loaded my bag into the trunk, George handed me a small envelope.

"For you to take. Maybe it will help," he said.

I opened it and let slide into my palm a small charm, a brilliant blue eye trimmed in silver, a talisman seen everywhere in Greece. The eye protects its wearer by reflecting evil back at the person or spirit wishing harm.

"You're too much," I told him and pulled him in for a final hug. *"Efharisto."*

"You're welcome, Garifalitsa," he said. In hearing my name in Greek again, in *his* saying my Greek name, a warm wave rushed from the tips of my ears down to my feet, the kind of surge I'd felt countless times when my panic began. But it wasn't that at all. Instead, I felt awash with love.

On the way to the airport, I sat exhausted in the back seat and stared at the distant mountains, trying to memorize their every bump and ridge. Leaving Greece felt like a necessary breakup: I'd fallen in love with it, but I also had to go home. Home. That was the first time I thought of Tallahassee as a place I could be settled. Not settled into an apartment but settled into myself. I knew that the moment I returned—after a proper night's sleep—I would call my mother and say simply, "Come here. I can't express what's happened over the phone." And three days later she'd arrive. Curbside at our regional airport, she'd hug me before holding me at arm's length and say, "My god, Lisa. You *look* different."

A month after that, I'd hop a plane for Philadelphia to join my family for both a reunion and a celebration of my grandmother's eighty-fifth birthday. Mike would pick me up, and together we'd drive to Long Beach Island, just the two of us.

It would be the first time we'd been alone in six years.

"It's weird," he'd say. "Do you remember how good Dad was with kids?"

I'd look at Mike, at his crooked nose and unkempt facial hair. He was a father. My little brother—a father with a car seat in the back of his Saturn to prove it.

"He could make anyone laugh," he'd add.

"Yeah, he could charm the pants off a nudist." *He was such a good man.*

The traffic would continue at a firm four miles per hour, and in that steady inching, we'd turn to the details of it all.

"How do you not think about the bad shit all the time?" I'd ask.

"I don't know. But we don't have the same memories." He'd be right.

We'd talk about Greece, the family, our father, our feelings. It would be a conversation with dimension, with depth, and it would feel like a salve to our six-year-old wounds. Finally, we'd talk—really talk—about the thing we should have been talking about all along.

"Maybe we could catch up more often now," Mike would suggest. "You know, like we used to."

"I'd like to try," I'd say. "Hell, we should try."

∞

I didn't know those reconciliations were coming. Not in the back of the cab, the Athenian countryside still whipping by, but my body felt full, quiet. It was a quiet I'd been waiting for my entire life. I'd traveled all over Greece, a young woman on the go, but at some point, I'd grown still, reverent. I closed my eyes to remember that feeling forever when the driver yanked me out of my reverie.

"You know what it is about the Greek people?" he half yelled. "They want to be lied to."

"Excuse me?" I asked in Greek.

"These people, they want lies. The lies are easier to believe, so this is what they wish to hear."

"What do you mean?" I asked, and he continued rambling. After a moment, I realized he wasn't speaking to me but was talking back to some political program on the radio. A man fed up with the state of his country. I laughed, and he glanced at me in the rearview mirror. With those words, the last I'd hear in Greece, I smiled at his unintended gift: a much-needed bit of absolution.

Dreamy-eyed and exhausted, I turned again to watch the land. Beyond the mountains—out where the peaks seamlessly blended blue-pink with dusky sky—lay a future, my future: a tenure-track job, medication, marriage, sobriety. I couldn't see any of that clearly, not yet, but it was out there—beyond my taxi driver, beyond Greece, beyond my father. Beyond all of it, waiting in the great blue-pink, stood some future me: calm and grinning and ready for a better life.

ACKNOWLEDGMENTS

My unwavering gratitude to:

My agent, Rayhané Sanders, for her patience, belief, laughter, and excellent notes.

Selena James for believing in me and this book, as well as the whole team at Little A.

Emily Murdock Baker for her terrific editorial insight.

Everyone at Hedgebrook, especially my unbelievably fierce and talented coven: Mira Jacob, Piyali Bhattacharya, Vero González, Yaccaira Salvatierra, Ashley M. Jones, and Amanda Leduc.

The beta readers and friends who stuck with and encouraged me throughout this interminable project, including Avni Vyas, Anna Claire Hodge, Tarfia Faizullah, Chris Mink, Spencer Wise, John Beardsley, Adam Cluley, Kyle Harrington, and anyone I may have forgotten in this moment.

Erin Elizabeth Smith, who offered me time at SAFTA more than once with open arms and kick-ass animals. And everyone who shared residency time, space, and energy with me.

Mary Lombardo-Graves, who kindly let me whisper my problems to her horses anytime I needed.

Andy Landis, the surprise connection I wasn't expecting at an Airbnb. And hell, Lars too.

The University of Evansville for supporting my work through various grants and awards. I would not have been able to spend time at residencies without that.

My UE colleagues, who never doubted this book would happen.

Ron Mitchell at *Southern Indiana Review* for publishing my work and nominating it for *Best American Essays*, Jonathan Franzen for choosing it, and Robert Atwan for being such a gracious editor.

Other editors and journals that have published my work on this topic over the past decade: *New Orleans Review*, *Salt Hill*, *Brevity*, *Hippocampus*, *Harpur Palate*, *Chautauqua*, the *Briar Cliff Review*, the *Citron Review*, *Press 53*, and the Hearst publications *Esquire*, *Cosmopolitan*, *Elle*, and *Good Housekeeping*.

Lidia Yuknavitch, Louise Glück, Dan Chaon, Jo Ann Beard, Kelly Sundberg, Julianna Baggott, Gabe Mac, and Diane Roberts for their kindness and generosity toward my work.

My students.

My teachers.

My mother and brother, who never asked for a memoirist to put their lives on the page, for understanding the creative process and what drives us to do what we must.

My nieces for being the best humans on the planet.

My incredible Little E for being the most wonderful mentee a Big could have wished for.

Christie for many hours on the phone digging into the darkness and laughing at the light, for always checking in, for being her lovely self. Also for the Instant Pot.

My grandmother, who assisted financially every time my dedication to working on this book pushed me ever closer to broke.

Everyone in Greece who helped me, a stranger, find what she was looking for: Mitsos, Anna, Greg and Anna, and especially Stelios. I could not have done this without your generosity and hospitality.

My Greek family. I thank and love you and am so sorry I lied. I hope you will understand why and forgive me. George, we must reunite. Soon.

Lindsay Sproul for being there, encouraging me, and the hikes and swimming on the phone.

Alex Marzano-Lesnevich for sitting at the Hedgebrook picnic table as the sun went down (and a small rabbit lost their mind) to talk to me about life after a memoir. Plus all the talking after that.

Erin Belieu, who gave me a home when I most needed one and taught me the importance of the phrase "Eyes on the prize."

Olivia Johnson, my chosen sister, greatest cheerleader, killer reader, and confidante. We're overdue for a night at Club Chaka.

And J, the greatest therapist I've ever known. Thank you for believing my voice matters and making me believe it too. Thank you for helping me recognize the gifts of trauma.

ABOUT THE AUTHOR

Lisa Nikolidakis's work has been selected for *The Best American Essays 2016* (edited by Jonathan Franzen) and she has won numerous prizes and awards for both her fiction and nonfiction, including the Annie Dillard, the Orlando, and the Lamar York prizes. Born in Philadelphia and raised in New Jersey, Nikolidakis presently teaches creative writing, photographs animals, and writes. For more information, visit www.lisanikolidakis.com.